SAS® Applications Guide

1 9 8 7 E D I T I O N

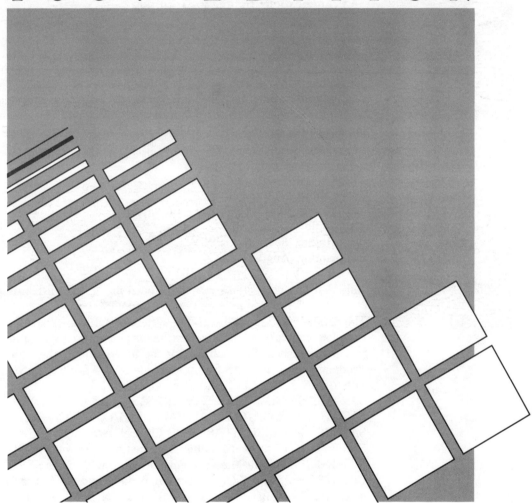

SAS Institute Inc.
SAS Campus Drive
Cary, NC 27513

Brenda C. Kalt edited the *SAS Applications Guide, 1987 Edition.*
Stephenie P. Joyner is the series editor for the SAS Applications Guide
Series. Writers were **Deborah S. Blank, Anne Corrigan, Stephenie P.
Joyner, Brenda C. Kalt, J. Robin Keller, Carol W. Myrick, Marian
Saffer,** and **Judith K. Whatley.** Copyediting was performed by **J. Chris
Parker.**

The correct bibliographic citation for this manual is as follows:
SAS Institute Inc. *SAS® Applications Guide, 1987 Edition.* Cary, NC:
SAS Institute Inc., 1987. 252 pp.

SAS® Applications Guide, 1987 Edition

1st printing, March 1987
2nd printing, May 1987
3rd printing, May 1988
4th printing, April 1989
5th printing, February 1990
6th printing, August 1991

Note that text corrections may have been made at each printing.

The SAS® System is an integrated system of software providing
complete control over data access, management, analysis, and
presentation. Base SAS software is the foundation of the SAS System.
Products within the SAS System include SAS/ACCESS; SAS/AF;
SAS/ASSIST; SAS/CPE; SAS/DMI; SAS/ETS; SAS/FSP; SAS/GRAPH;
SAS/IML; SAS/IMS-DL/I; SAS/OR; SAS/QC; SAS/REPLAY-CICS;
SAS/SHARE; SAS/STAT; SAS/CALC; SAS/CONNECT; SAS/DB2;
SAS/EIS; SAS/INSIGHT; SAS/PH-Clinical; SAS/SQL-DS; and
SAS/TOOLKIT™ software. Other SAS Institute products are
SYSTEM 2000® Data Management Software, with basic SYSTEM 2000,
CREATE; Multi-User; QueX; Screen Writer; and CICS interface
software; NeoVisuals® software; JMP; JMP IN; JMP SERVE; and
JMP Ahead™ software; SAS/RTERM® software; the SAS/C® Compiler,
and the SAS/CX® Compiler. MultiVendor Architecture™ and MVA™ are
trademarks of SAS Institute Inc. *SAS Communications; SAS Training;
SAS Views;* and the SASware Ballot® are published by SAS Institute Inc.
All trademarks above are registered trademarks or trademarks, as
indicated by their mark, of SAS Institute Inc.

A footnote must accompany the first use of each Institute registered
trademark or trademark and must state that the referenced trademark
is used to identify products or services of SAS Institute Inc.

The Institute is a private company devoted to the support and further
development of its software and related services.

Contents

Credits

SAS Applications Guide, 1987 Edition was adapted for Version 5 and Version 6 from the *SAS Applications Guide, 1980 Edition*. The original book was edited by **Kathryn A. Council**; **John P. Sall** contributed text and examples for chapters 4, 5, 10, 11, and 12; **Ginger B. Sall** chapter 7; and **Jane T. Helwig**, chapter 1.

Technical support for the *SAS Applications Guide, 1987 Edition* was provided by **Margaret L. Adair, Douglas R. Austin, Eric Brinsfield, Gloria N. Cappy, Rusti M. Ludwick, Susan Marshall, Sally Painter, Toby Trott,** and **Gwen G. Wiggs.**

Preface

About This Book
The *SAS Applications Guide, 1987 Edition* is a collection of examples that illustrate how you can use base SAS software to solve a variety of data entry, analysis, management, and report generation problems. The examples came from suggestions by base SAS software users and are designed to provide detailed answers to questions about using the SAS System more efficiently. Because this book describes a broad range of topics and discusses each in extensive detail, new and experienced SAS users will find it a valuable tool in their programming activities.

Each chapter is self-contained and provides an in-depth look at a data-handling task you can perform with base SAS software. General topics related to the task are discussed and specific programming techniques are provided to help you accomplish the results you want. Read through the table of contents to find the chapters that focus on your specific needs. You may find that other chapters offer additional information and solutions that will make your programming tasks easier. Use the following chapter descriptions as a starting point:

Chapter 1, "Reading Data," discusses reading data into SAS data sets with the INPUT statement.

Chapter 2, "Recoding Variables," covers creating new variables and modifying old ones with programming statements and SAS functions.

Chapter 3, "Reshaping Your Data," describes how to create new and modified SAS data sets with the SET statement and other program statements.

Chapter 4, "Merging SAS Data Sets," describes how to combine two or more SAS data sets with the MERGE statement.

Chapter 5, "Updating and Editing SAS Data Sets," discusses two approaches to changing values and adding observations to SAS data sets.

Chapter 6, "Writing Reports," covers SAS software features for displaying information either with minimal programming or to exact formatting specifications.

Chapter 7, "Managing SAS Data Libraries," discusses SAS data libraries and how to manage them with the APPEND, CONTENTS, COPY, and DATASETS procedures.

Chapter 8, "Diagnosing Errors," describes some of the most common errors in SAS programming and how to detect them by examining log and procedure output.

Chapter 9, "Working with External Files," discusses reading and writing external files with the INFILE, INPUT, FILE, and PUT statements.

Chapter 10, "Processing Large Data Sets with SAS Software," describes ways to approach SAS programs when the size of your data sets makes the use of computer resources an important consideration.

Chapter 11, "Writing Programs That Write Other Programs," discusses using the DATA step to write other programs automatically (either SAS programs or programs in another language).

What You Need to Know

The *SAS Applications Guide, 1987 Edition* was written for a wide range of users. Some topics are simple, and some are relatively advanced. You need at least the level of knowledge in the *SAS Introductory Guide, Third Edition*, or the *SAS Introductory Guide for Personal Computers, Version 6 Edition*, to use this book effectively.

Version 5 Users

You should have access to the *SAS User's Guide: Basics, Version 5 Edition* and to one of the following manuals and technical reports, depending on your operating system:

□ AOS/VS SAS users: SAS Technical Report P-159, "Using the SAS System, Version 5, under AOS/VS"

□ CMS SAS users: *SAS Companion for the CMS Operating System, 1986 Edition*

□ OS SAS users: *SAS Companion for OS Operating Systems and TSO, 1984 Edition*

□ PRIMOS SAS users: SAS Technical Report P-160, "Using the SAS System, Version 5, under PRIMOS"

□ VMS SAS users: *SAS Companion for the VMS Operating System, 1986 Edition*

□ VSE SAS users: *SAS Companion for the VSE Operating System, 1983 Edition* and SAS Technical Report P-132, "Enhancements and Updates in SAS Release 82.4 under VSE."

Version 6 Users

If you are using the SAS System under PC DOS, Version 6, you should have access to the *SAS Introductory Guide for Personal Computers, Version 6 Edition*, the *SAS Language Guide for Personal Computers, Version 6 Edition*, and the *SAS Procedures Guide for Personal Computers, Version 6 Edition*. You will find most of the examples in this book useful, although a few describe features that are not needed when using personal computers. If you do not know whether a feature used in a particular example is available in the SAS System for personal computers, consult one of these three reference manuals.

Conventions Used in This Book

The sample applications described in the following chapters are complete SAS programs that you can replicate on your system. The data for the examples have been included for this purpose. When studying the examples and their output, you should note the following:

□ When you see a libref or fileref in a sample program, assume that it is defined correctly. In order to duplicate examples in your environment, you must define such names according to the rules for your operating system, whether in control language or with SAS statements. (A libref is the first-level name of a SAS file. A fileref is a symbolic name for an external file and is used in an INFILE or FILE statement.)

□ All output was produced with these SAS system option settings:

NONUMBER
NODATE
LINESIZE=80 | 120
NOOPLIST

□ Primary descriptions of SAS features used in the sample applications can be found in the *SAS User's Guide: Basics, Version 5 Edition* or the *SAS Language Guide for Personal Computers, Version 6 Edition* and the *SAS Procedures Guide for Personal Computers, Version 6 Edition.*

□ In general, the sample applications are designed to execute on a Version 5 SAS System under any operating system. Exceptions to this are noted where appropriate. Most of the examples are also useful under Version 6 of the SAS System for personal computers. However, this book does not attempt to distinguish between Version 5 and Version 6 usages.

□ Control language needed to set up and execute the examples is not shown because control language requirements are different for each operating system. Refer to the appropriate SAS documentation for details on operating system specifics in your environment.

Contributing Suggestions for Applications

If you have applications you would like to see documented in future volumes in the Applications Guide series, please write your suggestions on a photocopy of the **Your Turn** page at the end of this book. You may want to attach an outline or detailed description of your application, as well as hardcopy of the SAS code used in the example.

x

1 Reading Data

The DATA step reads data into a SAS data set. This chapter describes the basics of data input and retrieval, and illustrates some more challenging situations such as working with files that contain mixed records, hierarchical files, variable-length fields, and multiple record types.

How the DATA Step Works

The statements in a SAS DATA step make up a loop. In the simplest case, if you do not use explicit OUTPUT and RETURN statements, the loop is executed once for each line of data that you read, an observation is written to the SAS data set being created, and SAS returns to the top of the loop for another execution. This automatic output and return at the end of simple DATA steps means that the two DATA steps below are equivalent:

```
DATA NEW;                    DATA NEW;
    INPUT A B C;                 INPUT A B C;
    CARDS;                       OUTPUT;
data lines                       RETURN;
;                                CARDS;
RUN;                         data lines
                             ;
                             RUN;
```

The INPUT Statement The INPUT statement is the key to data input and retrieval in SAS programs, and you need to know exactly what happens when SAS executes an INPUT statement. For example, in the previous DATA step

- □ SAS goes to the source of the input data and gets a line of data. In this case, the data follow the CARDS statement in the program stream.
- □ SAS reads information from the line into the SAS variables A, B, and C.
- □ SAS positions the column pointer ready to read the first column of the next line of data.

Usually, the INPUT statement contains instructions that locate the values of variables in the data line. Subsequent parts of this chapter explain these instructions. Later, this chapter also discusses features that let you change the sequence in which lines and variables are read; for example, you may not want SAS to go to the next line of data but to continue to read the current line.

The Source of Data　In the DATA step, you must tell SAS the source of your input data. You can either include the data in the SAS code by preceding it with a CARDS statement, or you can tell SAS and the operating system where to find the input lines in a disk or tape file with the INFILE statement.

The CARDS Statement　When SAS sees a CARDS statement, it expects to find the data lines described by the INPUT statement immediately after the CARDS statement. Since the only function of the CARDS statement is to notify SAS that the data lines accompany the DATA step, the CARDS statement is not an executable statement: SAS takes no direct action when this statement occurs. Instead, the CARDS statement only notifies SAS that the data lines follow the DATA step statements.

The INFILE Statement　Another statement used in the DATA step is the INFILE statement. The INFILE statement defines the external file that contains the raw data. Specifically, the INFILE statement supplies the fileref of the current input file. This statement is executable: each time SAS encounters an INFILE statement, the "current" input file becomes the one described in that INFILE statement.

If you keep in mind that the statements in the DATA step make up a program that is executed once for each observation, you will find it easier to write more complex SAS programs.

List, Column, and Formatted Input

Specifications in an INPUT statement give SAS information about the way the raw data are organized. The instructions used determine how SAS inputs the data records. There are three main styles of input in SAS programming: list, column, and formatted. The one you use depends on what the records look like.

List Input　With list input, you just list the names of the variables in the order they appear on the data line. Follow the variable name with a dollar sign $ when the field contains character data. When SAS sees the list of variables after the keyword INPUT, it scans over the input data line until it finds the first nonblank column, reads the value up to the next blank, and assigns that value to the first variable in the list for the observation being built. The next nonblank field becomes the value of the next variable, and so on. Here is an example of a DATA step with a simple list INPUT statement:

```
DATA ZIPCODE;
   INPUT CITY $ STATE $ ZIP;
   CARDS;
CANTON OHIO 44701
CHICAGO ILLINOIS 60007
CYPRESS FLORIDA 32432
N.Y. N.Y. 10012
;
PROC PRINT;
   TITLE 'DATA SET ZIPCODE';
RUN;
```

The SAS data set is shown in **Output 1.1.**

Output 1.1
Data Set Created Using
List Input

```
                    DATA SET ZIPCODE

          OBS   CITY      STATE      ZIP

           1    CANTON    OHIO       44701
           2    CHICAGO   ILLINOIS   60007
           3    CYPRESS   FLORIDA    32432
           4    N.Y.      N.Y.       10012
```

Using the free-format list style for entering data lines at a terminal is convenient since your data need not be in the same column positions on every line. Keep in mind the following rules for using list input:

☐ Each data value on the input line must be separated from the next by at least one blank.
☐ You must give a name to every field on the input line since SAS makes a one-to-one match between the fields and the variable names given in the INPUT statement. (You can, however, ignore all fields after a given point.)
☐ If data are missing for a variable, a period must be coded to hold the position.
☐ Only standard character and numeric values can be read with list input.
☐ Character values can be no longer than eight characters and may not contain embedded blanks.

Note that the last two limitations above can be overcome through the use of format modifiers, discussed in a subsequent section.

Column Input   If your data contain standard character and numeric values in the same column location on each line, then you can use column input. This style of input requires you to follow each variable name with its column location in the INPUT statement. Specify the beginning column, a dash, and the ending column of the field containing the value. SAS looks in the specified columns for the value of the variable in the observation being built.

Column input has some advantages over list input:

☐ Any field in the input line can be a variable in the data set. You can reread portions of a variable or read the same field several times.

☐ You can select any subset of data you want to read and read it in any order.

☐ If a field is blank, SAS reads it as a missing value.

☐ Character values can be up to 200 characters long and can contain embedded blanks.

Character values read with column input are trimmed of leading blanks before they are written to the SAS data set. If you want to maintain leading blanks in a character field, you can use the $CHAR. informat and formatted input (see **Formatted Input**, below) instead of column input.

Numeric values read with column input are like all numeric values; regardless of input style, these values can have any length and are stored in SAS data sets as double-precision floating point numbers. SAS finds the numeric value anywhere in the field between the columns you specify.

☐ Numeric data values can fill any consecutive positions in the field.

☐ They can contain a decimal in one of the positions.

☐ They can be preceded by a $+$ or $-$ sign.

☐ They can be coded in scientific or E notation.

☐ Numeric values cannot contain embedded blanks.

Below are five columns of input lines containing numeric data. All of the values appear in the SAS data set as 98 in double-precision floating point representation.

```
            column

          1  2  3  4  5
         _____

             9  8  .  0
                   9  8
          9  8  .  0
          9  .  8  E  1
             +  9  8
         _____
```

With column input, you can optionally specify the number of decimal places. When a data value contains a decimal, SAS reads the value with the decimal located exactly as it appears in the data. However, if the value contains no decimal point, SAS stores the data value with the decimal point placed according to what you specify in the INPUT statement. For example, consider the following numeric values for a variable RESPONSE. The INPUT statement for reading the data is as follows:

```
INPUT RESPONSE 1-5 .2;
```

The use of .2 in this INPUT statement calls for two decimal places for each data value, unless the data value already has a decimal point in it.

Raw data for variable RESPONSE	Resulting values for RESPONSE in SAS data set

column

1 2 3 4 5

1 1 2 0	11.20
1 1 2 . 0	112.00
1 1 2	1.12

Formatted Input The third style of input lets you read data in virtually any form. (The form specification is called an informat.) Formatted input combines all the features of column input with the flexibility of reading data stored in internal formats such as binary and packed. Since formatted input lets you control an input pointer across the line of raw data, you can use pointer controls to scan repeating fields or fields located in data-defined locations.

In the following examples, you can see how formatted input contrasts with column input when the same data are read using both techniques. The following INPUT statement uses column input to read data containing several sequences of repeating fields:

```
INPUT P 1-3 PH 4 FIELD1 13 STREAM1 14 TIME1 15
             FIELD2 16 STREAM2 17 TIME2 18
             FIELD3 19 STREAM3 20 TIME3 21
             . . .
             FIELD10 40 STREAM10 41 TIME10 42;
```

The two variables P and PH are located in the first four columns of each record. These two variables are followed by a sequence of ten repeating fields, each consisting of the three variables FIELD, STREAM, and TIME. By using formatted input to read the data, the INPUT statement is shortened from ten lines to three:

```
INPUT P 1-3 PH 4 @13 (FIELD1-FIELD10) (1. +2)
                 @14 (STREAM1-STREAM10) (1. +2)
                 @15 (TIME1-TIME10) (1. +2);
```

What does this INPUT statement do?

□ It reads in the P and PH variables like the first INPUT statement does.

□ It reads in all the FIELD variables starting at column 13, reading for a length of 1, then skipping the next two columns.

□ It reads in the STREAM and TIME variables in the same manner.

Format Modifiers

The three styles of input—list, column, and formatted—allow you to read data from the simplest to the most complex files. If your data are free-format and you can use list input to read them, then you should, since list input is the easiest to specify. Two format modifiers, the colon : and the ampersand &, give you added flexibility when you are reading data with list input.

: Format Modifier Sometimes data meet the requirements of list input except that some numeric variables are in a special form; for example, a variable DATE may use seven columns of space in the form DDMMMYY. Or, a character value may have more than eight characters. You can use the colon format modifier to read the variables in other forms but still use list input.

Like any format modifier, the colon appears just before the informat you want to use to read the variable's value. When SAS sees a colon, SAS uses the informat that you specify for the variable rather than the standard numeric or character informat of length eight. Except for this difference, the data value is read like any other value using list input; SAS stops reading the field when it encounters a blank.

Suppose you want to enter some election data. Some of the character values are as long as 10 bytes:

```
1956 EISENHOWER STEVENSON
1960 KENNEDY NIXON
1964 JOHNSON GOLDWATER
1968 NIXON HUMPHREY
1972 NIXON MCGOVERN
1976 CARTER FORD
1980 REAGAN CARTER
1984 REAGAN MONDALE
```

You can read the data into a SAS data set with these statements:

```
DATA ELECT1;
   INPUT YEAR WINNER : $12. LOSER : $12.;
   CARDS;
data lines
;
PROC PRINT;
   TITLE 'ELECTION DATA FROM ELECT1';
RUN;
```

The resulting data set is shown in **Output 1.2.**

Output 1.2
Character Data Input with
Colon Format Modifier

```
                       ELECTION DATA FROM ELECT1

             OBS    YEAR      WINNER        LOSER

              1     1956    EISENHOWER    STEVENSON
              2     1960    KENNEDY       NIXON
              3     1964    JOHNSON       GOLDWATER
              4     1968    NIXON         HUMPHREY
              5     1972    NIXON         MCGOVERN
              6     1976    CARTER        FORD
              7     1980    REAGAN        CARTER
              8     1984    REAGAN        MONDALE
```

If you read the election data with ordinary list input,

```
DATA ELECT2;
   INPUT YEAR WINNER $ LOSER $;
   CARDS;
data lines
;
PROC PRINT;
   TITLE 'ELECTION DATA FROM ELECT2';
RUN;
```

the variables WINNER and LOSER are truncated to a length of 8 bytes, as shown in **Output 1.3**.

Output 1.3
Character Data Read with
Ordinary List Input

```
                       ELECTION DATA FROM ELECT2

             OBS    YEAR     WINNER      LOSER

              1     1956    EISENHOW    STEVENSO
              2     1960    KENNEDY     NIXON
              3     1964    JOHNSON     GOLDWATE
              4     1968    NIXON       HUMPHREY
              5     1972    NIXON       MCGOVERN
              6     1976    CARTER      FORD
              7     1980    REAGAN      CARTER
              8     1984    REAGAN      MONDALE
```

An INPUT statement containing formats not preceded by a colon tells SAS to use ordinary formatted input. Thus, the following statements produce **Output 1.4**:

```
DATA ELECT3;
   INPUT YEAR WINNER $12. LOSER $12.;
   CARDS;
data lines
;
PROC PRINT;
   TITLE 'ELECTION DATA FROM ELECT3';
RUN;
```

Output 1.4
Character Data Read with
Ordinary Formatted Input

```
                          ELECTION DATA FROM ELECT3

                 OBS    YEAR    WINNER           LOSER

                  1     1956    EISENHOWER S      TEVENSON
                  2     1960    KENNEDY NIXO      N
                  3     1964    JOHNSON GOLD      WATER
                  4     1968    NIXON HUMPHR      EY
                  5     1972    NIXON MCGOVE      RN
                  6     1976    CARTER FORD
                  7     1980    REAGAN CARTE      R
                  8     1984    REAGAN MONDA      LE
```

In this case, SAS fills up the WINNER variable with twelve
characters for each value, including blanks as characters.

The INPUT statement above uses list input to read the YEAR values
and formatted input to read WINNER and LOSER values. You can
combine any of the three input methods in one INPUT statement.

& Format Modifier

If you want to use list input to read character data containing
embedded blanks, you can use the ampersand format modifier as long
as one value is separated from the next one in the input line with at
least two blanks.

The ampersand follows the variable name and tells SAS to look for
two blanks to end the field. If the data value contains one embedded
blank, like JOE JONES, then the blank between JOE and JONES will
not end the field; only two consecutive blanks can do that.

If the data value is longer than eight characters, you also need to
include an informat. (You do not need a colon in this case because an
ampersand also performs the function of a colon.)

The following data contain character variables that have blanks in
the values:

```
GROUP-M  RALEIGH
INT WIDGET   CHICAGO
SURFACE  MADISON
B. SMITH   LOS ANGELES
LACOR   LOS ANGELES
GTARCO   CHICAGO
```

These statements read the data and create a SAS data set:

```
DATA COMPANY;
   INPUT COMPANY & $12. CITY & $12.;
   CARDS;
data lines
;
PROC PRINT;
   TITLE 'COMPANY DATA INPUT WITH &';
RUN;
```

Output 1.5 shows what data set COMPANY looks like when it is
printed out.

Output 1.5
Character Values with
Embedded Blanks Read
Using &

```
                    COMPANY DATA INPUT WITH &

            OBS     COMPANY      CITY

             1      GROUP-M      RALEIGH
             2      INT WIDGET   CHICAGO
             3      SURFACE      MADISON
             4      B. SMITH     LOS ANGELES
             5      LACOR        LOS ANGELES
             6      GTARCO       CHICAGO
```

Without the ampersand, use the following statements to produce the data set shown in **Output 1.6**:

```
DATA COMPANY;
   INPUT COMPANY : $12. CITY : $12.;
   CARDS;
data lines
;
PROC PRINT;
   TITLE 'COMPANY DATA INPUT WITHOUT &';
RUN;
```

Output 1.6
Character Values with
Embedded Blanks Read
without &

```
                    COMPANY DATA INPUT WITHOUT &

            OBS     COMPANY      CITY

             1      GROUP-M      RALEIGH
             2      INT          WIDGET
             3      SURFACE      MADISON
             4      B.           SMITH
             5      LACOR        LOS
             6      GTARCO       CHICAGO
```

Keep in mind that both colon and ampersand format modifiers tell SAS to use list input to read the data lines. SAS scans over blanks to read the values. If you specify only a colon, SAS looks for one blank to end the field. If you use the ampersand, SAS looks for two blanks (although you may use more than two). SAS takes the width you give after the colon or the ampersand as the width of the variable in the data set.

Two Input Files

Use of the INFILE statement presents many possibilities for reading data. For example, you can read data from two or more input files in a single DATA step.

Suppose you want to read variables A, B, and C from an input file whose fileref is FIRST, and variables X, Y, and Z from another input file whose fileref is SECOND. In this case, both files contain the same number of records. You want the observations in the SAS data set to contain the six variables A, B, C, X, Y, and Z:

```
DATA NEW;
    INFILE FIRST;
    INPUT A B C;
    INFILE SECOND;
    INPUT X Y Z;
PROC PRINT;
    TITLE 'TWO INPUT FILES WITH THE SAME NUMBER OF RECORDS';
RUN;
```

If the input file described by FIRST has these lines,

```
1 2 3
4 5 6
7 8 9
```

and the file described by SECOND has these lines,

```
11 22 33
44 55 66
77 88 99
```

then the resulting data set is shown in **Output 1.7.**

Output 1.7
Two Input Files Read into
One Data Set

```
         TWO INPUT FILES WITH THE SAME NUMBER OF RECORDS

         OBS     A     B     C     X     Y     Z

          1      1     2     3     11    22    33
          2      4     5     6     44    55    66
          3      7     8     9     77    88    99
```

When End-of-File Is Reached

Each time SAS gets a new input line, it checks to see if any more lines remain to be read. Regardless of the results of this check, SAS continues to the next statement in the DATA step; but when the check shows that the current observation is the last one in the input file, SAS sets the automatic end-of-file value to 1.

When the INPUT statement is executed the next time, it cannot get a new line. The INPUT statement fails, and SAS ends the DATA step immediately.

You can use the EOF= option of the INFILE statement to name a statement label that SAS should go to when the end-of-file is reached. You can also use the END= option of the INFILE statement to define a variable whose value is the end-of-file indicator. (Note that you cannot use END= for data that you input with a CARDS statement, but only EOF= .)

Two Files with a Different Number of Records

In the previous example, what happens if the input file FIRST has five records instead of three? Everything progresses nicely the first three times through the DATA step. The fourth time through the DATA step, the first file contains more records, but the second file has reached end-of-file. Thus, the second INPUT statement fails, and SAS automatically ends the DATA step. Data set NEW again contains three records built by combining the first three records in each input file.

To get around this problem, use automatic end-of-file variables and execute an INPUT statement only when the corresponding end-of-file value is not set. Stop building the data set if both end-of-file variables are set.

```
DATA NEW;
    IF EOF1 AND EOF2 THEN STOP;
    INFILE FIRST END=EOF1;
    IF ¬EOF1 THEN INPUT A B C;
    INFILE SECOND END=EOF2;
    IF ¬EOF2 THEN INPUT X Y Z;
PROC PRINT;
    TITLE 'TWO INPUT FILES WITH DIFFERENT NUMBERS OF RECORDS';
RUN;
```

Executing this SAS program for the files containing five and three input lines produces five observations in data set NEW; for observations 4 and 5, the variables X, Y, and Z have missing values. **Output 1.8** shows the data set.

Output 1.8
Data Set from Two Different Files with Different Numbers of Records

```
TWO INPUT FILES WITH DIFFERENT NUMBERS OF RECORDS

OBS     A     B     C     X     Y     Z

 1      1     2     3    11    22    33
 2      4     5     6    44    55    66
 3      7     8     9    77    88    99
 4     10    11    12     .     .     .
 5     13    14    15     .     .     .
```

Why is the STOP statement necessary? In the DATA step above, you must tell SAS to stop building the data set when both files are at end-of-file. Otherwise, although the IF conditions will fail when end-of-file is reached, the INPUT statements never fail, and the step never ends. Instead a data set containing six observations is produced; the sixth observation has missing values for all the variables. An error message indicates that the step has gone into an endless loop.

Variable Number of Lines

A line of data in a SAS data set is called an observation. Often, the amount of information for observations in a data set will vary. For example, in a data set that contains the dates that patients visited a clinic, some people may have many visits to a clinic while others have only one.

Rectangular Data Sets and Missing Data

Even when the amount of information varies among observations, each observation in a SAS data set contains the same number of variables. SAS data sets are rectangular, as illustrated by **Figure 1.1**.

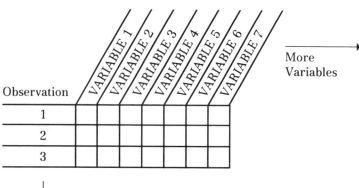

Figure 1.1
Rectangular Data Set Structure

If you have ten variables for observation 1 and only five for observation 2, you must have ten variables in your data set. The remaining five variables for observation 2 will contain an indication that the data are missing. If there are as many as ten visit dates for each patient record, you must include ten visit variables in your SAS data set, even though many observations will have fewer than ten values.

Using an Array

In SAS, an array is a set of variables.* Each variable of the array has a value associated with it for different observations. This section discusses two examples involving arrays. The first example illustrates the use of an array to read raw data into a new SAS data set. The second example contains an array that reorganizes information from an existing SAS data set. Both are examples of the clinic visit problem.

---

* In many programming languages, by contrast, an array identifies a single variable that may contain several values.

Array Example 1 The first example below reads raw data into a SAS data set using the array VISIT. Each line of raw data contains a patient identification number and a date that the patient visited the clinic. The data are to be grouped by patient identification number (ID) so that all the visit dates for one patient are together. The maximum number of visits is ten. You want to end up with a SAS data set with eleven variables for each observation—one ID and ten visit dates, some of which may have missing values.

```
DATA CLINIC;
    INFILE CARDS EOF=STOP;
    ARRAY VISIT{10} VISIT1-VISIT10;
    DO I=1 TO 10 WHILE(ID=NEXTID);
        INPUT ID 1-3 @5 VISIT{I} MMDDYY8.;
        INPUT NEXTID 1-3 @@;
        END;
    DROP NEXTID I;
    STOP: OUTPUT;
    CARDS;
111 10/01/87
111 02/01/87
111 03/01/87
111 04/01/87
222 01/15/87
333 02/07/87
333 02/14/87
333 02/21/87
444 03/12/87
444 04/21/87
444 04/28/87
444 05/05/87
444 05/12/87
444 05/19/87
444 05/26/87
;
PROC PRINT;
    FORMAT VISIT1-VISIT10 DATE7.;
    TITLE 'CLINIC VISIT DATES BY ID - EXAMPLE1';
RUN;
```

The resulting data set is in **Output 1.9.**

Output 1.9 *Array Example 1—Clinic Visits by Patient ID*

```
                                CLINIC VISIT DATES BY ID - EXAMPLE 1

OBS    VISIT1      VISIT2      VISIT3     VISIT4    VISIT5    VISIT6     VISIT7    VISIT8   VISIT9   VISIT10   ID

 1     01OCT87     01FEB87     01MAR87    01APR87     .         .          .         .        .        .      111
 2     15JAN87        .           .          .        .         .          .         .        .        .      222
 3     07FEB87     14FEB87     21FEB87        .        .         .          .         .        .        .      333
 4     12MAR87     21APR87     28APR87    05MAY87   12MAY87   19MAY87    26MAY87      .        .        .      444
```

What happens as each statement in this step is executed?

DATA CLINIC;

The DATA statement begins the DATA step and gives the name CLINIC to the new data set being created.

INFILE CARDS EOF = STOP;

The EOF= option gives the label STOP to the statement SAS should go to when end-of-file is reached.

ARRAY VISIT{10} VISIT1-VISIT10;

The ARRAY statement sets up an array containing the ten variables for the clinic visit dates. The array's name is VISIT.

DO I = 1 TO 10 WHILE(ID = NEXTID);

The DO statement begins a DO loop; the variable I is the indexing variable. The DO statement tells SAS to execute the statements within the DO loop up to ten times or until the WHILE clause becomes false. The first time through the DO loop, I's value is one; the fifth time through, I's value is five, and so on. The DO statement's function in this DATA step is to read values into the appropriate variables in the array VISIT.

The WHILE clause is evaluated at the top of the DO loop. For the first execution of the loop, the variables ID and NEXTID are both set to missing, so the WHILE condition is true. During subsequent executions of the DO loop, the WHILE condition is tested, as explained in the discussion of the statement

```
INPUT NEXTID 1-3 @@;
```

INPUT ID 1-3 @5 VISIT{I} MMDDYY8.;

For the first input line with a given ID value, this INPUT statement reads the ID value, then the first visit date using the MMDDYY8. informat. VISIT is an array name, and thus the current value of the index variable I determines which of the ten VISIT variables is assigned the visit date value. When I's value is 1, using the array reference VISIT{I} in a SAS statement refers to the first element of the array, VISIT1; likewise, when I's value is 6, using the reference VISIT{I} refers to the sixth element, VISIT6. In other words, each time SAS sees an array reference in a SAS statement, it finds the current value of the index variable and substitutes the corresponding element of the array into the SAS statement.

When the record being read is not the first with a given ID value, then this INPUT statement rereads the value of NEXTID (read on the previous pass through the DO loop) as ID, and then reads the next visit date. (See the following description of the next INPUT statement for more about NEXTID and the input line being reread.)

Note that in the output data set, the array variables are the first variables in each observation, followed by ID. Although the INPUT statement specifies the variables to be read as ID and VISIT{I}, the array VISIT was set up before ID, so the variables are defined first.

INPUT NEXTID 1-3 @@;

This INPUT statement, with its double trailing @@, is central to understanding the example. Normally, when a double trailing @@ appears at the end of an INPUT statement, SAS holds on to the current data line until another INPUT statement is executed that does not end with @@. (If a double trailing @@ appears at the end of an INPUT statement that uses list input, SAS releases the line after reading all the values on the line.) Executing this statement results in SAS reading the first value in the data line as the value of NEXTID and keeping the pointer on that line so that the next INPUT statement executed does not read in a new line.

NEXTID's value is the ID value from the input data line that is held. ID's value is the ID value from the previous data line. Whenever the two values are different, you know that the previous data line is the last for an ID value. When the DO loop executes again, the WHILE condition is tested. If the WHILE condition is true, the next INPUT statement executed is the first statement in the DO group; it rereads the value of NEXTID into the variable ID. If the WHILE condition is false, that is, if ID does not equal NEXTID, the observation is output. The next execution of the DATA step begins reading the same data line that the previous execution read (because of @@), so that no data are lost.

END;

This END statement ends the DO loop. SAS increments I's value by 1 and goes back to the top of the DO loop. If I is 10 or less and the WHILE condition is true, the statements in the loop are executed again.

DROP NEXTID I;

This statement prevents the variables NEXTID and I from being written to data set CLINIC. (These variables are used during the DATA step but are not written to the output data set.) Note that when an index variable is specified in a DO statement, SAS adds it to the new data set unless a DROP statement eliminates it.

STOP: OUTPUT;

The OUTPUT statement causes an observation to be written to the data set if the WHILE condition is false, that is, when ID does not equal NEXTID. In addition, because of the statement label STOP, SAS goes to this statement when it reaches end-of-file.

When the INPUT statement

```
INPUT ID 1-3 @5 VISIT(I) MMDDYY8.;
```

reads the last line of data, the next INPUT statement will attempt to read a nonexistent data line. SAS goes to the statement labeled STOP and outputs an observation. It is not unusual to have one or more statements in your SAS program that are only needed to handle exceptional conditions such as the first or last execution.

CARDS;

The CARDS statement signals that the data lines follow in the program stream.

Array Example 2   The second example of the clinic visit problem works from the premise that a SAS data set containing patient IDs and visit dates already exists. PROC PRINT is used to print the data set:

```
PROC PRINT DATA=NEWCLIN;
   FORMAT DATE MMDDYY8.;
   TITLE 'DATA SET NEWCLIN';
RUN;
```

The SAS data set is arranged as shown in **Output 1.10** with a patient ID and a date on each line.

Output 1.10
Data Set NEWCLIN

```
                    DATA SET NEWCLIN

        OBS    ID       DATE

         1     777    03/13/87
         2     777    03/06/87
         3     888    03/17/87
         4     888    03/23/87
         5     777    03/28/87
         6     888    04/16/87
         7     888    04/02/87
         8     777    04/17/87
         9     777    05/22/87
        10     777    05/01/87
        11     777    06/12/87
        12     777    07/17/87
        13     555    06/09/87
        14     555    08/09/87
        15     777    08/14/87
        16     555    09/09/87
        17     777    09/11/87
        18     666    12/16/87
```

This example organizes the data for each patient's visits by reading the SAS data set (NEWCLIN) into an array:

```
PROC SORT DATA=NEWCLIN;
    BY ID DATE;
DATA SUMMARY;
    ARRAY VISIT{10} VISIT1-VISIT10;
    DO I=1 TO 10 UNTIL(LAST.ID);
        SET NEWCLIN;
        BY ID;
        VISIT{I}=DATE;
        END;
    DROP DATE I;
PROC PRINT;
    FORMAT VISIT1-VISIT10 DATE7.;
    TITLE 'DATA SET SUMMARY';
RUN;
```

The resulting data set is in **Output 1.11**.

Output 1.11 *Array Example 2—Clinic Visit Dates Chronologically by ID*

DATA SET SUMMARY

OBS	VISIT1	VISIT2	VISIT3	VISIT4	VISIT5	VISIT6	VISIT7	VISIT8	VISIT9	VISIT10	ID
1	09JUN87	09AUG87	09SEP87	.	.	.	.	.	.	.	555
2	16DEC87	.	.	.	.	.	.	.	.	.	666
3	06MAR87	13MAR87	28MAR87	17APR87	01MAY87	22MAY87	12JUN87	17JUL87	14AUG87	11SEP87	777
4	17MAR87	23MAR87	02APR87	16APR87	.	.	.	.	.	.	888

Here is a summary of what the statements in this example do:

PROC SORT DATA=NEWCLIN;
    BY ID DATE;

These statements invoke the SORT procedure to sort the data set NEWCLIN by the ID variable. DATE sorts clinic visit dates chronologically within ID.

DATA SUMMARY;

DATA SUMMARY begins a new DATA step. This step will create a new data set SUMMARY from the sorted version of the NEWCLIN data set.

ARRAY VISIT{10} VISIT1-VISIT10;

As in the previous example, the ARRAY statement sets up an array containing the ten variables with the clinic visit dates. The array's name is VISIT.

DO I = 1 TO 10 UNTIL(LAST.ID);

The DO statement begins a DO loop with the variable I as the indexing variable. As before, the DO statement tells SAS to execute the statements within the DO loop up to ten times, or until the UNTIL condition becomes true. The first time through the DO loop, I's value is 1; the fifth time through, I's value is 5, and so on.

The UNTIL clause is evaluated at the bottom of the loop, so the loop is always executed at least once. LAST.ID (discussed next) indicates the last observation for that ID.

SET NEWCLIN;
BY ID;

The SET statement identifies the data set NEWCLIN as the data set from which SAS should read observations. BY ID; evaluates each ID to see if it is still in the BY group. BY ID; also creates the FIRST. and LAST. BY variables FIRST.ID and LAST.ID.

VISIT{I} = DATE;

For each occurrence of the same ID value, SAS reads the value of the DATE variable into VISIT. SAS keeps reading DATE values into VISIT for each ID until I is equal to 10, or until the value of LAST.ID is 1, filling in with missing values if there are less than ten visits for any ID. The last observation with a given ID makes the UNTIL clause true at the end of that iteration. SAS automatically outputs an observation.

END;

This END statement ends the DO loop.

DROP DATE I;

This statement prevents the variables DATE and I from being written to the data set SUMMARY.

PROC PRINT;
  FORMAT VISIT1-VISIT10 DATE7.;

PROC PRINT prints the data set SUMMARY. The variables VISIT1-VISIT10 are displayed according to the DATE7. format.

Files Containing Mixed Records

A file of mixed records contains records that have several formats. A typical goal with such a mixed file is to produce several SAS data sets, each corresponding to a particular record type. To handle a mixed file, you need several INPUT statements, one for each record type you want to read.

The Trailing @ and Double Trailing @@

The trailing @ is an important tool in reading files with mixed records. When an INPUT statement ends in a trailing @, the next INPUT statement in the current DATA step execution reads the same input data line, rather than getting a new one. When an INPUT statement contains a single trailing @, executing a RETURN or a DELETE statement or beginning a new execution of the DATA step releases the line so that the next INPUT statement gets a new line.

When an INPUT statement contains a double trailing @@, the next INPUT statement continues to read the current data line, whether or not that next INPUT statement is in the same execution of the DATA step. SAS releases the line when

- □ there are no more data on the line to read.
- □ you execute a null INPUT statement, that is, one without any specifications at all, for example,

```
INPUT;
```

This condition releases the line immediately after the INPUT statement is executed.
- □ you execute an INPUT statement to read in additional variables without a trailing @ or @@. The line is released immediately.
- □ you execute an INPUT statement with a trailing @. The line is released at the end of the current DATA step execution.

Different Variables in Each Data Set

Suppose you have a file containing data about students at a state university. Information for each student—the student's name and home address—is stored in a single record. Some of the students are residents of the state, and others are nonresidents. For in-state students, the county is included in the home address. The data are stored in a file called STUDENTS. You want to read records for out-of-state students into a SAS data set called OUTSTATE and data for in-state students into the SAS data set INSTATE.

Here are some sample records from the file STUDENTS:

NAME	STREET	CITY	STATE	COUNTY
ALVAREZ, N	541 ANYSTREET AV	PRINCETON	NJ	
BRODSKY, B	919 SOMESTREET TER	RALEIGH	NC	WAKE
BURKE, R	45 ANYLANE AVE	SOUTHFIELD	MA	
CROSS, J	12-4 SOMELANE RD	FARMINGTON	NC	BRUNSWICK
DAVITO, F	1056 N ANYROAD PL	HIGH POINT	NC	DAVIDSON
FLEMING, J	212 SOMEDRIVE ST	CHAPEL HILL	NC	ORANGE
KIRBY, N	9 ANYPLACE APT 8	SANTA FE	NM	
LOVE, T	770 ANYCIRCLE CT	DURHAM	NC	DURHAM
MURRAY, P	923 ANYDRIVE RD	WESTON	CA	

These statements will create the two new SAS data sets:

```
DATA INSTATE(DROP=STATE)
    OUTSTATE(KEEP=NAME STREET CITY STATE);
  INFILE STUDENTS;
  INPUT @47 STATE $2. @;
  IF STATE='NC' THEN DO;
     INPUT @1 NAME $12. @14 STREET $18. @34 CITY $11.
           @54 COUNTY $9.;
     OUTPUT INSTATE;
     END;
  ELSE DO;
     INPUT @1 NAME $12. @14 STREET $18. @34 CITY $11.;
     OUTPUT OUTSTATE;
     END;
PROC PRINT DATA=INSTATE;
   TITLE 'IN-STATE STUDENTS';
PROC PRINT DATA=OUTSTATE;
   VAR NAME STREET CITY STATE;
   TITLE 'OUT-OF-STATE STUDENTS';
RUN;
```

The new data sets are shown in **Output 1.12**.

Output 1.12
Data Sets with Different Variables Created from One File

```
                          IN-STATE STUDENTS

   OBS      NAME          STREET            CITY         COUNTY

    1    BRODSKY, A    919 SOMESTREET TER   RALEIGH      WAKE
    2    CROSS, J      12-4 SOMELANE RD     FARMINGTON   BRUNSWICK
    3    DAVITO, F     1056 N ANYROAD PL    HIGH POINT   DAVIDSON
    4    FLEMING, J    212 SOMEDRIVE ST     CHAPEL HILL  ORANGE
    5    LOVE, T       770 ANYCIRCLE CT     DURHAM       DURHAM
```

```
                        OUT-OF-STATE STUDENTS

     OBS      NAME          STREET            CITY         STATE

      1    ALVAREZ, N    541 ANYSTREET AV   PRINCETON     NJ
      2    BURKE, R      45 ANYLANE AVE     SOUTHFIELD    MA
      3    KIRBY, N      9 ANYPLACE APT 8   SANTA FE      NM
      4    MURRAY, P     923 ANYDRIVE RD    WESTON        CA
```

The DATA statement includes two data set names: INSTATE and OUTSTATE. After the INSTATE data set name, DROP=STATE prevents the STATE variable from being included in the data set INSTATE. The KEEP= data set option following OUTSTATE lists the variables that the data set OUTSTATE is to contain. Normally, every variable mentioned in the DATA step will be included in all the data sets being created in the step.

The INFILE statement identifies the input file.

The first INPUT statement reads the variable STATE beginning in column 47 of each record. This INPUT statement ends in a trailing @, telling SAS not to read a new data line for the next INPUT statement.

The DO groups, one for the records in which STATE is NC and one for the records in which STATE is not NC, are used to read the data and output the observations to the new SAS data sets INSTATE and OUTSTATE. The OUTPUT statements write the data to the two data sets.

Note that the INSTATE data set observations contain the variables NAME, STREET, CITY, and COUNTY, but not STATE. The OUTSTATE data set observations contain the NAME, STREET, CITY, and STATE variables. Normally, STATE would be the first variable printed in the OUTSTATE data set since it was the first variable input. However, the VAR statement is used to rearrange the way variables are printed so that PROC PRINT prints STATE last.

After these SAS data sets are created, you can analyze the records easily using SAS procedures.

Hierarchical Files

A hierarchical file contains "nested" records and is a special case of a mixed file. A good example of a hierarchical file is the Public Use Sample of the U.S. Department of the Census. A diagram of a hierarchical file is provided by **Figure 1.2**.

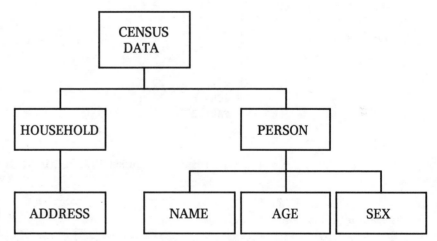

Figure 1.2
Hierarchical File Structure

Suppose you want to read a hierarchical file that contains two levels of hierarchy—households and people. You want to create one observation for each person and include information from the household record. For example, say the household record contains a field giving the address of the house. You want to read the address from the household record, then read in each person record, output it to a SAS data set, and include the address in the observation.

```
DATA PEOPLE(DROP=TYPE);
   RETAIN ADDRESS;
   INFILE CENSUS;
   INPUT @1 TYPE $ @;
   IF TYPE='H' THEN DO;
      INPUT @3 ADDRESS $20.;
      RETURN;
      END;
   ELSE IF TYPE='P' THEN DO;
      INPUT @3 NAME $10. AGE 2. +1 SEX $1.;
      OUTPUT;
      END;
   PROC PRINT;
   TITLE 'DATA SET PEOPLE';
RUN;
```

If the file described by fileref CENSUS contains these records,

```
H 321 S. MAIN ST
P MARY E     21 F
P WILLIAM M 23 M
P SUSAN K    3 F
H 324 S. MAIN ST
P THOMAS H  79 M
P WALTER S  46 M
P ALICE A   42 F
P JOY       20 F
P JOHN S    16 M
P PAUL R    12 M
```

then the resulting data set PEOPLE is in **Output 1.13.**

Output 1.13
Census Data by Household
Address

```
                         DATA SET PEOPLE

       OBS      ADDRESS           NAME        AGE    SEX

        1     321 S. MAIN ST    MARY E        21     F
        2     321 S. MAIN ST    WILLIAM M     23     M
        3     321 S. MAIN ST    SUSAN K        3     F
        4     324 S. MAIN ST    THOMAS H      79     M
        5     324 S. MAIN ST    WALTER S      46     M
        6     324 S. MAIN ST    ALICE A       42     F
        7     324 S. MAIN ST    JOY           20     F
        8     324 S. MAIN ST    JOHN S        16     M
        9     324 S. MAIN ST    PAUL R        12     M
```

Again, a trailing @ is used to read a record and check its type. Because of the RETAIN statement, the value of ADDRESS is included in each observation in the data set.

If the record is of type H, SAS reads the value of ADDRESS from the record and returns to the top of the step for another record. If the record is of type P, SAS reads the person record and outputs it to the SAS data set. The most recently read ADDRESS value appears in the observation.

Repeated Fields

It is not unusual to have a file containing records with a variable number of repeated fields. If the record contains a field that gives the number of times the segment is repeated, you can read this number, then use the value in a DO group to read in the repeated segments.

For example, suppose you have a file similar to the hierarchical file above, except that each record contains all the information about each household, including the name, age, and sex of each person in the house. Since each household contains a different number of individuals, there are a variable number of these "person-segments" in each record. The record contains a field that gives the number of person-segments included. You can read this file and create a SAS data set in two ways: each observation in the SAS data set corresponds to a household, each person to a variable; or each observation in the SAS data set corresponds to a person, with the household information contained in each observation.

The first approach requires that you know the maximum number of person-segments contained in any record. Then, each observation in the SAS data set contains that many person variables; the variables contain missing values when the number of persons in the household is less than the maximum number.

If you use the second approach, you repeat the address in each observation, and there are more observations (but fewer variables) in the SAS data set.

Two records from the file RESIDENTS are shown below.

```
321 S.MAIN ST  3  MARY E    21 F WILLIAM M 23 M SUSAN K    3 F
324 S.MAIN ST  6  THOMAS H  79 M WALTER S  46 M ALICE A   42 F JOY      20 F JOHN S   16 M PAUL R   12 M
```

You can use this DATA step to read the file and create the first type of SAS data set. The program assumes that no household has more than ten persons.

```
DATA HOUSES;
   INFILE DATAIN;
   ARRAY NAME{10} $10 NAME1-NAME10;
   ARRAY AGE{10} AGE1-AGE10;
   ARRAY SEX{10} $ SEX1-SEX10;
   INPUT ADDRESS $15. NUM 2. +1 a;
   DO I=1 TO NUM;
      INPUT NAME{I} $10. AGE{I} 2. +1 SEX{I} $1. +1 a;
      END;
   DROP I;
PROC PRINT;
   TITLE 'DATA SET HOUSES';
RUN;
```

The resulting data set is shown in **Output 1.14.**

Output 1.14 *Census Data by Household*

```
                                        DATA SET HOUSES

                                   N                                                          A
                                   N                                                          D
          N         N     N   N   N     N NNNA                              A       S         D
          A         A     A   A   A     A AAAMA A    A  A  A  AAAAGSSSSSSSSSE         R
    O M       M       M     M   M   M     M MMMEG  G    G  G  G  GGGGEEEEEEEEEEX         E       N
    B E       E       E     E   E   E     E EEE1E  E    E  E  E  EEEE1XXXXXXXX1         S       U
    S 1       2       3     4   5   6     7 8901 2    3  4  5  67890123456790         S       M

    1 MARY E   WILLIAM M SUSAN K                 21 23 3  .  .  . . . . . . F M F          321 S.MAIN ST 3
    2 THOMAS H WALTER S  ALICE A JOY JOHN S PAUL R  79 46 42 20 16 12 . . . . M M F F M M  324 S.MAIN ST 6
```

Data set HOUSES contains as many observations as the input file contains records. Each observation has ten name, age, and sex variables.

The first INPUT statement reads in the ADDRESS and NUM value. The trailing @ holds the record for the next INPUT statement.

Three ARRAY statements, one for each of the sets of variables NAME, AGE, and SEX, simplify the input of the repeated segments. When the value of I (the index variable) becomes equal to NUM (the number of person-segments), SAS outputs the observation and returns to the top of the DATA step for a new record. The DROP statement drops the I variable so that it is not included in the SAS data set HOUSES.

If you want each person to be an observation in your SAS data set, use the following statements:

```
DATA PERSON;
   INFILE DATAIN;
   RETAIN ADDRESS;
   INPUT ADDRESS $15. NUM 2. +1 @;
   DO I=1 TO NUM;
      INPUT NAME $10. AGE 2. +1 SEX $1. +1 @;
      OUTPUT;
      END;
   DROP I;
PROC PRINT;
   TITLE 'DATA SET PERSON';
RUN;
```

Data set PERSON is shown in **Output 1.15.**

Output 1.15
Census Data by Address and Occupant

```
                        DATA SET PERSON

        OBS     ADDRESS        NUM    NAME       AGE    SEX

         1    321 S.MAIN ST     3    MARY E       21     F
         2    321 S.MAIN ST     3    WILLIAM M    23     M
         3    321 S.MAIN ST     3    SUSAN K       3     F
         4    324 S.MAIN ST     6    THOMAS H     79     M
         5    324 S.MAIN ST     6    WALTER S     46     M
         6    324 S.MAIN ST     6    ALICE A      42     F
         7    324 S.MAIN ST     6    JOY          20     F
         8    324 S.MAIN ST     6    JOHN S       16     M
         9    324 S.MAIN ST     6    PAUL R       12     M
```

This data set contains more observations than data set HOUSES, created in the previous example, but has no missing data. By including the OUTPUT statement inside the DO loop, each person-segment becomes an observation in the data set.

The examples covered up to now are simple cases of some rather complex data retrieval problems. Advanced examples are discussed in the next section.

Variable-Length Fields

In addition to reading fields that repeat, you can read or skip fields of varying length. The next two examples use conditional input (the trailing @) to select only type 4 records from an external file named MASTER. The file contains employee records. The record for each department, indicated by the code 4, varies in length, depending on the number of employees in the department.

Skipping Variable-Length Fields

The following example reads the TYPE field in the file MASTER to determine if the record is a department record (type 4). You need to read fields that give information about the department, while skipping the fields that describe individual employees.

Three sample lines of data from the file MASTER are shown below.

```
019309 3902847 5859 84 95849 A9D03
04MARGARET A. THOMAS          10103THOMPSON 010180 MARTINI 051581 WATSON 021482 XXXXXXXXXX XXXXXXX750000
04GERALD R. WICHERSHAM        05901DONALDSON 062479 XXX 120000
```

Below are some SAS statements that read data from MASTER:

```
DATA DEPTSUM;
   INFILE MASTER;
   INPUT @2 TYPE 1. @;
   IF TYPE=4 THEN DO;
      INPUT @3  DEPTMGR  $30.
            @33 BUDGTCOL    3.
            @36 EMPLCNT     2.
            @BUDGTCOL PAYBUDGT 6.;
      OUTPUT;
      END;
PROC PRINT;
   TITLE 'DATA SET DEPTSUM';
RUN;
```

The first INPUT statement in this example reads the TYPE field. In the second INPUT statement

☐ DEPTMGR is the department manager.
☐ BUDGTCOL is the column for the total department salary budget.
☐ EMPLCNT is the number of employees in the department. Data for each employee—the employee's name and hire date—begin in column 38.
☐ the location of the PAYBUDGT data is stored in variable BUDGTCOL. @BUDGTCOL in the last line of the INPUT statement directs the pointer to the value for PAYBUDGT.

Data set DEPTSUM is shown in **Output 1.16**.

Output 1.16
Skipping Variable-Length
Fields

		DATA SET DEPTSUM			
OBS	TYPE	DEPTMGR	BUDGTCOL	EMPLCNT	PAYBUDGT
1	4	MARGARET A. THOMAS	101	3	750000
2	4	GERALD R. WICHERSHAM	59	1	120000

Reading Variable-Length Fields

Again using the file MASTER, suppose that you want to read the two types of data—name and date of hire—for each employee in a department. The number of employees for any department is stored in the EMPLCNT variable. Using this variable, you can construct a DO loop that reads the two fields of employee data—EMPLNAME and HIREDATE—on each iteration of the loop. Sample statements for this situation are below:

```
DATA EMPDATA;
   INFILE MASTER;
   INPUT @2 TYPE 1. @;
   IF TYPE=4 THEN DO;
      INPUT @3  DEPTMGR  $30.
            @36 EMPLCNT   2. @;

*Loop through employee data;

      DO I=1 TO EMPLCNT;
         INPUT EMPLNAME : $9. HIREDATE MMDDYY6. @;
         OUTPUT;
         END;
      END;
   DROP I;
PROC PRINT;
   FORMAT HIREDATE MMDDYY6.;
   TITLE 'DATA SET EMPDATA';
RUN;
```

In this example, the variable I is initialized to 1. The DO loop reads data for an employee on each iteration. When the number of iterations equals the value stored in EMPLCNT, the loop ends. Note that the value of I is not supposed to be included in the output data set—the I variable is thus dropped. The resulting data set is in **Output 1.17**.

Output 1.17
Reading Variable-Length
Fields

```
                              DATA SET EMPDATA

 OBS    TYPE    DEPTMGR                EMPLCNT    EMPLNAME    HIREDATE

  1      4      MARGARET A. THOMAS        3       THOMPSON    010180
  2      4      MARGARET A. THOMAS        3       MARTINI     051581
  3      4      MARGARET A. THOMAS        3       WATSON      021482
  4      4      GERALD R. WICHERSHAM      1       DONALDSON   062479
```

These examples are useful for reading selected information from large external files. The data, once read into a SAS data set, can then be reorganized, edited, printed, stored, or analyzed by other SAS procedures. Many of these procedures are discussed in subsequent chapters.

2 Recoding Variables

This chapter describes a variety of ways in which you can work with the variables in a SAS data set—using programming statements and SAS functions to create new variables and to modify old ones.

Classifying Numeric Variables into Categories

Suppose your data contain age values ranging from 1 to 49. You want to group values by decade so that observations with age values less than 10 are in one age group, those with age values between 10 and 19 are in another, and so on. The following age values are used in examples throughout this chapter:

```
.
1
3
7
9
12
17
21
27
30
31
36
41
43
49
51
```

Note that two values are out of the specified range. A missing value, shown in the first data line, is smaller than any numeric value. The value 51, in the last data line, is larger than the specified range.

IF-THEN/ELSE Statements

When you read the data into a SAS data set, you can use IF-THEN/ELSE statements to assign values to a new variable AGEGROUP, depending on the values of AGE:

```
DATA GROUP1;
   INPUT AGE;
   IF AGE>=0 & AGE<10 THEN AGEGROUP=0;
   ELSE IF AGE>=10 & AGE<20 THEN AGEGROUP=10;
   ELSE IF AGE>=20 & AGE<30 THEN AGEGROUP=20;
   ELSE IF AGE>=30 & AGE<40 THEN AGEGROUP=30;
   ELSE IF AGE>=40 & AGE<50 THEN AGEGROUP=40;
   CARDS;
data lines
;
PROC PRINT;
   TITLE 'DATA SET GROUP1';
RUN;
```

The SAS data set GROUP1 appears in **Output 2.1.**

Output 2.1
SAS Data Set GROUP1

```
                     DATA SET GROUP1

              OBS    AGE    AGEGROUP

               1      .         .
               2      1         0
               3      3         0
               4      7         0
               5      9         0
               6     12        10
               7     17        10
               8     21        20
               9     27        20
              10     30        30
              11     31        30
              12     36        30
              13     41        40
              14     43        40
              15     49        40
              16     51         .
```

You can use the value of AGEGROUP to look at an individual's age group rather than his age in years. For example, the following statements produce frequency counts of the number of people in each AGEGROUP category:

```
PROC FREQ;
   TABLES AGEGROUP;
   TITLE 'FREQUENCY TABLE1';
RUN;
```

The results are shown in tabular form in **Output 2.2.**

```
                          FREQUENCY TABLE1

                                        CUMULATIVE    CUMULATIVE
      AGEGROUP    FREQUENCY    PERCENT   FREQUENCY      PERCENT
      -----------------------------------------------------------
         .            2           .          .             .
         0            4         28.6         4           28.6
        10            2         14.3         6           42.9
        20            2         14.3         8           57.1
        30            3         21.4        11           78.6
        40            3         21.4        14          100.0
```

Efficiency hint

When the IF condition in IF-THEN/ELSE statements is true, the SAS System executes the statement following the THEN. If the condition is false, the ELSE statement is executed. If you list the IF conditions by likelihood of occurrence, SAS executes fewer ELSE statements, and you save computer time.

SELECT Statement for Recoding Value Ranges

Operating systems: CMS, OS, VM/PC, and VSE

You can also use the SELECT statement to assign values to a new variable. Use it when you want to execute a SAS statement for all and not just some of the observations in the SAS data set being created. Under CMS, OS, VM/PC, and VSE, you can use the following SELECT statement to produce the same results as the IF-THEN/ELSE statements shown earlier:

```
DATA GROUP2;
   INPUT AGE;
   SELECT;
      WHEN (AGE>=0 & AGE<10) AGEGROUP=0;
      WHEN (AGE>=10 & AGE<20) AGEGROUP=10;
      WHEN (AGE>=20 & AGE<30) AGEGROUP=20;
      WHEN (AGE>=30 & AGE<40) AGEGROUP=30;
      WHEN (AGE>=40 & AGE<50) AGEGROUP=40;
      OTHERWISE;
      END;
   CARDS;
data lines
;
PROC PRINT;
   TITLE 'DATA SET GROUP2';
RUN;
```

The results of this recoding are shown in **Output 2.3.**

Output 2.3
SAS Data Set GROUP2

```
                              DATA SET GROUP2

                      OBS     AGE     AGEGROUP

                       1       .          .
                       2       1          0
                       3       3          0
                       4       7          0
                       5       9          0
                       6      12         10
                       7      17         10
                       8      21         20
                       9      27         20
                      10      30         30
                      11      31         30
                      12      36         30
                      13      41         40
                      14      43         40
                      15      49         40
                      16      51          .
```

Bounded Expressions in IF Statements

When checking to see if the value of AGE lies within a range of values, you can surround the variable AGE in the IF statement with comparison operators:

```
DATA GROUP3;
   INPUT AGE;
   IF  0<=AGE<10 THEN AGEGROUP=0;
   ELSE IF 10<=AGE<20 THEN AGEGROUP=10;
   ELSE IF 20<=AGE<30 THEN AGEGROUP=20;
   ELSE IF 30<=AGE<40 THEN AGEGROUP=30;
   ELSE IF 40<=AGE<50 THEN AGEGROUP=40;
   CARDS;
data lines
;
PROC PRINT;
   TITLE 'DATA SET GROUP3';
RUN;
```

The results are shown in **Output 2.4.**

Output 2.4
SAS Data Set GROUP3

```
                              DATA SET GROUP3

                      OBS     AGE     AGEGROUP

                       1       .          .
                       2       1          0
                       3       3          0
                       4       7          0
                       5       9          0
                       6      12         10
                       7      17         10
                       8      21         20
                       9      27         20
                      10      30         30
                      11      31         30
                      12      36         30
                      13      41         40
                      14      43         40
                      15      49         40
                      16      51          .
```

The results shown in **Output 2.4** are the same as for the earlier examples. An invalid AGE value—one not in the range 0 to 49—results in a missing value for AGEGROUP.

Descending Checks   You can also use the method of descending checks to do this recoding. In this case, do not use the ELSE statement since more than one of the IF conditions can be true for an observation. For the following example, the method of descending checks is preferable to using the ELSE statement. It is especially useful under the AOS/VS, PRIMOS, and VMS operating systems, which cannot use the SELECT method shown earlier.

```
DATA GROUP4;
   INPUT AGE;
   AGEGROUP=40;
   IF AGE<40 THEN AGEGROUP=30;
   IF AGE<30 THEN AGEGROUP=20;
   IF AGE<20 THEN AGEGROUP=10;
   IF AGE<10 THEN AGEGROUP=0;
   CARDS;
data lines
;
PROC PRINT;
   TITLE 'DATA SET AGEGROUP4';
RUN;
```

The results appear in **Output 2.5.**

Output 2.5
SAS Data Set GROUP4

```
                    DATA SET GROUP4

           OBS    AGE    AGEGROUP

            1       .        0
            2       1        0
            3       3        0
            4       7        0
            5       9        0
            6      12       10
            7      17       10
            8      21       20
            9      27       20
           10      30       30
           11      31       30
           12      36       30
           13      41       40
           14      43       40
           15      49       40
           16      51       40
```

With this method, an observation may be assigned an AGEGROUP value several times as each IF statement is evaluated. In fact, for an observation with an AGE value under 10, AGEGROUP is first set to 40 and then to 30, 20, 10, and finally 0. For any AGE value greater than 40, AGEGROUP is 40. If AGE is any value less than 10 (including missing), AGEGROUP is 0.

Logical Expressions

You can also use logical expressions for recoding. The IF statements in the preceding example are combined into one statement:

```
DATA GROUP5;
   INPUT AGE;
   AGEGROUP=10*(10<=AGE<20)+20*(20<=AGE<30)+
            30*(30<=AGE<40)+40*(40<=AGE<50);
   CARDS;
data lines
;
PROC PRINT;
   TITLE 'DATA SET GROUP5';
RUN;
```

The results are shown in **Output 2.6**.

Output 2.6
SAS Data Set GROUP5

```
                      DATA SET GROUP5

            OBS     AGE     AGEGROUP

             1       .         0
             2       1         0
             3       3         0
             4       7         0
             5       9         0
             6      12        10
             7      17        10
             8      21        20
             9      27        20
            10      30        30
            11      31        30
            12      36        30
            13      41        40
            14      43        40
            15      49        40
            16      51         0
```

This method relies on the fact that the SAS System evaluates logical expressions as either 1 (true) or 0 (false). For example, suppose the value of AGE is 13 for the current observation. The logical expression

```
(10<=AGE<20)
```

is 1 since AGE is greater than or equal to 10 and less than 20. SAS multiplies 1 by the number 10. The other logical expressions are false for this observation, and the resulting AGEGROUP value is 10.

You can use the following alternative method, for which more than one of the logical expressions may be true:

```
DATA GROUP6;
   INPUT AGE;
   AGEGROUP=10*(AGE>=10)+10*(AGE>=20)+10*(AGE>=30)
           +10*(AGE>=40);
   CARDS;
data lines
;
PROC PRINT;
   TITLE 'DATA SET GROUP6';
RUN;
```

The results are shown in **Output 2.7.**

```
                        DATA SET GROUP6

                OBS     AGE     AGEGROUP

                 1       .          0
                 2       1          0
                 3       3          0
                 4       7          0
                 5       9          0
                 6      12         10
                 7      17         10
                 8      21         20
                 9      27         20
                10      30         30
                11      31         30
                12      36         30
                13      41         40
                14      43         40
                15      49         40
                16      51         40
```

In the first example that uses logical expressions (data set GROUP5), AGEGROUP is 0 when AGE is out of the normal range. Thus, AGEGROUP is 0 for AGE values greater than or equal to 50 and for AGE values less than 10. In the second example (data set GROUP6), any AGE value less than 10 results in a 0 for AGEGROUP; any AGE value greater than or equal to 40 results in a 40 for AGEGROUP.

Clever coding

An easier way to accomplish this recoding is with the following shorthand expression:

```
DATA GROUP7;
   INPUT AGE;
   AGEGROUP=INT(AGE/10)*10;
   CARDS;
data lines
;
PROC PRINT;
   TITLE 'DATA SET GROUP7';
RUN;
```

The results appear in **Output 2.8.**

Output 2.8
SAS Data Set GROUP7

```
                      DATA SET GROUP7

              OBS     AGE     AGEGROUP

               1       .          .
               2       1          0
               3       3          0
               4       7          0
               5       9          0
               6      12         10
               7      17         10
               8      21         20
               9      27         20
              10      30         30
              11      31         30
              12      36         30
              13      41         40
              14      43         40
              15      49         40
              16      51         50
```

The SAS System first divides AGE by 10, yielding a number with one decimal place. For example, the AGE value 23 becomes 2.3. The INT function results in the integer portion of the number, in this case, 2. SAS then multiplies 2 by 10 to produce the AGEGROUP value 20. In this case, missing AGE values result in a missing value for AGEGROUP.

Redefining Input Fields

You can also recode as you read the variable values. Consider this DATA step:

```
DATA GROUP8;
   INPUT AGE 1-2 AGEGRP 1;
   AGEGROUP=AGEGRP*10;
   IF AGEGRP=. THEN AGEGROUP=0;
   CARDS;
 .
 2
13
24
36
47
51
;
PROC PRINT;
   TITLE 'DATA SET GROUP8';
RUN;
```

The results are shown in **Output 2.9.**

```
                          DATA SET GROUP8

              OBS     AGE     AGEGRP    AGEGROUP

               1       .         .          0
               2       2         .          0
               3      13         1         10
               4      24         2         20
               5      36         3         30
               6      47         4         40
               7      51         5         50
```

The INPUT statement causes the SAS System to read AGE's value from columns 1 and 2 of the input line. Then SAS reads the variable AGEGRP from column 1; AGEGRP contains the first digit of the variable AGE. (AGE values must be right-aligned in the first two columns of the input line so that when an AGE value is less than 10, column 1 is blank.)

The next statement multiplies the one-digit value of AGEGRP by 10, producing the AGEGROUP value. The IF statement checks for missing AGEGRP values (which occur when AGE is a single digit or missing) and sets the AGEGROUP value to 0 for those observations.

Classifying Character Variables into Categories

Suppose you use this INPUT statement to read the values of AGE:

```
INPUT AGE $CHAR2.;
```

Using the format $CHAR2. that maintains leading blanks in the value, the SAS System reads AGE from the first two columns of the input data line. With AGE defined as a character variable, you can use some special SAS features to recode its values.

Character Comparisons — Normally, when you compare two character values, SAS extends the shorter value with blanks to the length of the longer value for the comparison. For example, because AGE has a length of two characters, the SAS statement

```
IF AGE='4' THEN AGEGROUP=40;
```

is equivalent to

```
IF AGE='4 ' THEN AGEGROUP=40;
```

None of the AGE values meet this IF condition.

However, by using a colon after the comparison operator, you can prevent the SAS System from adding blanks to the end of the value in a comparison. SAS then truncates the longer value to the length of the shorter value for the comparison. For example, the SAS statement

```
IF AGE=:'4' THEN AGEGROUP=40;
```

compares the first character of AGE and 4. If AGE's value falls
between 40 and 49, AGEGROUP has a value of 40. SAS truncates and
extends values only during the comparison. The original values of
AGE retain their lengths.

The following statements recode the character values of AGE into
the new variable AGEGROUP:

```
DATA GROUP9;
   INPUT AGE $CHAR2.;
   IF AGE=:' ' THEN AGEGROUP=0;
   ELSE IF AGE=:'1' THEN AGEGROUP=10;
   ELSE IF AGE=:'2' THEN AGEGROUP=20;
   ELSE IF AGE=:'3' THEN AGEGROUP=30;
   ELSE IF AGE=:'4' THEN AGEGROUP=40;
   CARDS;
data lines
;
PROC PRINT;
   TITLE 'DATA SET GROUP9';
RUN;
```

The results are shown in **Output 2.10.**

Output 2.10
SAS Data Set GROUP9

```
                        DATA SET GROUP9

                OBS     AGE     AGEGROUP

                 1       .          0
                 2       2          0
                 3      13         10
                 4      24         20
                 5      36         30
                 6      47         40
                 7      51          .
```

If AGE has a missing value (a blank), the first IF statement is true,
and AGEGROUP is 0. However, AGEGROUP has a missing value if
AGE begins with a character other than blank, 1, 2, 3, or 4.

Substringing and
Concatenation

You can perform the recoding above more simply with the following
DATA step:

```
DATA GROUP10;
   INPUT AGE $CHAR2.;
   AGEGROUP=SUBSTR(AGE,1,1)||'0';
   CARDS;
 .
 2
13
24
36
47
51
;
PROC PRINT;
   TITLE 'DATA SET GROUP10';
RUN;
```

The results are shown in **Output 2.11**.

Output 2.11
SAS Data Set GROUP10

```
                    DATA SET GROUP10

         OBS    AGE     AGEGROUP

          1      .          0
          2      2          0
          3     13         10
          4     24         20
          5     36         30
          6     47         40
          7     51         50
```

Again, the recoding depends on the values of AGE being right-aligned in the input lines. The assignment statement uses the SUBSTR function to get the first digit of AGE. Then the concatenation operator || joins this first digit of AGE and the character 0, forming the new character variable AGEGROUP.

Recoding Many Variables: Arrays

Suppose your data set contains answers to eighteen questions. When the responses are coded, a 9 indicates that an answer has been left blank. You want to recode the 9s to a SAS missing value. Use these SAS statements:

```
DATA ALL;
   DROP I;
   INPUT QUEST1-QUEST18;
   ARRAY QUESTION{18} QUEST1-QUEST18;
   DO I=1 TO 18;
      IF QUESTION{I}=9 THEN QUESTION{I}=.;
      END;
   CARDS;
data lines
;
```

The array QUESTION has as elements the eighteen variables QUEST1-QUEST18. For each observation, SAS executes the statements between DO and END eighteen times, once for each of the variables QUEST1 through QUEST18. When one of these variables is 9, the assignment statement changes the 9 to a missing value.

To recode every value of 9 for all the numeric variables in a SAS data set, use these statements:

```
DATA CHANGE;
   INPUT A B C D E F;
   ARRAY EVERY(*) _NUMERIC_;
   DO J=1 TO DIM(EVERY);
      IF EVERY(J)=9 THEN EVERY(J)=.;
      END;
   DROP J;
   CARDS;
0 0 0 0 0 0
1 1 1 1 1 1
2 9 2 9 2 9
3 3 3 3 3 3
1 9 1 9 1 9
;
PROC PRINT;
   TITLE 'DATA SET CHANGE';
RUN;
```

The results appear in **Output 2.12.**

Output 2.12
SAS Data Set CHANGE

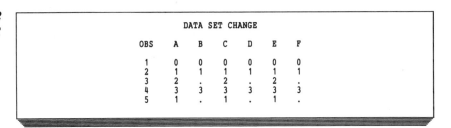

```
                      DATA SET CHANGE

          OBS    A    B    C    D    E    F

           1     0    0    0    0    0    0
           2     1    1    1    1    1    1
           3     2    .    2    .    2    .
           4     3    3    3    3    3    3
           5     1    .    1    .    1    .
```

The special word _NUMERIC_ tells the SAS System to include all numeric variables as elements of the array EVERY; the dimension of EVERY is the number of numeric variables.

Recoding Variable Values for Printing

When your only reason for recoding is to display the recoded values, use the FORMAT procedure to assign labels to the values of your variables. By assigning the same label to groups of values, you can change the display without changing the values in the data set. For example, the statements

```
PROC FORMAT;
    VALUE AGEFMT   0-9=' 0'
                  10-19='10'
                  20-29='20'
                  30-39='30'
                  40-49='40';
```

create a format called AGEFMT. You can use the value labels defined by AGEFMT. to print the AGE values. For example, these statements give you frequency counts on the grouped values:

```
PROC FREQ;
    TABLES AGE;
    FORMAT AGE AGEFMT.;
    TITLE 'FREQUENCY TABLE2';
RUN;
```

The results are shown in **Output 2.13.**

Output 2.13
Frequency Counts for
Grouped Values

```
                          FREQUENCY TABLE2

                                        CUMULATIVE   CUMULATIVE
      AGE    FREQUENCY    PERCENT       FREQUENCY     PERCENT
      ----------------------------------------------------------
       .         1          .              .            .
       0         4        26.7             4          26.7
      10         2        13.3             6          40.0
      20         2        13.3             8          53.3
      30         3        20.0            11          73.3
      40         3        20.0            14          93.3
      51         1         6.7            15         100.0
```

SAS uses the format AGEFMT. to print the values of AGE as age group categories; the frequency table shows the number in each category. (Some SAS procedures, such as FREQ, PLOT, and CHART, restrict the length of value labels to 16. This restriction applies only to the procedures that print the labels; PROC FORMAT allows a length of 40.) AGE values of missing (.) and 51 were not defined by PROC FORMAT and thus remain unformatted in the table.

**Recoding Only
Certain Values**

You may want to highlight certain values of a variable when you print them. Suppose you print a daily report for a bank that shows the current balance in each checking account. Any time a negative balance occurs, you want to print OVERDRAWN instead of the negative value. Use PROC FORMAT:

```
PROC FORMAT;
    VALUE ACCT LOW-<0='OVERDRAWN';
```

This VALUE statement assigns the label OVERDRAWN to all values from the lowest nonmissing value of BALANCE up to, but not including, 0. The actual amount is shown for all other values, including missing values. When a VALUE statement includes some but not all of a variable's values, using the format to print the variable produces a mixture of formatted and unformatted values.

Now use the format ACCT. to print the values of BALANCE:

```
PROC PRINT;
   FORMAT BALANCE ACCT.;
   TITLE 'DATA SET REPORT';
RUN;
```

Alternatively, you can use a PUT statement:

```
PUT BALANCE ACCT.;
```

The results of this recoding are shown in **Output 2.14.**

Output 2.14
SAS Data Set REPORT

```
                      DATA SET REPORT

          OBS      ACCTNUM      BALANCE

           1        889            .
           2       1234          456.9
           3       3534          67.34
           4       2033           0.24
           5       4909         2545.67
           6       2039        OVERDRAWN
           7       8029            0
           8       9942        OVERDRAWN
```

Recoding Numeric Values into Character Values and Vice Versa

You can use a format and the PUT function to create new character values with values equal to the value labels. The PUT function (similar to the PUT STRING feature in PL/I) has the form

```
PUT(argument,format.)
```

PUT causes SAS to "write" a value of *argument* (usually a variable name) using a *format* you specify. Either a SAS format or a format you have defined by PROC FORMAT can be used. Then use an assignment statement to assign the result to a variable. The statement

```
AGEGROUP=PUT(AGE,AGEFMT.);
```

causes the SAS System to "write" values of AGE using the AGEFMT. format and to assign the result to the character variable AGEGROUP. The results are shown in **Output 2.15.**

Output 2.15
SAS Data Set GROUP11

```
                         DATA SET GROUP11

                  OBS      AGE     AGEGROUP

                   1        .          .
                   2        1          0
                   3        3          0
                   4        7          0
                   5        9          0
                   6       12         10
                   7       17         10
                   8       21         20
                   9       27         20
                  10       30         30
                  11       31         30
                  12       36         30
                  13       41         40
                  14       43         40
                  15       49         40
                  16       51         51
```

Similarly, using an informat you specify, the INPUT function
"reads" a value. The form is

```
INPUT(argument,informat.)
```

where *argument* is usually a variable name. By using the INPUT
function with a numeric informat, you can read character values like
those in AGEGROUP and produce numeric values. Then use an
assignment statement to assign the result to a variable. The following
statement "reads" the values of AGEGROUP as numeric and assigns
the result to the numeric value AGEGRP:

```
AGEGRP=INPUT(AGEGROUP,2.);
```

The results are shown in **Output 2.16**.

Output 2.16
SAS Data Set GROUP12

```
                        DATA SET GROUP12

              OBS     AGE    AGEGROUP    AGEGRP

               1       .         .          .
               2       1         0          0
               3       3         0          0
               4       7         0          0
               5       9         0          0
               6      12        10         10
               7      17        10         10
               8      21        20         20
               9      27        20         20
              10      30        30         30
              11      31        30         30
              12      36        30         30
              13      41        40         40
              14      43        40         40
              15      49        40         40
              16      51        51         51
```

Recoding Multiple-Response Questions

In survey work, some questions permit more than one response. One way in which you can analyze responses to such questions is to make each possible combination of answers the values of a new variable. For example, consider the following question:

I use SAS software often for (circle all that apply)

a. retrieving data.
b. data management.
c. statistical analysis.
d. report writing.

Each respondent is asked to circle all the answers that apply. It is important for you to know how many find the report-writing features of the SAS System useful and to know how many use each combination of features.

From the question above, four variables result. If A is circled on the questionnaire, the variable A is coded as 1. If A is not circled, A is coded 0. The variables B, C, and D also have a value of 1 when the corresponding response is circled and 0 otherwise.

Using the statements below, you can examine the frequency distribution of combinations of these variables crossed with values of another variable, such as SEX:

```
PROC FREQ;
   TABLES SEX*A*B*C*D;
RUN;
```

However, the eight tables produced by these statements are difficult to study. To combine all the information into one table, create a single variable that represents each combination of A, B, C, and D. Consider a single variable ABCD formed by concatenating the variables A, B, C, and D. This is a binary number because it contains only 1s and 0s. You can transform a binary value to a decimal value with this equation:

$$\text{NEWVAR} = A(2^3) + B(2^2) + C(2^1) + D(2^0)$$

Consider this transformation as a SAS statement:

```
NEWVAR=A*2**3+B*2**2+C*2+D;
```

NEWVAR is the decimal equivalent of the binary number ABCD. The following table shows the values of A, B, C, and D that are represented by NEWVAR's values:

NEWVAR	A	B	C	D	Meaning
0	0	0	0	0	circled none of the responses
1	0	0	0	1	circled D only
2	0	0	1	0	circled C only
3	0	0	1	1	circled C and D
4	0	1	0	0	circled B only
5	0	1	0	1	circled B and D
6	0	1	1	0	circled B and C
7	0	1	1	1	circled B, C, and D
8	1	0	0	0	circled A only
9	1	0	0	1	circled A and D
10	1	0	1	0	circled A and C
11	1	0	1	1	circled A, C, and D
12	1	1	0	0	circled A and B
13	1	1	0	1	circled A, B, and D
14	1	1	1	0	circled A, B, and C
15	1	1	1	1	circled all responses

You can use PROC FORMAT to define labels for the values of NEWVAR:

```
PROC FORMAT;
    VALUE DECODE   0='NONE'
                   1='D ONLY'
                   2='C ONLY'
                      .
                      .
                      .
                  15='A, B, C, and D';
```

Then use a FORMAT statement with PROC FREQ:

```
PROC FREQ;
    TABLES NEWVAR*SEX;
    FORMAT NEWVAR DECODE.;
    TITLE 'FREQUENCY TABLE3';
RUN;
```

The number who responded to each of the possible combinations is shown in **Output 2.17.**

Output 2.17
Frequency Counts from
Consumer Survey

```
                              FREQUENCY TABLE3

                            TABLE OF NEWVAR BY SEX

             NEWVAR        SEX

             FREQUENCY  |
               PERCENT  |
               ROW PCT  |
               COL PCT  |F       |M       |   TOTAL
             -----------+--------+--------+
             NONE       |      1 |      0 |      1
                        |   5.56 |   0.00 |   5.56
                        | 100.00 |   0.00 |
                        |  11.11 |   0.00 |
             -----------+--------+--------+
             D ONLY     |      1 |      0 |      1
                        |   5.56 |   0.00 |   5.56
                        | 100.00 |   0.00 |
                        |  11.11 |   0.00 |
             -----------+--------+--------+
             C ONLY     |      0 |      1 |      1
                        |   0.00 |   5.56 |   5.56
                        |   0.00 | 100.00 |
                        |   0.00 |  11.11 |
             -----------+--------+--------+
             C AND D    |      0 |      1 |      1
                        |   0.00 |   5.56 |   5.56
                        |   0.00 | 100.00 |
                        |   0.00 |  11.11 |
             -----------+--------+--------+
             B ONLY     |      0 |      1 |      1
                        |   0.00 |   5.56 |   5.56
                        |   0.00 | 100.00 |
                        |   0.00 |  11.11 |
             -----------+--------+--------+
             B AND D    |      2 |      0 |      2
                        |  11.11 |   0.00 |  11.11
                        | 100.00 |   0.00 |
                        |  22.22 |   0.00 |
             -----------+--------+--------+
             B AND C    |      1 |      0 |      1
                        |   5.56 |   0.00 |   5.56
                        | 100.00 |   0.00 |
                        |  11.11 |   0.00 |
             -----------+--------+--------+
             B,C,AND D  |      1 |      1 |      2
                        |   5.56 |   5.56 |  11.11
                        |  50.00 |  50.00 |
                        |  11.11 |  11.11 |
             -----------+--------+--------+
             TOTAL             9        9       18
                           50.00    50.00   100.00

             (CONTINUED)
```

```
                              FREQUENCY TABLE3

                            TABLE OF NEWVAR BY SEX

             NEWVAR        SEX

             FREQUENCY  |
               PERCENT  |
               ROW PCT  |
               COL PCT  |F       |M       |   TOTAL
             -----------+--------+--------+
             A ONLY     |      0 |      1 |      1
                        |   0.00 |   5.56 |   5.56
                        |   0.00 | 100.00 |
                        |   0.00 |  11.11 |
             -----------+--------+--------+
             A AND D    |      0 |      1 |      1
                        |   0.00 |   5.56 |   5.56
                        |   0.00 | 100.00 |
                        |   0.00 |  11.11 |
             -----------+--------+--------+
             A AND C    |      0 |      1 |      1
                        |   0.00 |   5.56 |   5.56
                        |   0.00 | 100.00 |
                        |   0.00 |  11.11 |
```

```
-------------+--------+--------+
A, C, AND D  |    1 |     0 |      1
             | 5.56 |  0.00 |   5.56
             |100.00 |  0.00 |
             | 11.11 |  0.00 |
-------------+--------+--------+
A AND B      |    0 |     1 |      1
             | 0.00 |  5.56 |   5.56
             | 0.00 |100.00 |
             | 0.00 | 11.11 |
-------------+--------+--------+
A,B, AND D   |    1 |     0 |      1
             | 5.56 |  0.00 |   5.56
             |100.00 |  0.00 |
             | 11.11 |  0.00 |
-------------+--------+--------+
A,B, AND C   |    0 |     1 |      1
             | 0.00 |  5.56 |   5.56
             | 0.00 |100.00 |
             | 0.00 | 11.11 |
-------------+--------+--------+
A,B,C, AND D |    1 |     0 |      1
             | 5.56 |  0.00 |   5.56
             |100.00 |  0.00 |
             | 11.11 |  0.00 |
-------------+--------+--------+
TOTAL             9       9      18
               50.00   50.00  100.00
```

Recoding Arrays

Suppose you ask the following questions:

Circle the number(s) that correspond to the appliances you plan to purchase during the next year:

1. refrigerator
2. washing machine
3. dryer
4. dishwasher
5. food processor

Circle the number(s) that correspond to the appliance stores where you plan to shop for these items:

1. West Products, Inc.
2. ABC Appliance Mart
3. Horace's Wholesale Warehouse
4. Franklin's

What you want

You want to look at a table that shows, for each store, the number of appliances that might be sold there during the next year.

	West	ABC	Horace's	Franklin's
refrigerator				
washing machine				
dryer				
dishwasher				
food processor				

The data are coded so that five fields correspond to the first question. If a respondent circles the numbers 1, 3, and 5 from the list of appliances, fields 1, 3, and 5 are coded 1, and fields 2 and 4 are coded 0. Similarly, four fields correspond to the second question. The data lines (which begin with the customer's ID) look like this:

```
0001 0 1 1 0 1 0 1 0 1
0002 1 0 0 1 0 1 0 1 0
```

In a DATA step, you can input the appliance fields as variables P1-P5 and the store fields as variables S1-S4.

Because the response fields are contained in separate variables, the FREQ procedure cannot produce the table you want: it forms rows and columns from values of variables, not from different variables. With some recoding, however, you can create new variables from which PROC FREQ can produce the table. Consider these statements:

```
DATA TEMP;
   INPUT ID P1-P5 S1-S4;
   ARRAY P(5) P1-P5;
   ARRAY S(4) S1-S4;
   DO J=1 TO 5;
      IF P(J)=1 THEN DO I=1 TO 4;
         IF S(I)=1 THEN DO;
            PRODUCT=J;
            STORE=I;
            OUTPUT;
            END;
         END;
      END;
   KEEP ID PRODUCT STORE;
   CARDS;
0001 0 1 1 0 1 0 1 0 1
0002 1 0 0 1 0 1 0 1 0
;
PROC PRINT;
   TITLE 'DATA SET TEMP';
RUN;
```

The results are shown in **Output 2.18.**

Output 2.18
SAS Data Set TEMP

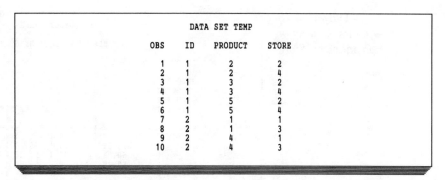

```
                         DATA SET TEMP

              OBS    ID    PRODUCT    STORE

               1      1       2         2
               2      1       2         4
               3      1       3         2
               4      1       3         4
               5      1       5         2
               6      1       5         4
               7      2       1         1
               8      2       1         3
               9      2       4         1
              10      2       4         3
```

The SAS System outputs a new observation to data set TEMP each time it finds a combination of P and S variables both equal to 1. In other words, when SAS finds a value of 1 for one of the variables P1-P5, it searches the variables S1 through S4 for a value of 1. When it finds a 1 for one of the S variables, it outputs an observation with two new variables: PRODUCT, the current value of the index variable J, and STORE, the current value of I. Therefore, when P1 is 1, J's value (and thus PRODUCT's value) is 1; when S3 is 1, I's value (and thus STORE's value) is 3.

The respondent with ID=0002 indicates that she plans to buy a refrigerator and a dishwasher in the next year and that she will shop at West and Horace's. For that observation, the variables P1, P4, S1, and S3 are all 1; all other variables are 0. Thus, the following combinations generate the four observations for ID=0002 in data set TEMP:

```
P1  S1
P1  S3
P4  S1
P4  S3
```

Use PROC FORMAT to establish value labels for PRODUCT and STORE, and then use PROC FREQ to produce the table you want:

```
PROC FORMAT;
   VALUE PRODFMT   1='REFRIG'
                   2='WASHER'
                   3='DRYER'
                   4='DISHWASHER'
                   5='FOOD PROC.';
   VALUE STFMT     1='WEST'
                   2='ABC'
                   3='HORACE''S'
                   4='FRANKLIN''S';
PROC FREQ;
   TABLES PRODUCT*STORE;
   FORMAT STORE STFMT. PRODUCT PRODFMT.;
   TITLE 'FREQUENCY TABLE4';
RUN;
```

The results appear in **Output 2.19.**

Output 2.19
Frequency Counts of
Product by Store

```
                              FREQUENCY TABLE4

                         TABLE OF PRODUCT BY STORE

     PRODUCT    STORE

     FREQUENCY  |
       PERCENT  |
       ROW PCT  |
       COL PCT  |WEST    |ABC     |HORACE'S|FRANKLIN|
                |        |        |        |'S      |   TOTAL
     -----------+--------+--------+--------+--------+
     REFRIG     |      1 |      0 |      1 |      0 |      2
                |  10.00 |   0.00 |  10.00 |   0.00 |  20.00
                |  50.00 |   0.00 |  50.00 |   0.00 |
                |  50.00 |   0.00 |  50.00 |   0.00 |
     -----------+--------+--------+--------+--------+
     WASHER     |      0 |      1 |      0 |      1 |      2
                |   0.00 |  10.00 |   0.00 |  10.00 |  20.00
                |   0.00 |  50.00 |   0.00 |  50.00 |
                |   0.00 |  33.33 |   0.00 |  33.33 |
     -----------+--------+--------+--------+--------+
     DRYER      |      0 |      1 |      0 |      1 |      2
                |   0.00 |  10.00 |   0.00 |  10.00 |  20.00
                |   0.00 |  50.00 |   0.00 |  50.00 |
                |   0.00 |  33.33 |   0.00 |  33.33 |
     -----------+--------+--------+--------+--------+
     DISHWASHER |      1 |      0 |      1 |      0 |      2
                |  10.00 |   0.00 |  10.00 |   0.00 |  20.00
                |  50.00 |   0.00 |  50.00 |   0.00 |
                |  50.00 |   0.00 |  50.00 |   0.00 |
     -----------+--------+--------+--------+--------+
     FOOD PROC. |      0 |      1 |      0 |      1 |      2
                |   0.00 |  10.00 |   0.00 |  10.00 |  20.00
                |   0.00 |  50.00 |   0.00 |  50.00 |
                |   0.00 |  33.33 |   0.00 |  33.33 |
     -----------+--------+--------+--------+--------+
     TOTAL            2        3        2        3       10
                  20.00    30.00    20.00    30.00   100.00
```

3 Reshaping Your Data

Before analyzing your data, you can change the arrangement of the values in the data set, using only certain observations or variables for your analysis, or combining information from several SAS data sets. This chapter describes several ways to reshape data by forming new SAS data sets from existing ones.

Subsetting Observations

The following SAS statements create data set CLASS:

```
DATA CLASS;
   INPUT NAME $ SEX $ AGE HEIGHT WEIGHT;
   CARDS;
data lines
;
PROC PRINT;
   TITLE 'DATA SET CLASS';
RUN;
```

The CLASS data set appears in **Output 3.1.**

Output 3.1
SAS Data Set CLASS

```
                          DATA SET CLASS

        OBS    NAME      SEX   AGE   HEIGHT   WEIGHT

          1    ALFRED     M     14    69.0    112.5
          2    ALICE      F     13    56.5     84.0
          3    BARBARA    F     13    65.3     98.0
          4    CAROL      F     14    62.8    102.5
          5    HENRY      M     14    63.5    102.5
          6    JAMES      M     12    57.3     83.0
          7    JANE       F     12    59.8     84.5
          8    JANET      F     15    62.5    112.5
          9    JEFFREY    M     13    62.5     84.0
         10    JOHN       M     12    59.0     99.5
         11    JOYCE      F     11    51.3     50.5
         12    JUDY       F     14    64.3     90.0
         13    LOUISE     F     12    56.3     77.0
         14    MARY       F     15    66.5    112.0
         15    PHILIP     M     16    72.0    150.0
         16    ROBERT     M     12    64.8    128.0
         17    RONALD     M     15    67.0    133.0
         18    THOMAS     M     11    57.5     85.0
         19    WILLIAM    M     15    66.5    112.0
```

Ways to Subset Observations

Suppose you want a subset of CLASS that contains only certain observations. There are several ways to create such a subset:

- □ a subsetting IF statement
- □ a DELETE statement
- □ an OUTPUT statement.

Subsetting IF Statement

Use a subsetting IF statement in your DATA step to give a condition that must be met to add an observation to the new data set. Use the subsetting IF statement when it is easier to specify a condition for including observations. For example, to use the subsetting IF to include only those observations from CLASS that have a SEX value of M, use the following SAS statements:

```
DATA MALES;
   SET CLASS;
   IF SEX='M';
PROC PRINT;
   TITLE 'DATA SET MALES';
RUN;
```

The MALES data set is shown in **Output 3.2.**

Output 3.2
SAS Data Set MALES

```
                        DATA SET MALES

      OBS    NAME      SEX    AGE    HEIGHT    WEIGHT

        1    ALFRED     M      14     69.0      112.5
        2    HENRY      M      14     63.5      102.5
        3    JAMES      M      12     57.3       83.0
        4    JEFFREY    M      13     62.5       84.0
        5    JOHN       M      12     59.0       99.5
        6    PHILIP     M      16     72.0      150.0
        7    ROBERT     M      12     64.8      128.0
        8    RONALD     M      15     67.0      133.0
        9    THOMAS     M      11     57.5       85.0
       10    WILLIAM    M      15     66.5      112.0
```

DELETE Statement

The subsetting IF statement

```
IF SEX='M';
```

is equivalent to the statement

```
IF SEX¬='M' THEN DELETE;
```

The DELETE statement indicates which observations not to add to the new data set. You usually use the DELETE statement when it is easier to specify a condition for excluding observations from the data set. For example, to delete all males from the CLASS data set to form a new data set, FEMALES, use these statements:

```
DATA FEMALES;
   SET CLASS;
   IF SEX='M' THEN DELETE;
PROC PRINT;
   TITLE 'DATA SET FEMALES';
RUN;
```

The FEMALES data set appears in **Output 3.3.**

Output 3.3
SAS Data Set FEMALES

```
                    DATA SET FEMALES

    OBS    NAME      SEX    AGE    HEIGHT    WEIGHT

     1     ALICE      F     13      56.5      84.0
     2     BARBARA    F     13      65.3      98.0
     3     CAROL      F     14      62.8     102.5
     4     JANE       F     12      59.8      84.5
     5     JANET      F     15      62.5     112.5
     6     JOYCE      F     11      51.3      50.5
     7     JUDY       F     14      64.3      90.0
     8     LOUISE     F     12      56.3      77.0
     9     MARY       F     15      66.5     112.0
```

Are these statements identical?

When the variable SEX has only two values, M and F, the statements

```
IF SEX='F';
```

and

```
IF SEX='M' THEN DELETE;
```

have the same effect. But what if some observations contain incorrect or missing SEX values? The subsetting IF statement above prevents observations with any value other than F from being added to the new data set. But the IF-THEN statement prevents only observations with a SEX value of M from being added; observations with any other SEX value (including incorrect or missing values) are added to the new data set. Thus, these two statements are not always equivalent. See **Creating Multiple Data Sets** later in this chapter for other ways to accommodate incorrect or missing values.

OUTPUT Statement

You can use the OUTPUT statement to explicitly add an observation to a new data set. If you do not include an OUTPUT statement in a DATA step, SAS automatically writes the current observation to the new data set when it

□ executes a RETURN statement
□ reaches the end of the statements in that step.

When an OUTPUT statement does appear in a DATA step, SAS no longer automatically outputs observations. Instead, SAS adds an observation to a new data set only when it executes an OUTPUT statement.

Here is an example of using the OUTPUT statement to create a subset of 12-year-olds:

```
DATA AGE12;
   SET CLASS;
   IF AGE=12 THEN OUTPUT;
PROC PRINT;
   TITLE 'DATA SET AGE12';
RUN;
```

Substituting the statement

```
IF AGE=12;
```

produces the same results in this example since only observations where AGE=12 are added to the data set. **Output 3.4** shows the new data set.

Output 3.4
Data Set Created by
Selecting a Variable

```
                         DATA SET AGE12

          OBS    NAME     SEX    AGE    HEIGHT    WEIGHT

           1     JAMES     M      12     57.3      83.0
           2     JANE      F      12     59.8      84.5
           3     JOHN      M      12     59.0      99.5
           4     LOUISE    F      12     56.3      77.0
           5     ROBERT    M      12     64.8     128.0
```

A Comparison of Subsetting IF, DELETE, and OUTPUT

Here are some guidelines for using the subsetting IF, DELETE, and OUTPUT statements.

□ Use the subsetting IF statement when it is easier to specify a condition for including observations in the data set.
□ Use the DELETE statement when it is easier to specify a condition for excluding observations from the data set.
□ Use the OUTPUT statement when you need to control the normal output of observations.

What happens when each of these statements is executed?

□ When SAS executes a subsetting IF statement and the IF condition is false, it immediately stops executing statements for the current observation and returns to the top of the DATA step. The observation is not added to the data set being built. When the IF condition is true for an observation, SAS continues to the next statement in the DATA step.
□ When a DELETE statement is executed, SAS acts as it does when the condition in a subsetting IF statement is false: it immediately stops executing statements for the current observation and returns to the top of the DATA step. The observation is not added to the data set being built.

□ When SAS executes an OUTPUT statement, it immediately adds the current observation to the data set being built and continues to the next statement in the DATA step.

OBS= and FIRSTOBS= for Subsetting

To base your subset on a sequence of observations rather than on variable values, use the OBS= and FIRSTOBS= options.

You can limit the number of observations that SAS reads from a data set by using the OBS= option after the data set name in a SET statement. Give the number of the last observation to be read. For example, these statements form a new data set from the first eight observations in CLASS:

```
DATA FIRST8;
   SET CLASS(OBS=8);
PROC PRINT;
   TITLE 'DATA SET FIRST8';
RUN;
```

The FIRST8 data set is shown in **Output 3.5**.

Output 3.5
Using the OBS= Option
to Limit the Number of
Observations in a Data Set

```
                        DATA SET FIRST8

      OBS   NAME      SEX   AGE   HEIGHT   WEIGHT

       1    ALFRED     M     14    69.0     112.5
       2    ALICE      F     13    56.5      84.0
       3    BARBARA    F     13    65.3      98.0
       4    CAROL      F     14    62.8     102.5
       5    HENRY      M     14    63.5     102.5
       6    JAMES      M     12    57.3      83.0
       7    JANE       F     12    59.8      84.5
       8    JANET      F     15    62.5     112.5
```

Think of OBS= as if it were LASTOBS. Because OBS=8, the eighth observation is the last one the SAS System reads from data set CLASS. To begin the subset in the middle of the original data set, use the FIRSTOBS= data set option. Give the observation number of the first observation to be read from the data set. For example, these statements form data set AFTER10 starting with the eleventh observation in CLASS:

```
DATA AFTER10;
   SET CLASS(FIRSTOBS=11);
PROC PRINT;
   TITLE 'DATA SET AFTER10';
RUN;
```

The AFTER10 data set appears in **Output 3.6**.

Output 3.6
Using the FIRSTOBS=
Option to Subset
a Data Set

```
                        DATA SET AFTER10

    OBS    NAME      SEX    AGE    HEIGHT    WEIGHT

     1     JOYCE      F      11     51.3      50.5
     2     JUDY       F      14     64.3      90.0
     3     LOUISE     F      12     56.3      77.0
     4     MARY       F      15     66.5     112.0
     5     PHILIP     M      16     72.0     150.0
     6     ROBERT     M      12     64.8     128.0
     7     RONALD     M      15     67.0     133.0
     8     THOMAS     M      11     57.5      85.0
     9     WILLIAM    M      15     66.5     112.0
```

Using FIRSTOBS=
and OBS=
Together

To select observations from the middle of a SAS data set, use
FIRSTOBS= and OBS= together. These statements select the eighth
through the sixteenth observations from CLASS:

```
DATA MIDDLE;
    SET CLASS(FIRSTOBS=8 OBS=16);
PROC PRINT;
    TITLE 'DATA SET MIDDLE';
RUN;
```

The MIDDLE data set is shown in **Output 3.7.**

Output 3.7
Using the FIRSTOBS=
and OBS= Options to
Subset a Data Set

```
                        DATA SET MIDDLE

    OBS    NAME      SEX    AGE    HEIGHT    WEIGHT

     1     JANET      F      15     62.5     112.5
     2     JEFFREY    M      13     62.5      84.0
     3     JOHN       M      12     59.0      99.5
     4     JOYCE      F      11     51.3      50.5
     5     JUDY       F      14     64.3      90.0
     6     LOUISE     F      12     56.3      77.0
     7     MARY       F      15     66.5     112.0
     8     PHILIP     M      16     72.0     150.0
     9     ROBERT     M      12     64.8     128.0
```

Subsetting Variables

The sections above describe several ways of subsetting observations to
form new data sets. When your original data set is large and contains
many variables not needed for your analysis, you can select a subset
of the variables.

DROP and KEEP
Statements

Use the statements below in the DATA step to create a subset of
CLASS containing all the observations but without the HEIGHT and
WEIGHT variables:

```
DATA AGESEX;
    SET CLASS;
    DROP HEIGHT WEIGHT;
PROC PRINT;
    TITLE 'DATA SET AGESEX';
RUN;
```

The AGESEX data set appears in **Output 3.8**.

Output 3.8
Using the DROP Statement
to Subset a Data Set

```
                        DATA SET AGESEX

         OBS    NAME       SEX    AGE

          1     ALFRED      M      14
          2     ALICE       F      13
          3     BARBARA     F      13
          4     CAROL       F      14
          5     HENRY       M      14
          6     JAMES       M      12
          7     JANE        F      12
          8     JANET       F      15
          9     JEFFREY     M      13
         10     JOHN        M      12
         11     JOYCE       F      11
         12     JUDY        F      14
         13     LOUISE      F      12
         14     MARY        F      15
         15     PHILIP      M      16
         16     ROBERT      M      12
         17     RONALD      M      15
         18     THOMAS      M      11
         19     WILLIAM     M      15
```

The DROP statement tells SAS to drop the variables HEIGHT and
WEIGHT from the data set being created. You can also indicate which
variables to keep:

```
DATA AGESEX;
    SET CLASS;
    KEEP NAME AGE SEX;
RUN;
```

Listing a variable in a DROP or KEEP statement does not affect its
availability during the DATA step. In each of the examples creating
data set AGESEX, the variables HEIGHT and WEIGHT can be used in
programming statements in the step.

**DROP= and
KEEP= Options**

You can use DROP= and KEEP= as data set options. For example,
the following statements are equivalent to the statements in the
previous example:

```
DATA AGESEX(KEEP=NAME SEX AGE);
    SET CLASS;
RUN;
```

**DROP= and KEEP=
for an Input
Data Set**

When DROP= and KEEP= options are used in a DATA statement,
they limit the variables output to the new data set. You can also use
DROP= and KEEP= in SET, MERGE, and UPDATE statements to
limit the variables brought into the DATA step. These options are
useful for subsetting a large data set containing variables that you do

not need. For example, these statements use DROP= on CLASS, the data set used as input:

```
DATA AGESEX;
   SET CLASS(DROP=HEIGHT WEIGHT);
RUN;
```

AGESEX is created as before, but HEIGHT and WEIGHT are not available for use in programming statements in the step.

Refer to Chapter 10, "Processing Large Data Sets with SAS Software," for more examples using the DROP= and KEEP= options.

Changing Variable Names

You can use the RENAME statement or the RENAME= data set option to change a variable's name either as it comes into the DATA step or as it is output to a new data set. Suppose you want the variable SEX to be named GENDER in the new data set. If you use the RENAME= option in the DATA statement, you refer to the old name, SEX, in programming statements:

```
DATA NEW(RENAME=(SEX=GENDER));
   SET CLASS;
   IF SEX='F';
PROC PRINT;
   TITLE 'DATA SET NEW';
RUN;
```

The NEW data set appears in **Output 3.9.**

Output 3.9
Using the RENAME=
Option to Rename
a Variable

```
                        DATA SET NEW

OBS    NAME       GENDER    AGE    HEIGHT    WEIGHT

 1     ALICE        F        13     56.5      84.0
 2     BARBARA      F        13     65.3      98.0
 3     CAROL        F        14     62.8     102.5
 4     JANE         F        12     59.8      84.5
 5     JANET        F        15     62.5     112.5
 6     JOYCE        F        11     51.3      50.5
 7     JUDY         F        14     64.3      90.0
 8     LOUISE       F        12     56.3      77.0
 9     MARY         F        15     66.5     112.0
```

In data set NEW the variable containing the sex values has the name GENDER. An equivalent way to create the data set is to use the RENAME statement:

```
DATA NEW;
   SET CLASS;
   RENAME SEX=GENDER;
   IF SEX='F';
RUN;
```

To rename the variable and use its new name in programming statements, use the RENAME= option in the SET, MERGE, or UPDATE statement. For example, suppose you want to concatenate two data sets containing the same kinds of values. (See **Combining Data Sets,** later in this chapter, for more about the concatenation operation.) In one data set the name of the variable containing height values is HT; in the other data set, the variable is named HEIGHT. The statements below rename the variable HT to HEIGHT in data set ONE:

```
DATA BOTH;
   SET ONE(RENAME=(HT=HEIGHT)) TWO;
   HT_FT=HEIGHT/12;
PROC PRINT;
   TITLE 'DATA SET BOTH';
RUN;
```

The ONE, TWO, and BOTH data sets are shown in **Output 3.10**.

Output 3.10
SAS Data Sets ONE, TWO, and BOTH

```
                      DATA SET ONE

         OBS      NAME        HT

          1      BARBARA      65.3
          2      JEFFERY      62.5
          3      JUDY         64.3
          4      LOUISE       56.3
          5      ROBERT       64.8
          6      RONALD       67.0
```

```
                      DATA SET TWO

         OBS      NAME       HEIGHT

          1      ALICE        56.5
          2      JANE         59.8
          3      JANET        62.5
          4      PHILIP       72.0
          5      RONALD       67.0
```

```
                      DATA SET BOTH

         OBS      NAME       HEIGHT      HT_FT

          1      BARBARA      65.3      5.44167
          2      JEFFERY      62.5      5.20833
          3      JUDY         64.3      5.35833
          4      LOUISE       56.3      4.69167
          5      ROBERT       64.8      5.40000
          6      RONALD       67.0      5.58333
          7      ALICE        56.5      4.70833
          8      JANE         59.8      4.98333
          9      JANET        62.5      5.20833
         10      PHILIP       72.0      6.00000
         11      RONALD       67.0      5.58333
```

Combining Variable-Subsetting Tools

By combining the variable-subsetting tools discussed above, you can create a data set completely different from the original one. For example, consider these statements:

```
DATA SUBSET;
   KEEP NAME SEX AGE BIRTHYR;
   SET CLASS;
   RENAME SEX=GENDER;
   BIRTHYR=1986-AGE;
PROC PRINT;
   TITLE 'DATA SET SUBSET';
RUN;
```

Although the new data set SUBSET has all the observations from CLASS, it has different variables. Notice that the variable containing sex values is named GENDER, even though the name SEX is specified in the KEEP statement. When a DATA step includes both KEEP (or DROP) and RENAME statements, the KEEP (or DROP) action is taken before the RENAME. Thus, you must use the old variable name in the KEEP or DROP statement. This rule holds regardless of the positions of the two statements in the DATA step. **Output 3.11** shows the data set SUBSET.

Output 3.11
Subsetted SAS Data Set

```
                              DATA SET SUBSET

              OBS     NAME      GENDER   AGE   BIRTHYR

               1     ALFRED       M      14     1972
               2     ALICE        F      13     1973
               3     BARBARA      F      13     1973
               4     CAROL        F      14     1972
               5     HENRY        M      14     1972
               6     JAMES        M      12     1974
               7     JANE         F      12     1974
               8     JANET        F      15     1971
               9     JEFFREY      M      13     1973
              10     JOHN         M      12     1974
              11     JOYCE        F      11     1975
              12     JUDY         F      14     1972
              13     LOUISE       F      12     1974
              14     MARY         F      15     1971
              15     PHILIP       M      16     1970
              16     ROBERT       M      12     1974
              17     RONALD       M      15     1971
              18     THOMAS       M      11     1975
              19     WILLIAM      M      15     1971
```

Reshaping Variables to Observations

Another way you can change the shape of a data set is to create several observations from a single observation in the original data set. For example, consider data set TESTS (**Output 3.12**).

Output 3.12
SAS Data Set TESTS

```
                    DATA SET TESTS

    OBS    NAME    TEST1    TEST2    TEST3

     1     JIM      70       80       86
     2     JOHN     85       91       83
     3     JAMES    80       85       91
```

Repeated Measures Data

Data set TESTS includes three test scores for each observation. This arrangement of data, where some measure is repeated several times for each observation, is called repeated measures data. To get separate observations for each of the three test scores, use multiple OUTPUT statements. Then, eliminate the information you do not need with a DROP or KEEP statement and create a new variable, TEST, to identify the test number.

```
DATA MORE;
    SET TESTS;
    SCORE=TEST1;
    TEST=1;
    OUTPUT;
    SCORE=TEST2;
    TEST=2;
    OUTPUT;
    SCORE=TEST3;
    TEST=3;
    OUTPUT;
    KEEP NAME TEST SCORE;
PROC PRINT;
    TITLE 'DATA SET MORE';
RUN;
```

The resulting data set appears in **Output 3.13**.

Output 3.13
Data Set Showing Repeated Measures Data

```
                 DATA SET MORE

    OBS    NAME    SCORE    TEST

     1     JIM       70      1
     2     JIM       80      2
     3     JIM       86      3
     4     JOHN      85      1
     5     JOHN      91      2
     6     JOHN      83      3
     7     JAMES     80      1
     8     JAMES     85      2
     9     JAMES     91      3
```

When you want to reshape many variables into observations, this technique takes many statements. An explicitly subscripted ARRAY statement simplifies the process:

```
DATA MORE;
   ARRAY ALLTEST{3} TEST1-TEST3;
   SET TESTS;
   DO TEST=1 TO 3;
      SCORE=ALLTEST{TEST};
      OUTPUT;
      END;
   DROP TEST1-TEST3;
PROC PRINT;
   TITLE 'DATA SET MORE';
RUN;
```

The final result appears in **Output 3.14**.

Output 3.14
Data Set Resulting from
ARRAY Statement

```
                        DATA SET MORE

            OBS    NAME    TEST    SCORE

             1     JIM      1       70
             2     JIM      2       80
             3     JIM      3       86
             4     JOHN     1       85
             5     JOHN     2       91
             6     JOHN     3       83
             7     JAMES    1       80
             8     JAMES    2       85
             9     JAMES    3       91
```

Creating Multiple Data Sets

Suppose you want to separate observations into groups and put each group into a different SAS data set. You can do this in one DATA step by specifying several SAS data set names in the DATA statement.

The following DATA step divides CLASS into two data sets, one listing the males and the other the females:

```
DATA MALES FEMALES;
   SET CLASS;
   IF SEX='F' THEN OUTPUT FEMALES;
   ELSE IF SEX='M' THEN OUTPUT MALES;
   ELSE PUT 'PROBLEM OBSERVATION '_ALL_;
PROC PRINT DATA=FEMALES;
   TITLE 'DATA SET FEMALES';
PROC PRINT DATA=MALES;
   TITLE 'DATA SET MALES';
RUN;
```

Each observation in CLASS with SEX equal to F is added to data set FEMALES (see **Output 3.15**). If SEX does not equal F, the observation is added to MALES (see **Output 3.16**).

Output 3.15
SAS Data Set FEMALES

```
                        DATA SET FEMALES

          OBS    NAME       SEX    AGE    HEIGHT    WEIGHT

           1     ALICE       F     13      56.5      84.0
           2     BARBARA     F     13      65.3      98.0
           3     CAROL       F     14      62.8     102.5
           4     JANE        F     12      59.8      84.5
           5     JANET       F     15      62.5     112.5
           6     JOYCE       F     11      51.3      50.5
           7     JUDY        F     14      64.3      90.0
           8     LOUISE      F     12      56.3      77.0
           9     MARY        F     15      66.5     112.0
```

Output 3.16
SAS Data Set MALES

```
                        DATA SET MALES

          OBS    NAME       SEX    AGE    HEIGHT    WEIGHT

           1     ALFRED      M     14      69.0     112.5
           2     HENRY       M     14      63.5     102.5
           3     JAMES       M     12      57.3      83.0
           4     JEFFREY     M     13      62.5      84.0
           5     JOHN        M     12      59.0      99.5
           6     PHILIP      M     16      72.0     150.0
           7     ROBERT      M     12      64.8     128.0
           8     RONALD      M     15      67.0     133.0
           9     THOMAS      M     11      57.5      85.0
          10     WILLIAM     M     15      66.5     112.0
```

The following statements show an alternative way to divide a data set if you prefer to use the SELECT statement:

```
DATA FEMALES MALES;
   SET CLASS;
   SELECT(SEX);
      WHEN ('F') OUTPUT FEMALES;
      WHEN ('M') OUTPUT MALES;
      OTHERWISE PUT 'PROBLEM OBSERVATION '_ALL_;
      END;
RUN;
```

Putting an Observation into Several Data Sets

Suppose that in addition to the MALES and FEMALES data sets, you want to create a data set of all the 14-year-olds. You can use these statements:

```
DATA FEMALES MALES AGE14;
   SET CLASS;
   IF SEX='F' THEN OUTPUT FEMALES;
   IF SEX='M' THEN OUTPUT MALES;
   IF AGE=14 THEN OUTPUT AGE14;
PROC PRINT DATA=FEMALES;
   TITLE 'DATA SET FEMALES';
PROC PRINT DATA=MALES;
   TITLE 'DATA SET MALES';
PROC PRINT DATA=AGE14;
   TITLE 'DATA SET AGE14';
RUN;
```

The three resulting data sets appear in **Output 3.17**.

Output 3.17
SAS Data Sets FEMALES,
MALES, and AGE14

```
                        DATA SET FEMALES

           OBS   NAME      SEX   AGE   HEIGHT   WEIGHT

            1    ALICE      F    13     56.5     84.0
            2    BARBARA    F    13     65.3     98.0
            3    CAROL      F    14     62.8    102.5
            4    JANE       F    12     59.8     84.5
            5    JANET      F    15     62.5    112.5
            6    JOYCE      F    11     51.3     50.5
            7    JUDY       F    14     64.3     90.0
            8    LOUISE     F    12     56.3     77.0
            9    MARY       F    15     66.5    112.0
```

```
                        DATA SET MALES

           OBS   NAME      SEX   AGE   HEIGHT   WEIGHT

            1    ALFRED     M    14     69.0    112.5
            2    HENRY      M    14     63.5    102.5
            3    JAMES      M    12     57.3     83.0
            4    JEFFREY    M    13     62.5     84.0
            5    JOHN       M    12     59.0     99.5
            6    PHILIP     M    16     72.0    150.0
            7    ROBERT     M    12     64.8    128.0
            8    RONALD     M    15     67.0    133.0
            9    THOMAS     M    11     57.5     85.0
           10    WILLIAM    M    15     66.5    112.0
```

```
                        DATA SET AGE14

           OBS   NAME      SEX   AGE   HEIGHT   WEIGHT

            1    ALFRED     M    14     69.0    112.5
            2    CAROL      F    14     62.8    102.5
            3    HENRY      M    14     63.5    102.5
            4    JUDY       F    14     64.3     90.0
```

When you create more than one data set, remember to give a data set name in the OUTPUT statement. If no data set name is given, SAS adds the observations to all the data sets being created.

Specifying Variables for New Data Sets

To include different variables in each of the data sets being created, use the DROP= and KEEP= data set options:

```
DATA HTWT(KEEP=NAME HEIGHT WEIGHT) AGSX(KEEP=NAME AGE SEX);
   SET CLASS;
PROC PRINT DATA=HTWT;
   TITLE 'DATA SET HTWT';
PROC PRINT DATA=AGSX;
   TITLE 'DATA SET AGSX';
RUN;
```

The two data sets, HTWT and AGSX (**Output 3.18**), include all the observations from CLASS but different sets of variables.

Output 3.18
SAS Data Sets HTWT and AGSX

```
                       DATA SET HTWT

          OBS    NAME       HEIGHT    WEIGHT

           1     ALFRED      69.0     112.5
           2     ALICE       56.5      84.0
           3     BARBARA     65.3      98.0
           4     CAROL       62.8     102.5
           5     HENRY       63.5     102.5
           6     JAMES       57.3      83.0
           7     JANE        59.8      84.5
           8     JANET       62.5     112.5
           9     JEFFREY     62.5      84.0
          10     JOHN        59.0      99.5
          11     JOYCE       51.3      50.5
          12     JUDY        64.3      90.0
          13     LOUISE      56.3      77.0
          14     MARY        66.5     112.0
          15     PHILIP      72.0     150.0
          16     ROBERT      64.8     128.0
          17     RONALD      67.0     133.0
          18     THOMAS      57.5      85.0
          19     WILLIAM     66.5     112.0
```

```
                       DATA SET AGSX

          OBS    NAME       SEX    AGE

           1     ALFRED      M      14
           2     ALICE       F      13
           3     BARBARA     F      13
           4     CAROL       F      14
           5     HENRY       M      14
           6     JAMES       M      12
           7     JANE        F      12
           8     JANET       F      15
           9     JEFFREY     M      13
          10     JOHN        M      12
          11     JOYCE       F      11
          12     JUDY        F      14
          13     LOUISE      F      12
          14     MARY        F      15
          15     PHILIP      M      16
          16     ROBERT      M      12
          17     RONALD      M      15
          18     THOMAS      M      11
          19     WILLIAM     M      15
```

Combining Data Sets

Base SAS software has several ways to combine observations from more than one SAS data set. This section describes the concatenation and interleave operations that use the SET statement. The MERGE and UPDATE statements are described in the next two chapters.

Concatenating SAS Data Sets

The concatenation operation appends up to fifty data sets, one after another, in the order they are specified. The following statements concatenate the MALES and FEMALES data sets:

```
DATA JOIN;
   SET MALES FEMALES;
PROC PRINT;
   TITLE 'DATA SET JOIN';
RUN;
```

Data set JOIN (**Output 3.19**) contains all the observations from data set MALES, followed by all the observations from data set FEMALES.

You can also use the APPEND procedure to add observations from one SAS data set to the end of another SAS data set. See the *SAS User's Guide: Basics, Version 5 Edition* for details.

Output 3.19
Concatenating Two
Data Sets

```
                        DATA SET JOIN

        OBS    NAME      SEX   AGE   HEIGHT   WEIGHT

         1     ALFRED     M     14    69.0    112.5
         2     HENRY      M     14    63.5    102.5
         3     JAMES      M     12    57.3     83.0
         4     JEFFREY    M     13    62.5     84.0
         5     JOHN       M     12    59.0     99.5
         6     PHILIP     M     16    72.0    150.0
         7     ROBERT     M     12    64.8    128.0
         8     RONALD     M     15    67.0    133.0
         9     THOMAS     M     11    57.5     85.0
        10     WILLIAM    M     15    66.5    112.0
        11     ALICE      F     13    56.5     84.0
        12     BARBARA    F     13    65.3     98.0
        13     CAROL      F     14    62.8    102.5
        14     JANE       F     12    59.8     84.5
        15     JANET      F     15    62.5    112.5
        16     JOYCE      F     11    51.3     50.5
        17     JUDY       F     14    64.3     90.0
        18     LOUISE     F     12    56.3     77.0
        19     MARY       F     15    66.5    112.0
```

Several Copies of a Data Set

You can use the concatenation operation to create a new data set containing several copies of the observations in a data set. For example, the following statements result in a data set containing three copies of the CLASS observations:

```
DATA REPEAT;
   SET CLASS CLASS CLASS;
RUN;
```

Interleaving SAS Data Sets

The interleave operation brings data sets together in sorted order; a BY statement specifies the sorting variable(s). Up to fifty SAS data sets can be interleaved; SAS concatenates the data sets within each BY group. Remember to first sort the data sets by the variable(s) specified in the BY statement if the data are not already in that order.

```
PROC SORT DATA=FEMALES;
   BY AGE;
PROC SORT DATA=MALES;
   BY AGE;
DATA NTRLEAVE;
   SET MALES FEMALES;
   BY AGE;
PROC PRINT;
   TITLE 'DATA SET NTRLEAVE';
RUN;
```

The NTRLEAVE data set is shown in **Output 3.20**.

Output 3.20
Interleaving Two Data Sets

```
                        DATA SET NTRLEAVE

      OBS    NAME      SEX    AGE    HEIGHT    WEIGHT

        1    THOMAS     M     11     57.5       85.0
        2    JOYCE      F     11     51.3       50.5
        3    JAMES      M     12     57.3       83.0
        4    JOHN       M     12     59.0       99.5
        5    ROBERT     M     12     64.8      128.0
        6    JANE       F     12     59.8       84.5
        7    LOUISE     F     12     56.3       77.0
        8    JEFFREY    M     13     62.5       84.0
        9    ALICE      F     13     56.5       84.0
       10    BARBARA    F     13     65.3       98.0
       11    ALFRED     M     14     69.0      112.5
       12    HENRY      M     14     63.5      102.5
       13    CAROL      F     14     62.8      102.5
       14    JUDY       F     14     64.3       90.0
       15    RONALD     M     15     67.0      133.0
       16    WILLIAM    M     15     66.5      112.0
       17    JANET      F     15     62.5      112.5
       18    MARY       F     15     66.5      112.0
       19    PHILIP     M     16     72.0      150.0
```

The data sets MALES and FEMALES contain the same variables, but what happens when you join data sets with different variables? In that case, the resulting data set contains all the variables in the data sets being joined, plus any variables created in the step. Consider these data sets, CLASS1 and CLASS2, both in order of NAME:

```
DATA CLASS1;
   INPUT NAME $ AGE;
   CARDS;
ANN   10
BOB   13
TOM   14
;
RUN;
```

and

```
DATA CLASS2;
    INPUT NAME $ ID AGE;
    CARDS;
MARY    203  13
MIKE    101  14
SUSAN   115  12
;
RUN;
```

These statements

```
DATA NEW;
    SET CLASS1 CLASS2;
    BY NAME;
PROC PRINT;
    TITLE 'DATA SET NEW';
RUN;
```

produce data set NEW, shown in **Output 3.21.**

Output 3.21
Joined Data Sets with
Different Variables

```
                    DATA SET NEW

            OBS    NAME    AGE    ID

             1     ANN     10      .
             2     BOB     13      .
             3     MARY    13     203
             4     MIKE    14     101
             5     SUSAN   12     115
             6     TOM     14      .
```

The variable ID appears in the new data set with missing values for observations from CLASS1.

Interleaving is used most often with data sets that are already in sorted order. If your data sets must be sorted before you can interleave them, it might be more efficient to concatenate the data sets and sort the result, since then only one sort is required. The result is the same.

Note: although the term *merge* is often used to mean *interleave*, SAS reserves merge for a matching operation, described in Chapter 4, "Merging SAS Data Sets."

Two SET Statements

Two SET statements in a DATA step let you join observations, much as you do with MERGE. The first SET statement brings in an observation from one data set. The next SET statement joins that observation with an observation from another data set, and so on. Unlike MERGE, building of the new data set stops when any of the data sets being joined runs out of observations. If the data sets contain the same variables, the observation coming in from the last data set provides the values for the variable in the new observation.

Pairing Observations
Data set FEMALES contains nine observations; data set MALES contains ten. You want to pair the observations from the two data sets and produce one data set containing nine sets of partners. The two data sets contain the same variable names, but in the new data set you want the female NAME variable to be called FEMNAME and the female AGE variable to be called FEMAGE:

```
DATA MATCHUP;
   SET MALES;
   SET FEMALES(RENAME=(NAME=FEMNAME AGE=FEMAGE));
   DROP SEX HEIGHT WEIGHT;
PROC PRINT;
   TITLE 'DATA SET MATCHUP';
RUN;
```

The resulting data set appears in **Output 3.22.**

Output 3.22
Data Set with Males and Females Matched

```
                          DATA SET MATCHUP

          OBS    NAME      AGE    FEMNAME    FEMAGE

           1     THOMAS    11     JOYCE       11
           2     JAMES     12     JANE        12
           3     JOHN      12     LOUISE      12
           4     ROBERT    12     ALICE       13
           5     JEFFREY   13     BARBARA     13
           6     ALFRED    14     CAROL       14
           7     HENRY     14     JUDY        14
           8     RONALD    15     JANET       15
           9     WILLIAM   15     MARY        15
```

FEMNAME and FEMAGE appear in data set MATCHUP along with the values of NAME and AGE from the MALES data set. MATCHUP contains nine observations because the pairing process stops when FEMALES runs out of observations.

You can also use the MERGE operation, described in Chapter 4, "Merging SAS Data Sets," for this application:

```
DATA MATCHUP2;
   MERGE MALES FEMALES(RENAME=(NAME=FEMNAME AGE=FEMAGE));
   DROP SEX HEIGHT WEIGHT;
PROC PRINT;
   TITLE 'DATA SET MATCHUP2';
RUN;
```

In this case, data set MATCHUP2 contains ten observations; the tenth has missing values for FEMNAME and FEMAGE. **Output 3.23** shows the resulting data set.

Output 3.23
Merged Data Set

```
                        DATA SET MATCHUP2

            OBS    NAME      AGE    FEMNAME    FEMAGE

             1     THOMAS    11     JOYCE      11
             2     JAMES     12     JANE       12
             3     JOHN      12     LOUISE     12
             4     ROBERT    12     ALICE      13
             5     JEFFREY   13     BARBARA    13
             6     ALFRED    14     CAROL      14
             7     HENRY     14     JUDY       14
             8     RONALD    15     JANET      15
             9     WILLIAM   15     MARY       15
            10     PHILIP    16                 .
```

Putting Values into Observations

Suppose you calculate summary values using a SAS procedure, and you want to include those summary values in every observation in a data set. Typically, the summary values are contained in a single observation of a SAS data set created by a PROC step.

```
PROC MEANS DATA=CLASS;
   VAR HEIGHT WEIGHT;
   OUTPUT OUT=SUMMARY MEAN=MHEIGHT MWEIGHT;
PROC PRINT;
   TITLE 'DATA SET SUMMARY';
RUN;
```

The MEANS procedure calculates the mean height and weight values for the observations in the CLASS data set and creates a new data set called SUMMARY. **Output 3.24** shows that the single observation in SUMMARY contains two variables, MHEIGHT and MWEIGHT.

Output 3.24
Data Set Resulting from
Using PROC MEANS

```
                  DATA SET SUMMARY

         OBS     MHEIGHT     MWEIGHT

          1      62.3368     100.026
```

You can use two SET statements to combine the observation from SUMMARY with each observation in CLASS.

```
DATA TOGETHER;
   IF _N_=1 THEN SET SUMMARY;
   SET CLASS;
   HTDIFF=HEIGHT-MHEIGHT;
   WTDIFF=WEIGHT-MWEIGHT;
PROC PRINT;
   TITLE 'DATA SET TOGETHER';
RUN;
```

The resulting data set appears in **Output 3.25**.

Output 3.25
Combined Data Sets

```
                              DATA SET TOGETHER

   OBS   MHEIGHT   MWEIGHT   NAME      SEX   AGE   HEIGHT   WEIGHT   HTDIFF    WTDIFF

    1    62.3368   100.026   ALFRED     M    14    69.0     112.5     6.663    12.474
    2    62.3368   100.026   ALICE      F    13    56.5      84.0    -5.837   -16.026
    3    62.3368   100.026   BARBARA    F    13    65.3      98.0     2.963    -2.026
    4    62.3368   100.026   CAROL      F    14    62.8     102.5     0.463     2.474
    5    62.3368   100.026   HENRY      M    14    63.5     102.5     1.163     2.474
    6    62.3368   100.026   JAMES      M    12    57.3      83.0    -5.037   -17.026
    7    62.3368   100.026   JANE       F    12    59.8      84.5    -2.537   -15.526
    8    62.3368   100.026   JANET      F    15    62.5     112.5     0.163    12.474
    9    62.3368   100.026   JEFFREY    M    13    62.5      84.0     0.163   -16.026
   10    62.3368   100.026   JOHN       M    12    59.0      99.5    -3.337    -0.526
   11    62.3368   100.026   JOYCE      F    11    51.3      50.5   -11.037   -49.526
   12    62.3368   100.026   JUDY       F    14    64.3      90.0     1.963   -10.026
   13    62.3368   100.026   LOUISE     F    12    56.3      77.0    -6.037   -23.026
   14    62.3368   100.026   MARY       F    15    66.5     112.0     4.163    11.974
   15    62.3368   100.026   PHILIP     M    16    72.0     150.0     9.663    49.974
   16    62.3368   100.026   ROBERT     M    12    64.8     128.0     2.463    27.974
   17    62.3368   100.026   RONALD     M    15    67.0     133.0     4.663    32.974
   18    62.3368   100.026   THOMAS     M    11    57.5      85.0    -4.837   -15.026
   19    62.3368   100.026   WILLIAM    M    15    66.5     112.0     4.163    11.974
```

What happens in the DATA step?

☐ The IF-THEN statement brings in the observation from data set SUMMARY. The value of the automatic variable _N_ is the number of times SAS has begun executing the DATA step. Since _N_ equals 1 only on the first execution of the DATA step, the first SET statement is executed only once, and the variables from data set SUMMARY retain their values throughout processing of the DATA step.

☐ The next SET statement brings in an observation from data set CLASS. HTDIFF and WTDIFF are computed using the values of HEIGHT and WEIGHT from this CLASS observation and the values MHEIGHT and MWEIGHT from the SUMMARY observation. SAS outputs the observation, returns for the next observation in CLASS, and so on, until there are no more observations in CLASS.

Combining Subtotals with Each Detail Record

To determine the average age for each sex in the CLASS data set, you first sort by SEX. Then, you can use the MEANS procedure to calculate the average age for each sex:

```
PROC SORT DATA=CLASS;
   BY SEX;
PROC MEANS DATA=CLASS;
   VAR AGE;
   BY SEX;
   OUTPUT OUT=AVERAGE MEAN=AVE_AGE;
PROC PRINT DATA=AVERAGE;
   TITLE 'DATA SET AVERAGE';
RUN;
```

The AVERAGE data set is shown in **Output 3.26.**

Output 3.26
SAS Data Set AVERAGE

```
                        DATA SET AVERAGE

                  OBS    SEX    AVE_AGE

                   1      F     13.2222
                   2      M     13.4000
```

Next, you can combine the average ages with the CLASS data set by merging CLASS with AVERAGE and then compute the difference between AGE and AVE_AGE:

```
DATA NEWCLASS;
   MERGE CLASS AVERAGE;
   BY SEX;
   DIFF=AGE-AVE_AGE;
PROC PRINT DATA=NEWCLASS;
   TITLE 'DATA SET NEWCLASS';
RUN;
```

The NEWCLASS data set appears in **Output 3.27**.

Output 3.27
Merged Data Sets

```
                              DATA SET NEWCLASS

      OBS    NAME      SEX    AGE    HEIGHT    WEIGHT    AVE_AGE     DIFF

       1     ALICE      F     13      56.5      84.0     13.2222    -0.2222
       2     BARBARA    F     13      65.3      98.0     13.2222    -0.2222
       3     CAROL      F     14      62.8     102.5     13.2222     0.7778
       4     JANE       F     12      59.8      84.5     13.2222    -1.2222
       5     JANET      F     15      62.5     112.5     13.2222     1.7778
       6     JOYCE      F     11      51.3      50.5     13.2222    -2.2222
       7     JUDY       F     14      64.3      90.0     13.2222     0.7778
       8     LOUISE     F     12      56.3      77.0     13.2222    -1.2222
       9     MARY       F     15      66.5     112.0     13.2222     1.7778
      10     ALFRED     M     14      69.0     112.5     13.4000     0.6000
      11     HENRY      M     14      63.5     102.5     13.4000     0.6000
      12     JAMES      M     12      57.3      83.0     13.4000    -1.4000
      13     JEFFREY    M     13      62.5      84.0     13.4000    -0.4000
      14     JOHN       M     12      59.0      99.5     13.4000    -1.4000
      15     PHILIP     M     16      72.0     150.0     13.4000     2.6000
      16     ROBERT     M     12      64.8     128.0     13.4000    -1.4000
      17     RONALD     M     15      67.0     133.0     13.4000     1.6000
      18     THOMAS     M     11      57.5      85.0     13.4000    -2.4000
      19     WILLIAM    M     15      66.5     112.0     13.4000     1.6000
```

Reading from a Data Set Twice: Leads and Lags

Suppose you have data on a company's book sales. The monthly sales totals seem erratic, and you want to "smooth" them by averaging each month's sales with the sales figures for the previous month and for the following month. **Output 3.28** shows the BOOKS data set.

```
                         DATA SET BOOKS

                  OBS      MONTH     SALES

                   1        JAN      23848
                   2        FEB      34212
                   3        MAR      46211
                   4        APR      19215
                   5        MAY      20408
                   6        JUN      32411
```

The LAG function can get the sales figure for the preceding month. To get the sales figure for the following month, use another SET statement with the same data set name. With this SET statement, use FIRSTOBS=2 to make the second observation the first one read. That SET statement is always one observation ahead of the other SET statement.

```
DATA SMOOTH(KEEP=MONTH SALES SMSALES);
   IF ENDLEAD¬=1 THEN DO;
      SET BOOKS(FIRSTOBS=2) END=ENDLEAD;
      NEXTMON=SALES;
      END;
   SET BOOKS;
   SMSALES=MEAN(LAG(SALES),SALES,NEXTMON);
PROC PRINT;
   TITLE 'DATA SET SMOOTH';
RUN;
```

When the same data set name appears on more than one SET statement, SAS keeps track of its position in each data set separately. The first time through the DATA step, the first SET statement gets the second observation from BOOKS. SAS assigns the SALES value in that observation to the variable NEXTMON. Executing the second SET statement gets the first observation from BOOKS.

The smoothing is done in the last statement. The LAG function gets the value of SALES in the previous observation (for the first observation, it is missing), and the MEAN function calculates the mean sales for the previous, current, and following months. The SMSALES value for JUN is based on the previous and current months since the NEXTMON value is missing. **Output 3.29** shows the result.

```
                        DATA SET SMOOTH

              OBS    MONTH    SALES    SMSALES

               1      JAN     23848    29030.0
               2      FEB     34212    34757.0
               3      MAR     46211    33212.7
               4      APR     19215    28611.3
               5      MAY     20408    24011.3
               6      JUN     32411    26409.5
```

Where You Are in the Data Set

Direct Access of SAS Data Sets

You can access SAS data sets directly rather than sequentially by using the POINT= and NOBS= options in the SET statement. Use the following statements to select every third male from the MALES data set:

```
DATA MALES3;
   DO NUMBER=1 TO TOTAL BY 3;
      SET MALES POINT=NUMBER NOBS=TOTAL;
      OUTPUT;
      END;
   STOP;
PROC PRINT;
   TITLE 'DATA SET MALES3';
RUN;
```

Output 3.30 shows the resulting data set. See more sampling examples later in Chapter 10, "Processing Large Data Sets with SAS Software."

Output 3.30
Observations Read by
Direct Access

```
                        DATA SET MALES3

      OBS    NAME     SEX    AGE    HEIGHT    WEIGHT

       1    THOMAS     M      11     57.5      85.0
       2    ROBERT     M      12     64.8     128.0
       3    HENRY      M      14     63.5     102.5
       4    PHILIP     M      16     72.0     150.0
```

Searching for a Particular Value

You can also use two SET statements to search for a particular value in the data set and then reread the data set for all other observations with that value:

```
DATA TALL;
   RETAIN HIGH 0;
   DO UNTIL(LAST);
      SET CLASS END=LAST;
      IF HEIGHT>HIGH THEN HIGH=HEIGHT;
      END;
   X=HIGH-6;
   DO UNTIL(FINAL);
      SET CLASS END=FINAL;
      IF HEIGHT>=X THEN OUTPUT;
      END;
   DROP HIGH X;
PROC PRINT;
   TITLE 'DATA SET TALL';
RUN;
```

The resulting data set appears in **Output 3.31.**

Output 3.31
SAS Data Set TALL

```
                          DATA SET TALL

         OBS    NAME      SEX    AGE    HEIGHT    WEIGHT

          1     MARY       F      15     66.5     112.0
          2     ALFRED     M      14     69.0     112.5
          3     PHILIP     M      16     72.0     150.0
          4     RONALD     M      15     67.0     133.0
          5     WILLIAM    M      15     66.5     112.0
```

Multiple SET Statements: Direct Access

Suppose a small data set contains all the observations you need to locate in a larger data set. For example, suppose that a data set, MALES2 (**Output 3.32**), contains all the males from data set CLASS and a variable that identifies the observation number of the person in CLASS. The CLASS data set with ID variable added is shown in **Output 3.33**.

Output 3.32
SAS Data Set MALES2

```
                     DATA SET MALES2

         OBS    NAME       SEX    ID

          1     ALFRED      M      1
          2     HENRY       M      5
          3     JAMES       M      6
          4     JEFFREY     M      9
          5     JOHN        M     10
          6     PHILIP      M     15
          7     ROBERT      M     16
          8     RONALD      M     17
          9     THOMAS      M     18
         10     WILLIAM     M     19
```

Output 3.33
CLASSID Data Set Showing ID Variable

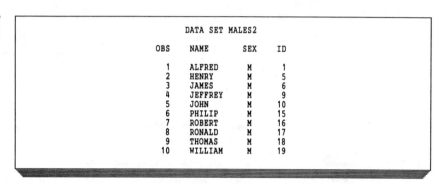

```
                        DATA SET CLASSID

    OBS    NAME      SEX    AGE    HEIGHT    WEIGHT    ID

     1     ALFRED     M      14     69.0     112.5      1
     2     ALICE      F      13     56.5      84.0      2
     3     BARBARA    F      13     65.3      98.0      3
     4     CAROL      F      14     62.8     102.5      4
     5     HENRY      M      14     63.5     102.5      5
     6     JAMES      M      12     57.3      83.0      6
     7     JANE       F      12     59.8      84.5      7
     8     JANET      F      15     62.5     112.5      8
     9     JEFFREY    M      13     62.5      84.0      9
    10     JOHN       M      12     59.0      99.5     10
    11     JOYCE      F      11     51.3      50.5     11
    12     JUDY       F      14     64.3      90.0     12
    13     LOUISE     F      12     56.3      77.0     13
    14     MARY       F      15     66.5     112.0     14
    15     PHILIP     M      16     72.0     150.0     15
    16     ROBERT     M      12     64.8     128.0     16
    17     RONALD     M      15     67.0     133.0     17
    18     THOMAS     M      11     57.5      85.0     18
    19     WILLIAM    M      15     66.5     112.0     19
```

The following SAS code reads an observation from the MALES2 data set and selects the corresponding observation from CLASSID, based on the value of ID in MALES2. It then selects observations with AGE less than or equal to 14. Data set CHECK therefore contains males with ages less than or equal to 14. The DATA step stops executing when MALES2 runs out of observations.

```
DATA CHECK;
   SET MALES2;
   SET CLASSID POINT=ID;
   IF AGE<=14;
   KEEP NAME AGE;
PROC PRINT;
   TITLE 'DATA SET CHECK';
RUN;
```

The resulting output appears in **Output 3.34**.

Output 3.34
MALES Data Set with
Selected Ages

```
                          DATA SET CHECK

                   OBS     NAME       AGE

                    1      ALFRED      14
                    2      HENRY       14
                    3      JAMES       12
                    4      JEFFREY     13
                    5      JOHN        12
                    6      ROBERT      12
                    7      THOMAS      11
```

FIRST., LAST., and IN= Variables

When a BY statement appears in a DATA step, SAS makes available the FIRST. and LAST. variables for each variable in the BY statement. FIRST. and LAST. let you know if you are processing the first or last observation of a BY group.

When you are tallying the number of males and the number of females, you must first sort the CLASS data set by SEX:

```
PROC SORT DATA=CLASS;
   BY SEX;
DATA SUBSET;
   SET CLASS(KEEP=SEX);
   BY SEX;
   IF FIRST.SEX THEN COUNT=0;
   COUNT+1;
   IF LAST.SEX;
PROC PRINT DATA=SUBSET;
   TITLE 'SUBSET DATA SET WITH COUNT FOR SEX';
RUN;
```

The result is shown in **Output 3.35**.

Output 3.35
Accumulated Totals for
Each Sex

```
                SUBSET DATA SET WITH COUNT FOR SEX

                   OBS    SEX    COUNT

                    1      F       9
                    2      M      10
```

In addition, when you read one or more SAS data sets in a DATA step, you can set up a variable to indicate which data sets contributed information to the current observation. Specify the IN= variable in parentheses after the name of the data set in the SET statement:

```
SET MALES(IN=M) FEMALES(IN=F);
```

The variables FIRST., LAST., and IN= can be used in programming statements in the DATA step although they cannot be output to the data set being created. To output their values, you must assign them to other variables.

Two BY Variables　The next example interleaves the MALES and FEMALES data sets by AGE and SEX. The values of FIRST., LAST., and IN= variables are assigned to new variables and are thus output to the new data set.

　　There are two BY variables, so there are two FIRST. variables, FIRST.AGE and FIRST.SEX, and two LAST. variables, LAST.AGE and LAST.SEX.

```
DATA EXAMINE;
    SET MALES(IN=M) FEMALES(IN=F);
    BY AGE SEX;
    FIRSTAGE=FIRST.AGE;
    LASTAGE=LAST.AGE;
    FIRSTSEX=FIRST.SEX;
    LASTSEX=LAST.SEX;
    INMALE=M;
    INFEMALE=F;
PROC PRINT;
    TITLE 'DATA SET EXAMINE';
RUN;
```

The resulting data set appears in **Output 3.36.**

```
                              DATA SET EXAMINE
                                           F       F             I
                                           I   L   I   L         N
                                           R   A   R   A   I     F
                                   H     W S   S   S   S   N     E
                                   E     E T   T   T   T   M     M
                       N           I     I A   A   A   A   A     A
  O   N       S   A    G     W     G A   S A   S   S   S   L     L
  B   A       E   G    H     E     H G   T A   S   E   E   E     E
  S   M       X   E    T     I     T E   E S   E   X   X   E     E
      E                      G                 E       X
  1   JOYCE    F   11   51.3  50.5  1   0   1   1   0   1
  2   THOMAS   M   11   57.5  85.0  0   1   1   1   1   0
  3   JANE     F   12   59.8  84.5  1   0   1   0   0   1
  4   LOUISE   F   12   56.3  77.0  0   0   0   1   0   1
  5   JAMES    M   12   57.3  83.0  0   0   1   0   1   0
  6   JOHN     M   12   59.0  99.5  0   0   0   0   1   0
  7   ROBERT   M   12   64.8 128.0  0   1   0   1   1   0
  8   ALICE    F   13   56.5  84.0  1   0   1   0   0   1
  9   BARBARA  F   13   65.3  98.0  0   0   0   1   0   1
 10   JEFFREY  M   13   62.5  84.0  0   1   1   1   1   0
 11   CAROL    F   14   62.8 102.5  1   0   1   0   0   1
 12   JUDY     F   14   64.3  90.0  0   0   0   1   0   1
 13   ALFRED   M   14   69.0 112.5  0   0   1   0   1   0
 14   HENRY    M   14   63.5 102.5  0   1   0   1   1   0
 15   JANET    F   15   62.5 112.5  1   0   1   0   0   1
 16   MARY     F   15   66.5 112.0  0   0   0   1   0   1
 17   RONALD   M   15   67.0 133.0  0   0   1   0   1   0
 18   WILLIAM  M   15   66.5 112.0  0   1   0   1   1   0
 19   PHILIP   M   16   72.0 150.0  1   1   1   1   1   0
```

SEX is a character variable, so the data value F sorts before M. Therefore, observations from FEMALES come into data set EXAMINE before the MALES observations even though the MALES data set is mentioned first.

Consider the observation for JOYCE. It is the first observation to have an AGE value of 11, so FIRST.AGE is 1. JOYCE is also the first and the last observation in that age group to have the SEX value F, so both FIRST.SEX and LAST.SEX are 1. It is not the last observation with AGE 11, so LAST.AGE equals 0. And since JOYCE is from the FEMALES data set, F is 1 and M is 0.

END= Variable

Specify the END= variable on the SET statement to determine when you are processing the last observation from all the SAS data sets being input. The variable has the value 1 when the last observation is being processed. If you are reading more than one SAS data set, only the last observation read from all the data sets has a value of 1 for the END= variable.

END= in Concatenating and Interleaving

If you want to know the last observation read in the concatenation example, use these statements:

```
DATA JOIN;
    SET MALES FEMALES END=LAST;
    IF LAST THEN LASTCODE='*';
PROC PRINT;
    TITLE 'DATA SET JOIN';
RUN;
```

The resulting data set is shown in **Output 3.37**.

Output 3.37
Data Set JOIN with
LASTCODE Variable

```
                              DATA SET JOIN

        OBS     NAME     SEX   AGE    HEIGHT    WEIGHT    LASTCODE

         1      THOMAS    M    11      57.5      85.0
         2      JAMES     M    12      57.3      83.0
         3      JOHN      M    12      59.0      99.5
         4      ROBERT    M    12      64.8     128.0
         5      JEFFREY   M    13      62.5      84.0
         6      ALFRED    M    14      69.0     112.5
         7      HENRY     M    14      63.5     102.5
         8      RONALD    M    15      67.0     133.0
         9      WILLIAM   M    15      66.5     112.0
        10      PHILIP    M    16      72.0     150.0
        11      JOYCE     F    11      51.3      50.5
        12      JANE      F    12      59.8      84.5
        13      LOUISE    F    12      56.3      77.0
        14      ALICE     F    13      56.5      84.0
        15      BARBARA   F    13      65.3      98.0
        16      CAROL     F    14      62.8     102.5
        17      JUDY      F    14      64.3      90.0
        18      JANET     F    15      62.5     112.5
        19      MARY      F    15      66.5     112.0        *
```

Only the last observation has a LASTCODE value of *. This observation is the last one from FEMALES; LASTCODE is blank (missing) for all other observations.

In the interleave operation below, the last observation comes from the MALES data set.

```
DATA INTERL;
    SET MALES FEMALES END=FINIS;
    BY AGE;
    IF FINIS THEN LASTCODE='*';
PROC PRINT;
    TITLE 'DATA SET INTERL';
RUN;
```

The resulting data set is shown in **Output 3.38**.

Output 3.38
SAS Data Set INTERL with
LASTCODE Variable

```
                             DATA SET INTERL

        OBS     NAME     SEX   AGE    HEIGHT    WEIGHT    LASTCODE

         1      THOMAS    M    11      57.5      85.0
         2      JOYCE     F    11      51.3      50.5
         3      JAMES     M    12      57.3      83.0
         4      JOHN      M    12      59.0      99.5
         5      ROBERT    M    12      64.8     128.0
         6      JANE      F    12      59.8      84.5
         7      LOUISE    F    12      56.3      77.0
         8      JEFFREY   M    13      62.5      84.0
         9      ALICE     F    13      56.5      84.0
        10      BARBARA   F    13      65.3      98.0
        11      ALFRED    M    14      69.0     112.5
        12      HENRY     M    14      63.5     102.5
        13      CAROL     F    14      62.8     102.5
        14      JUDY      F    14      64.3      90.0
        15      RONALD    M    15      67.0     133.0
        16      WILLIAM   M    15      66.5     112.0
        17      JANET     F    15      62.5     112.5
        18      MARY      F    15      66.5     112.0
        19      PHILIP    M    16      72.0     150.0        *
```

END= for Outputting Totals

The END= specification is also useful when you are accumulating totals and want to output those totals after reading the last observation.

Interleave the two data sets, MALES and FEMALES, by AGE. Count the number of different AGE values and the number of observations in the combined data set. Output totals when you reach the last observation.

```
DATA COUNT;
    SET MALES FEMALES END=FINIS;
    BY AGE;
    COUNTAGE+FIRST.AGE;
    N+1;
    IF FINIS THEN OUTPUT;
PROC PRINT;
    TITLE 'DATA SET COUNT';
RUN;
```

The resulting output is shown in **Output 3.39.**

Output 3.39
Interleaving and Counting
by AGE Variable

```
                      DATA SET COUNT

  OBS    NAME    SEX   ·AGE   HEIGHT   WEIGHT   COUNTAGE   N

   1    PHILIP    M     16      72      150        6      19
```

The variable COUNTAGE accumulates the number of different AGE values by adding the value of FIRST.AGE. Since FIRST.AGE is 1 each time a new AGE group starts, there are as many 1s for FIRST.AGE as there are different AGE values. N accumulates the total number of observations. Only one observation is output. It contains all the variables in the MALES data set plus COUNTAGE and N. If you want the resulting observation to contain only the new variables, use a KEEP statement.

Placement of END= Check

You can use the value of the END= variable in programming statements before the SET statement.

```
DATA ALL;
    IF FINIS THEN OUTPUT;
    SET MALES(IN=M) FEMALES(IN=F) END=FINIS;
    BY AGE;
    COUNTAGE+FIRST.AGE;
    MALES+M;
    FEMALES+F;
    TOTAL+1;
    KEEP COUNTAGE MALES FEMALES TOTAL;
PROC PRINT;
    TITLE 'DATA SET ALL';
RUN;
```

The resulting data set is shown in **Output 3.40.**

Output 3.40
Data Set ALL Showing
Result of END= Variable

```
                          DATA SET ALL

        OBS     COUNTAGE     MALES     FEMALES     TOTAL

         1         6          10          9          19
```

When SAS reads the last observation, FINIS is 1. This value is retained until SAS tries to execute the SET statement again, an execution that will fail because there are no more data to be processed.

Even if there are no data in MALES and FEMALES, ALL has one observation with missing values for all the variables. The rule is that the END= variable has a value of 1 when the next execution of the SET, MERGE, or UPDATE fails because there are no data.

Reshaping Observations to Variables

Converting from repeated measures to repeated observations was discussed earlier in this chapter. But how do you go in the other direction to convert repeated observations to single observations with repeated measures? Each observation in data set MORE (**Output 3.41**) contains a TEST number and a SCORE for that test.

Output 3.41
SAS Data Set MORE

```
                       DATA SET MORE

           OBS     NAME     TEST     SCORE

            1      JIM        1        70
            2      JIM        2        80
            3      JIM        3        86
            4      JOHN       1        85
            5      JOHN       2        91
            6      JOHN       3        83
            7      JAMES      1        80
            8      JAMES      2        85
            9      JAMES      3        91
```

To combine three observations into one, use these statements:

```
PROC SORT DATA=MORE;
   BY NAME;
DATA TESTS(KEEP=NAME TEST1-TEST3);
   ARRAY COMBINE{3} TEST1-TEST3;
   DO TEST=1 TO 3;
      SET MORE;
      BY NAME;
      COMBINE{TEST}=SCORE;
      IF LAST.NAME THEN RETURN;
      END;
PROC PRINT;
   TITLE 'DATA SET TESTS';
RUN;
```

The TESTS data set is shown in **Output 3.42**.

Output 3.42
Data Set Converted from
Repeated Observations to
One Observation

		DATA SET TESTS		
OBS	TEST1	TEST2	TEST3	NAME
1	80	85	91	JAMES
2	70	80	86	JIM
3	85	91	83	JOHN

The DO loop is executed three times or until LAST.NAME is 1. Then SAS outputs an observation and returns to the top of the DATA step. Each time SAS reads an observation, the value of TEST (the index variable for the DO loop) determines the element of the array that takes SCORE's value. After SAS reads all observations for a NAME, it outputs one observation to TESTS.

4 Merging SAS® Data Sets

You can use SAS software's merge operation to combine information from several data sets. You should understand the basics of the merge operation as described in the *SAS User's Guide: Basics, Version 5 Edition*. This chapter briefly reviews match-merging with an example, then covers more advanced merge techniques.

The final section of this chapter contains some merge exercises for you to solve. Hints for solving some of the exercises are provided at the end of the chapter.

Merging Multiple Data Sets

Match-Merge Example

Consider the two data sets CLASS and LIBRARY (**Output 4.1**).

Output 4.1
SAS Data Sets CLASS and LIBRARY

```
                         DATA SET CLASS

          OBS   NAME      SEX   AGE   HEIGHT   WEIGHT

            1   ALFRED     M    14     69.0    112.5
            2   ALICE      F    13     56.5     84.0
            3   BARBARA    F    13     65.3     98.0
            4   CAROL      F    14     62.8    102.5
            5   HENRY      M    14     63.5    102.5
            6   JAMES      M    12     57.3     83.0
            7   JANE       F    12     59.8     84.5
            8   JANET      F    15     62.5    112.5
            9   JEFFREY    M    13     62.5     84.0
           10   JOHN       M    12     59.0     99.5
           11   JOYCE      F    11     51.3     50.5
           12   JUDY       F    14     64.3     90.0
           13   LOUISE     F    12     56.3     77.0
           14   MARY       F    15     66.5    112.0
           15   PHILIP     M    16     72.0    150.0
           16   ROBERT     M    12     64.8    128.0
           17   RONALD     M    15     67.0    133.0
           18   THOMAS     M    11     57.5     85.0
           19   WILLIAM    M    15     66.5    112.0
```

```
                        DATA SET LIBRARY

          OBS      NAME      DATE    TEXTBOOK

           1     BARBARA      2      ENGLISH
           2     CAROL        2      SCIENCE
           3     CAROL        3      ENGLISH
           4     DONALD       1      ART
           5     JAMES        4      ARITHMETIC
           6     JOYCE        5      SEWING
           7     MARY         2      ART
           8     PHILIP       1      MECHANICS
           9     WILLIAM      2      SCIENCE
```

CLASS is a roster of students in a school classroom; LIBRARY is a record of textbooks checked from the library. Both data sets have been sorted by the common variable NAME; LIBRARY is sorted by DATE within NAME.

For each student in the class, what is the most recently checked out textbook?

For each student in data set CLASS, you must look through the LIBRARY data set for an observation with a matching value of NAME.

Nonmatches   Even though some students in the class—like ALFRED—have never been to the library, you want them in the answer. However, you do not want observations from LIBRARY that have no match in CLASS; DONALD has been to the library but is not part of the class.

Multiple   A name can appear more than once in the LIBRARY data set; for
Occurrences   instance, CAROL has been to the library twice. The most recently checked out book is the last in the BY group, so select the observation only if LAST.NAME is 1.

These statements produce a data set that answers the question about the most recently checked out textbook for each student:

```
DATA NEWCLASS;
   MERGE CLASS(IN=C) LIBRARY;
   BY NAME;
   IF C & LAST.NAME;
PROC PRINT;
   TITLE 'DATA SET NEWCLASS';
RUN;
```

NEWCLASS looks like the CLASS data set with two new variables. Students in CLASS who have not been to the library have missing values for DATE and TEXTBOOK. DONALD, who is not in the class, is not in the result, and CAROL appears only once. See **Output 4.2** for the resulting data set.

Output 4.2
SAS Data Set NEWCLASS

```
                            DATA SET NEWCLASS

     OBS    NAME      SEX    AGE    HEIGHT    WEIGHT    DATE    TEXTBOOK

       1    ALFRED     M      14     69.0     112.5      .
       2    ALICE      F      13     56.5      84.0      .
       3    BARBARA    F      13     65.3      98.0      2     ENGLISH
       4    CAROL      F      14     62.8     102.5      3     ENGLISH
       5    HENRY      M      14     63.5     102.5      .
       6    JAMES      M      12     57.3      83.0      4     ARITHMETIC
       7    JANE       F      12     59.8      84.5      .
       8    JANET      F      15     62.5     112.5      .
       9    JEFFREY    M      13     62.5      84.0      .
      10    JOHN       M      12     59.0      99.5      .
      11    JOYCE      F      11     51.3      50.5      5     SEWING
      12    JUDY       F      14     64.3      90.0      .
      13    LOUISE     F      12     56.3      77.0      .
      14    MARY       F      15     66.5     112.0      2     ART
      15    PHILIP     M      16     72.0     150.0      1     MECHANICS
      16    ROBERT     M      12     64.8     128.0      .
      17    RONALD     M      15     67.0     133.0      .
      18    THOMAS     M      11     57.5      85.0      .
      19    WILLIAM    M      15     66.5     112.0      2     SCIENCE
```

For each library transaction, what is the age and sex of the person checking out the book?

In this case, students who have never been to the library are the nonmatches from CLASS; they are not needed in the result. But you want all the students who have been to the library, even if they are not in the CLASS data set. Some students have been to the library more than once, so multiple occurrences appear in LIBRARY; but again, you want all the observations in LIBRARY. The KEEP= data set option lets you keep only the variables you need from CLASS:

```
DATA NEWLIB;
    MERGE LIBRARY(IN=L) CLASS(KEEP=NAME AGE SEX);
    BY NAME;
    IF L;
PROC PRINT;
    TITLE 'DATA SET NEWLIB';
RUN;
```

The resulting data set appears in **Output 4.3.**

Output 4.3
SAS Data Set NEWLIB

```
                        DATA SET NEWLIB

     OBS      NAME      DATE    TEXTBOOK      SEX    AGE

       1    BARBARA      2      ENGLISH        F     13
       2    CAROL        2      SCIENCE        F     14
       3    CAROL        3      ENGLISH        F     14
       4    DONALD       1      ART                   .
       5    JAMES        4      ARITHMETIC     M     12
       6    JOYCE        5      SEWING         F     11
       7    MARY         2      ART            F     15
       8    PHILIP       1      MECHANICS      M     16
       9    WILLIAM      2      SCIENCE        M     15
```

NEWLIB is a copy of the LIBRARY data set but with two new variables. DONALD is in the result, but students who have not been to the library are excluded; both CAROL observations appear. The new data set includes a subset of variables from CLASS; HEIGHT and WEIGHT are omitted.

Both questions above are answered using the same data sets. In the first example, you begin with the observations in CLASS and look for a match in LIBRARY; in the second, you go first to LIBRARY, then match in CLASS.

Three-Way Merge
Whether you merge two data sets or fifty, it is important that you understand the techniques SAS uses in each merge operation. The execution logic is described in detail in the *SAS User's Guide: Basics, Version 5 Edition*. For example, consider what happens when you merge three data sets.

Suppose a company has suggestion boxes in each of its three food service areas—the cafeteria (CAFE), the snack bar (SNACK), and the vending machines (VENDING). Suggestions for each food area are given coded sequential numbers, then sorted by employee name. The data sets are shown in **Output 4.4.**

Output 4.4
SAS Data Sets CAFE, SNACK, and VENDING

```
                        DATA SET CAFE

            OBS     NAME       PLACE     CNUM

             1      ANDERSON   CAFE      C1
             2      COOPER     CAFE      C2
             3      DIXON      CAFE      C3
             4      FREDERIC   CAFE      C4
             5      FREDERIC   CAFE      C5
             6      PALMER     CAFE      C6
             7      RANDALL    CAFE      C7
             8      RANDALL    CAFE      C8
             9      SMITH      CAFE      C9
            10      SMITH      CAFE      C10
            11      SMITH      CAFE      C11
```

```
                        DATA SET SNACK

            OBS     NAME       PLACE     SNUM

             1      BARRETT    SNACK     S1
             2      COOPER     SNACK     S2
             3      DANIELS    SNACK     S3
             4      DIXON      SNACK     S4
             5      DIXON      SNACK     S5
             6      FREDERIC   SNACK     S6
             7      GARY       SNACK     S7
             8      HODGE      SNACK     S8
             9      HODGE      SNACK     S9
            10      PALMER     SNACK     S10
            11      RANDALL    SNACK     S11
            12      RANDALL    SNACK     S12
            13      SMITH      SNACK     S13
            14      SMITH      SNACK     S14
            15      SMITH      SNACK     S15
            16      SMITH      SNACK     S16
            17      SPENCER    SNACK     S17
            18      SPENCER    SNACK     S18
```

```
                         DATA SET VENDING

                 OBS      NAME        PLACE       VNUM

                   1     CARTER      VENDING      V1
                   2     DANIELS     VENDING      V2
                   3     GARY        VENDING      V3
                   4     GARY        VENDING      V4
                   5     HODGE       VENDING      V5
                   6     PALMER      VENDING      V6
                   7     RANDALL     VENDING      V7
                   8     RANDALL     VENDING      V8
                   9     SMITH       VENDING      V9
                  10     SMITH       VENDING      V10
                  11     SPENCER     VENDING      V11
                  12     SPENCER     VENDING      V12
                  13     SPENCER     VENDING      V13
                  14     SPENCER     VENDING      V14
```

What is the maximum number of complaints made for any single food service?

You can answer this question by merging the three data sets. To see how the different combinations of matches, nonmatches, and multiples work in the three-way merge, save the values of the IN=, and FIRST. and LAST. variables.

```
DATA ALL;
    MERGE CAFE(IN=CAFEIN) SNACK(IN=SNACKIN)
          VENDING(IN=VENDIN);
    BY NAME;
    CIN=CAFEIN;
    SIN=SNACKIN;
    VIN=VENDIN;
    FIRST=FIRST.NAME;
    LAST=LAST.NAME;
PROC PRINT;
    TITLE 'DATA SET ALL';
RUN;
```

Data set ALL is shown in **Output 4.5.**

Output 4.5
SAS Data Set ALL

```
                              DATA SET ALL

 OBS   NAME      PLACE     CNUM   SNUM   VNUM   CIN   SIN   VIN   FIRST   LAST

  1   ANDERSON   CAFE      C1                    1     0     0     1       1
  2   BARRETT    SNACK            S1             0     1     0     1       1
  3   CARTER     VENDING                 V1      0     0     1     1       1
  4   COOPER     SNACK     C2     S2             1     1     0     1       1
  5   DANIELS    VENDING          S3     V2      0     1     1     1       1
  6   DIXON      SNACK     C3     S4             1     1     0     1       0
  7   DIXON      SNACK     C3     S5             1     1     0     0       1
  8   FREDERIC   SNACK     C4     S6             1     1     0     1       0
  9   FREDERIC   CAFE      C5     S6             1     1     0     0       1
 10   GARY       VENDING          S7     V3      0     1     1     1       0
 11   GARY       VENDING          S7     V4      0     1     1     0       1
 12   HODGE      VENDING          S8     V5      0     1     1     1       0
 13   HODGE      SNACK            S9     V5      0     1     1     0       1
 14   PALMER     VENDING   C6     S10    V6      1     1     1     1       1
 15   RANDALL    VENDING   C7     S11    V7      1     1     1     1       0
 16   RANDALL    VENDING   C8     S12    V8      1     1     1     0       1
 17   SMITH      VENDING   C9     S13    V9      1     1     1     1       0
 18   SMITH      VENDING   C10    S14    V10     1     1     1     0       0
 19   SMITH      SNACK     C11    S15    V10     1     1     1     0       0
```

(continued on next page)

```
(continued from previous page)
  20   SMITH      SNACK      C11   S16   V10   1    1    1    0    1
  21   SPENCER    VENDING          S17   V11   0    1    1    1    0
  22   SPENCER    VENDING          S18   V12   0    1    1    0    0
  23   SPENCER    VENDING          S18   V13   0    1    1    0    0
  24   SPENCER    VENDING          S18   V14   0    1    1    0    1
```

This example includes a variety of situations:

□ one observation from one data set (ANDERSON, BARRETT, CARTER)
□ one observation from each of two data sets (COOPER, DANIELS)
□ one observation from one data set, two observations from another (DIXON, FREDERICK, GARY, HODGE)
□ one observation from all three data sets (PALMER)
□ two observations from all three data sets (RANDALL)
□ a different number of observations from all three data sets (SMITH)
□ three observations from two data sets (SPENCER).

Multiple Observations

When data sets have several observations with the same BY value, the first observation from each data set is joined, then the second, and so on, until all the data sets run out of observations for that BY value. When a data set has no more observations for a BY value, variables appearing just on that data set retain their values from that data set's previous observation.

For each BY value, the resulting data set contains as many observations as the maximum number of observations for that BY value in any of the input data sets. SMITH has four observations in the SNACK data set, and less than four in all other data sets, so ALL contains four observations for SMITH. Thus, the maximum number of complaints an employee makes for a service is the number of observations for that employee in the output data set. Count the complaints for each employee using a sum statement and output the total at the end of the BY group:

```
DATA COUNTUP;
   MERGE CAFE SNACK VENDING;
   BY NAME;
   COUNT+1;
   IF LAST.NAME;
   OUTPUT;
   COUNT=0;
   KEEP NAME COUNT;
PROC PRINT;
   TITLE 'DATA SET COUNTUP';
RUN;
```

The result appears in **Output 4.6.**

Output 4.6
SAS Data Set COUNTUP

```
                      DATA SET COUNTUP

             OBS    NAME        COUNT

              1     ANDERSON      1
              2     BARRETT       1
              3     CARTER        1
              4     COOPER        1
              5     DANIELS       1
              6     DIXON         2
              7     FREDERIC      2
              8     GARY          2
              9     HODGE         2
             10     PALMER        1
             11     RANDALL       2
             12     SMITH         4
             13     SPENCER       4
```

For each employee, what is the number of suggestions made about each food service, the maximum number made for any of them, and the total of suggestions made?

To answer this question, you need the number of observations each data set contributes. But IN= values are retained within a BY group; once an IN= variable becomes 1, it stays 1 for the remainder of the BY group. One way to answer the question is to reset the IN= variables to 0 after reading each observation. Then, if you read new data from that data set, the IN= variable is reset to 1.

These statements merge the three data sets and answer the question:

```
DATA COUNTALL;
   MERGE CAFE(IN=C) SNACK(IN=S) VENDING(IN=V);
   BY NAME;
   CCOUNT+C;
   SCOUNT+S;
   VCOUNT+V;
   C=0;
   S=0;
   V=0;
   IF LAST.NAME;
   MAXCOUNT=MAX(CCOUNT,SCOUNT,VCOUNT);
   TOTCOUNT=SUM(CCOUNT,SCOUNT,VCOUNT);
   OUTPUT;
   CCOUNT=0;
   SCOUNT=0;
   VCOUNT=0;
   KEEP NAME CCOUNT SCOUNT VCOUNT MAXCOUNT TOTCOUNT;
PROC PRINT;
   TITLE 'DATA SET COUNTALL';
RUN;
```

The result is shown in **Output 4.7.**

```
                         DATA SET COUNTALL

 OBS    NAME      CCOUNT    SCOUNT    VCOUNT    MAXCOUNT    TOTCOUNT

  1    ANDERSON     1         0         0          1           1
  2    BARRETT      0         1         0          1           1
  3    CARTER       0         0         1          1           1
  4    COOPER       1         1         0          1           2
  5    DANIELS      0         1         1          1           2
  6    DIXON        1         2         0          2           3
  7    FREDERIC     2         1         0          2           3
  8    GARY         0         1         2          2           3
  9    HODGE        0         2         1          2           3
 10    PALMER       1         1         1          1           3
 11    RANDALL      2         2         2          2           6
 12    SMITH        3         4         2          4           9
 13    SPENCER      0         2         4          4           6
```

A better way to answer this question is to interleave the three data
sets. Then you do not have to set the IN= variables to 0 after each
observation:

```
DATA INTER;
    SET CAFE(IN=C) SNACK(IN=S) VENDING(IN=V);
    BY NAME;
    CCOUNT+C;
    SCOUNT+S;
    VCOUNT+V;
    IF LAST.NAME;
    MAXCOUNT=MAX(CCOUNT,SCOUNT,VCOUNT);
    TOTCOUNT=SUM(CCOUNT,SCOUNT,VCOUNT);
    OUTPUT;
    CCOUNT=0;
    SCOUNT=0;
    VCOUNT=0;
    KEEP NAME CCOUNT SCOUNT VCOUNT MAXCOUNT TOTCOUNT;
PROC PRINT;
    TITLE 'DATA SET INTER';
RUN;
```

The result appears in **Output 4.8.**

```
                          DATA SET INTER

 OBS    NAME      CCOUNT    SCOUNT    VCOUNT    MAXCOUNT    TOTCOUNT

  1    ANDERSON     1         0         0          1           1
  2    BARRETT      0         1         0          1           1
  3    CARTER       0         0         1          1           1
  4    COOPER       1         1         0          1           2
  5    DANIELS      0         1         1          1           2
  6    DIXON        1         2         0          2           3
  7    FREDERIC     2         1         0          2           3
  8    GARY         0         1         2          2           3
  9    HODGE        0         2         1          2           3
 10    PALMER       1         1         1          1           3
 11    RANDALL      2         2         2          2           6
 12    SMITH        3         4         2          4           9
 13    SPENCER      0         2         4          4           6
```

Combining Data Sets That Lack a Common Variable

If you need to combine several data sets that lack a common variable, you can sometimes merge them two at a time. For example, suppose you had these data sets: CITIES, FIRMS, and PRODUCTS (**Output 4.9**).

Output 4.9
SAS Data Sets CITIES, FIRMS, and PRODUCTS

```
                          DATA SET CITIES

               OBS     CITY           POP

                1      CHICAGO        5000000
                2      LOS ANGELES    4000000
                3      RALEIGH         160000
                4      MADISON         200000
                5      PORTLAND        500000
```

```
                          DATA SET FIRMS

               OBS     COMPANY        CITY

                1      GROUP-M        RALEIGH
                2      INT WIDGET     CHICAGO
                3      SURFACE        MADISON
                4      B. SMITH       LOS ANGELES
                5      LACOR          LOS ANGELES
                6      GTARCO         CHICAGO
```

```
                          DATA SET PRODUCTS

               OBS     PRODUCT     COMPANY

                1      GADGET      GROUP-M
                2      WIDGET      INT WIDGET
                3      MIRROR      SURFACO
                4      CLOCK       GTARCO
                5      GUITAR      GTARCO
                6      CLOCK       B. SMITH
```

The data sets lack a common variable, but both CITIES and FIRMS contain the variable CITY; FIRMS and PRODUCTS both contain the variable COMPANY.

What products are made in cities with populations over one million?

To answer this question, merge the data sets in two steps. First, sort and merge FIRMS and CITIES by CITY, deleting nonmatches such as cities that have no companies:

```
PROC SORT DATA=CITIES;
   BY CITY;
PROC SORT DATA=FIRMS;
   BY CITY;
DATA FIRMS2;
   MERGE FIRMS(IN=F) CITIES;
   BY CITY;
   IF F;
PROC PRINT;
   TITLE 'DATA SET FIRMS2';
RUN;
```

The resulting data set is shown in **Output 4.10.**

Output 4.10
SAS Data Set FIRMS2

```
                        DATA SET FIRMS2

         OBS     COMPANY       CITY          POP

          1      INT WIDGET    CHICAGO       5000000
          2      GTARCO        CHICAGO       5000000
          3      B. SMITH      LOS ANGELES   4000000
          4      LACOR         LOS ANGELES   4000000
          5      SURFACE       MADISON        200000
          6      GROUP-M       RALEIGH        160000
```

Next, sort and merge FIRMS2 and PRODUCTS by COMPANY.
Select those cities that have a population greater than one million and
keep only the variable PRODUCT.

```
PROC SORT DATA=FIRMS2;
   BY COMPANY;
PROC SORT DATA=PRODUCTS;
   BY COMPANY;
DATA PRODUCT2;
   MERGE PRODUCTS(IN=P) FIRMS2;
   BY COMPANY;
   IF P AND POP>1000000;
   KEEP PRODUCT;
PROC PRINT;
   TITLE 'DATA SET PRODUCT2';
RUN;
```

See **Output 4.11** for the resulting output.

Output 4.11
SAS Data Set PRODUCT2

```
              DATA SET PRODUCT2

         OBS       PRODUCT

          1        CLOCK
          2        CLOCK
          3        GUITAR
          4        WIDGET
```

To remove duplicate products in the list, sort the data set by
PRODUCT, then select one observation with each PRODUCT value:

```
PROC SORT DATA=PRODUCT2;
   BY PRODUCT;
DATA PRODUCT3;
   SET PRODUCT2;
   BY PRODUCT;
   IF FIRST.PRODUCT;
PROC PRINT;
   TITLE 'DATA SET PRODUCT3';
RUN;
```

Your answer is a unique list of products produced in cities of over one million in population (**Output 4.12**).

Output 4.12
SAS Data Set PRODUCT3

```
DATA SET PRODUCT3

OBS    PRODUCT

 1     CLOCK
 2     GUITAR
 3     WIDGET
```

Merging a Data Set with Itself

Consider SAS data set FLIGHTS, an airline schedule (**Output 4.13**).

Output 4.13
SAS Data Set FLIGHTS

```
                 DATA SET FLIGHTS

OBS    FROM       TO        DEPART    ARRIVE

 1     RALEIGH    ATLANTA     720       830
 2     ATLANTA    TAMPA       930      1030
 3     TAMPA      CHICAGO    1200      1330
 4     RALEIGH    CHICAGO    1000      1110
 5     CHICAGO    TAMPA       930      1045
 6     CHICAGO    RALEIGH    1400      1500
```

You can plan a trip from RALEIGH to TAMPA by matching the variables TO and FROM, even though there is no direct flight between the two cities.

Create two new data sets—each differently sorted versions of FLIGHTS. **Output 4.14** shows data sets LEG1 and LEG2.

```
PROC SORT DATA=FLIGHTS OUT=LEG1;
   BY FROM;
PROC SORT DATA=FLIGHTS OUT=LEG2;
   BY TO;
PROC PRINT DATA=LEG1;
   TITLE 'DATA SET LEG1';
PROC PRINT DATA=LEG2;
   TITLE 'DATA SET LEG2';
RUN;
```

Output 4.14
SAS Data Sets LEG1 and LEG2

```
                 DATA SET LEG1

OBS    FROM       TO        DEPART    ARRIVE

 1     ATLANTA    TAMPA       930      1030
 2     CHICAGO    TAMPA       930      1045
 3     CHICAGO    RALEIGH    1400      1500
 4     RALEIGH    ATLANTA     720       830
 5     RALEIGH    CHICAGO    1000      1110
 6     TAMPA      CHICAGO    1200      1330
```

```
                         DATA SET LEG2

         OBS      FROM       TO      DEPART    ARRIVE

          1     RALEIGH   ATLANTA      720       830
          2     TAMPA     CHICAGO     1200      1330
          3     RALEIGH   CHICAGO     1000      1110
          4     CHICAGO   RALEIGH     1400      1500
          5     ATLANTA   TAMPA        930      1030
          6     CHICAGO   TAMPA        930      1045
```

By matching the TO values of data set LEG2 with the FROM values of
data set LEG1, you get a list of all flights with one intermediate stop.
Rename FROM and TO to a common name, and change the names of
ARRIVE and DEPART on one of the data sets. Delete any nonmatches
and impossible flight schedules.

```
DATA CONNECT;
   MERGE LEG1(IN=INLEG1 RENAME=(FROM=VIA DEPART=DEPART2
             ARRIVE=ARRIVE2))
         LEG2(IN=INLEG2 RENAME=(TO=VIA));
   BY VIA;
   IF INLEG1 & INLEG2 & ARRIVE<DEPART2;
PROC PRINT;
   TITLE 'DATA SET CONNECT';
RUN;
```

The resulting flight schedule, data set CONNECT, is shown in
Output 4.15.

Output 4.15
SAS Data Set CONNECT

```
                          DATA SET CONNECT

 OBS    FROM       VIA     DEPART    ARRIVE     TO       DEPART2   ARRIVE2

  1    RALEIGH   ATLANTA     720       830    TAMPA        930      1030
  2    RALEIGH   CHICAGO    1000      1110    RALEIGH     1400      1500
  3    ATLANTA   TAMPA       930      1030    CHICAGO     1200      1330
  4    CHICAGO   TAMPA       930      1045    CHICAGO     1200      1330
```

Merge data set CONNECT with data set LEG1 to plan flights with two
connections:

```
PROC SORT DATA=CONNECT;
   BY TO;
DATA SCHEDULE;
   MERGE CONNECT(IN=INCON RENAME=(TO=VIA2))
         LEG1(IN=INLEG1 RENAME=(FROM=VIA2 DEPART=DEPART3
              ARRIVE=ARRIVE3));
   BY VIA2;
   IF INCON & INLEG1 & ARRIVE2<DEPART3;
PROC PRINT;
   TITLE 'DATA SET SCHEDULE';
RUN;
```

The resulting data set appears in **Output 4.16**.

Output 4.16
SAS Data Set SCHEDULE

```
                                          DATA SET SCHEDULE

                                          D    A                   D    A
                                          E    R                   E    R
                           D    A         P    R         V         P    R
                   F       E    R         A    I         I         A    I
           O       R    V  P    R    V    R    V         R    V    R    V
           B       O    I  A    I    I    T    E    T    T    E
           S       M    A  T    V    A    2    2    O    3    3

           1  CHICAGO  TAMPA    930  1045  CHICAGO  1200  1330  RALEIGH  1400  1500
           2  RALEIGH  ATLANTA  720   830  TAMPA     930  1030  CHICAGO  1200  1330
```

This technique lets you double the number of connections at each stage using two sorts and a merge. By merging a data set with itself, you can do things like the following:

☐ construct a family tree from records with variables for child, father, and mother

☐ solve symmetric networks; for example, identify roads between cities where each observation has its dual going in the other direction

☐ look at possible overlay structures for program modules based on information that tells which modules call which other modules.

Attaching Value Labels—Table Look-up

Suppose you have a set of data that contains numeric codes, and you want to print a label associated with each code. If you have only a few values, you can easily create a new variable using IF statements, or you can use the FORMAT procedure. The following are examples:

```
IF SEX=1 THEN SEXNAME='MALE  ';
ELSE IF SEX=2 THEN SEXNAME='FEMALE';
RUN;
```

or

```
PROC FORMAT;
    VALUE SEXNAME 1='MALE' 2='FEMALE';
RUN;
```

But hundreds or even thousands of such values require a lot of coding.

Suppose your data set contains city codes, and you want to print the corresponding city names. Construct a SAS data set CITY containing the codes and names (see **Output 4.17**).

Output 4.17
SAS Data Set CITY

```
                         DATA SET CITY

          OBS    CTCODE    CITY        CTABBREV

           1       1       BOSTON         BS
           2       2       CHICAGO        CH
           3       3       HOBOKEN        HB
           4       4       RALEIGH        RL
```

Another data set, A (**Output 4.18**), contains information about each employee in a company. One variable, CTCODE, contains a numeric code corresponding to the employee's home city.

Output 4.18
SAS Data Set A

```
                          DATA SET A

        OBS    NAME      POSITION    TENURE    CTCODE

         1    FOLEY       CLERK        5          2
         2    BRIGGS      PRES         11         1
         3    MARION      SEC          4          3
         4    DEBNAM      SEC          3          4
         5    ALLEN       VP           10         2
         6    FARLOW      SEC          9          3
         7    SHIPLEY     SALES        1          4
```

You want a list of information about each employee that shows the name of the city instead of the code. Form a SAS data set containing city names for each employee by merging data set A with the table of codes:

```
PROC SORT DATA=A;
   BY CTCODE;
DATA NEWA;
   MERGE A(IN=INA) CITY;
   BY CTCODE;
   IF INA;
   DROP CTCODE;
PROC PRINT;
   TITLE 'DATA SET NEWA';
RUN;
```

The resulting data set is shown in **Output 4.19.**

Output 4.19
SAS Data Set NEWA

```
                            DATA SET NEWA

      OBS    NAME      POSITION    TENURE    CITY       CTABBREV

       1    BRIGGS      PRES         11      BOSTON        BS
       2    FOLEY       CLERK        5       CHICAGO       CH
       3    ALLEN       VP           10      CHICAGO       CH
       4    MARION      SEC          4       HOBOKEN       HB
       5    FARLOW      SEC          9       HOBOKEN       HB
       6    DEBNAM      SEC          3       RALEIGH       RL
       7    SHIPLEY     SALES        1       RALEIGH       RL
```

Retrieving Data from a Master File

Suppose you have a very large master file sorted by employee number. Periodically, employees apply for promotion or transfer within the company. Given just a list of employee numbers, you need a report containing all the information in the master file about these employees so the promotion committee can review work histories of the applicants. **Output 4.20** shows the MASTER data set.

Output 4.20
SAS Data Set MASTER

```
                          DATA SET MASTER

       OBS    NAME        DEPT    EMPLOYEE     SAL     SEX

        1     DANIEL      811       2267      474.60    M
        2     LINN        815      10248      769.20    M
        3     CORNWALL    815       2688      246.26    F
        4     NAGEL       835       1370      664.60    M
        5     BAINHART    815       3057      444.80    M
        6     BALL        815       1931      592.26    M
        7     BRANDON     815       2200      805.65    M
        8     CARSON      811       6512      383.93    F
        9     MYER        835       7635      496.68    F
       10     RUSS        821       1376      469.90    M
       11     POWERS      811       1710      343.20    F
       12     MCWELON     840       4234      486.40    M
       13     RICHARDS    835       3416      313.80    F
       14     MOST        811       1445      202.00    F
       15     METRIK      821       1577      320.80    F
       16     KEITH       815       2983      279.36    F
       17     STUART      811       3571      342.40    M
       18     ROYAL       821       4225      255.50    F
       19     MANNING     815       2765      235.85    F
       20     BEST        840      15737      835.00    M
       21     THOMAS      821       1743      225.45    F
       22     BRIDGES     840       3936      334.43    M
       23     GREENE      821       1549      429.30    M
       24     JAMES       840       1949      708.80    M
       25     SMITH       811       9764      803.80    M
       26     WILLIAMS    811       1211      544.40    M
       27     ADAMS       821      11246      399.25    M
```

These statements read the employee numbers into a SAS data set, sort the data set, and merge it with the master file. Only observations in PROMO are output.

```
DATA PROMO;
   INPUT EMPLOYEE @@;
   CARDS;
10248 6512 3057 11246 7635 2983 15737
;
PROC SORT;
   BY EMPLOYEE;
PROC SORT DATA=MASTER;
   BY EMPLOYEE;
DATA EXTRACT;
   MERGE MASTER PROMO(IN=INP);
   BY EMPLOYEE;
   IF INP;
PROC PRINT;
   TITLE 'DATA SET EXTRACT';
RUN;
```

The resulting data set appears in **Output 4.21.**

```
                        DATA SET EXTRACT

    OBS     NAME        DEPT    EMPLOYEE     SAL     SEX

     1      KEITH       815       2983     279.36     F
     2      BAINHART    815       3057     444.80     M
     3      CARSON      811       6512     383.93     F
     4      MYER        835       7635     496.68     F
     5      LINN        815      10248     769.20     M
     6      ADAMS       821      11246     399.25     M
     7      BEST        840      15737     835.00     M
```

Handling Hierarchical Data with Merge

Hierarchical files store data so that each level of the hierarchy has an identifier indicating the level. For example, suppose you have a hierarchical file with the following three levels:

Level	Variables
STATE	STATE, STATEPOP
CITY	CITY, CITYPOP
FIRM	FIRM, SALES, EMPLOYS

Each record has a variable TYPE that identifies the level. For STATE records, TYPE is S; for CITY records, TYPE is C; and for FIRM records, TYPE is F. Here are the records from the file:

```
S  NY  18241
C  NEW YORK  9974
F  ARCON  48630  126000
F  NEXACO  26451  72766
S  CA  19953
C  LOS ANGELES  7042
F  PACIFIC OILFIELD  8462  26972
F  TRAVELERS PETROL.  5525  33600
C  SAN FRANCISCO  3109
F  MIDEAST OIL  19434  38397
F  ROYAL CONTAINER  2125  31619
S  IL  11113
C  CHICAGO  6978
F  AMERICAN TRACTOR  5488  97550
F  EXMARK  5300  47000
S  OHIO  10652
C  CLEVELAND  2064
F  WIDESPREAD OIL OHIO  2916  21062
F  COMMONWEALTH  2545  39593
C  CINCINNATI  1385
F  ROCKER AND RAMBLE  6512  52200
C  AKRON  679
F  GOODSTONE  5791  151263
F  FIREMARK  3939  113000
```

You can store the data from this hierarchical file in a SAS data set, a rectangular file, with these statements:

```
DATA HIER;
   RETAIN;
   INPUT TYPE $ a;
   DROP TYPE;
   SELECT (TYPE);
      WHEN ('S') INPUT STATE $ STATEPOP;
      WHEN ('C') INPUT CITY & $15. CITYPOP;
      WHEN ('F') DO;
         INPUT FIRM & $20. SALES EMPLOYS;
         OUTPUT;
         END;
      OTHERWISE;
      END;
PROC PRINT;
   TITLE 'DATA SET HIER';
RUN;
```

Data set HIER appears in **Output 4.22.**

Output 4.22
SAS Data Set HIER

```
                            DATA SET HIER

   OBS STATE STATEPOP CITY          CITYPOP FIRM              SALES EMPLOYS

     1 NY     18241    NEW YORK        9974  ARCON             48630 126000
     2 NY     18241    NEW YORK        9974  NEXACO            26451  72766
     3 CA     19953    LOS ANGELES     7042  PACIFIC OILFIELD   8462  26972
     4 CA     19953    LOS ANGELES     7042  TRAVELERS PETROL.  5525  33600
     5 CA     19953    SAN FRANCISCO   3109  MIDEAST OIL       19434  38397
     6 CA     19953    SAN FRANCISCO   3109  ROYAL CONTAINER    2125  31619
     7 IL     11113    CHICAGO         6978  AMERICAN TRACTOR   5488  97550
     8 IL     11113    CHICAGO         6978  EXMARK             5300  47000
     9 OHIO   10652    CLEVELAND       2064  WIDESPREAD OIL OHIO 2916 21062
    10 OHIO   10652    CLEVELAND       2064  COMMONWEALTH       2545  39593
    11 OHIO   10652    CINCINNATI      1385  ROCKER AND RAMBLE  6512  52200
    12 OHIO   10652    AKRON            679  GOODSTONE          5791 151263
    13 OHIO   10652    AKRON            679  FIREMARK           3939 113000
```

In this data set, the same value of STATEPOP appears in each observation for a given state. CITYPOP values are also repeated for several observations. By creating one SAS data set from this hierarchical file, you store redundant information and thus waste space. However, if you create a separate data set for each level of hierarchy, you reduce the space needed to store the data set.

```
PROC SORT;
   BY STATE CITY FIRM;
DATA STATE (KEEP=STATE STATEPOP)
     CITY (KEEP=CITY STATE CITYPOP)
     FIRM (KEEP=FIRM CITY SALES EMPLOYS);
   SET HIER;
   BY STATE CITY;
   IF FIRST.STATE THEN OUTPUT STATE;
   IF FIRST.CITY THEN OUTPUT CITY;
   OUTPUT FIRM;
PROC PRINT DATA=STATE;
   TITLE 'DATA SET STATE';
PROC PRINT DATA=CITY;
   TITLE 'DATA SET CITY';
PROC PRINT DATA=FIRM;
   TITLE 'DATA SET FIRM';
RUN;
```

The statements above produce the data sets shown in **Output 4.23**.

Output 4.23
SAS Data Sets STATE,
CITY, and FIRM

```
                        DATA SET STATE

             OBS     STATE    STATEPOP

              1       CA        19953
              2       IL        11113
              3       NY        18241
              4       OHIO      10652
```

```
                        DATA SET CITY

             OBS     STATE    CITY            CITYPOP

              1       CA      LOS ANGELES      7042
              2       CA      SAN FRANCISCO    3109
              3       IL      CHICAGO          6978
              4       NY      NEW YORK         9974
              5       OHIO    AKRON             679
              6       OHIO    CINCINNATI       1385
              7       OHIO    CLEVELAND        2064
```

```
                        DATA SET FIRM

     OBS    CITY           FIRM                  SALES    EMPLOYS

      1     LOS ANGELES    PACIFIC OILFIELD       8462     26972
      2     LOS ANGELES    TRAVELERS PETROL.      5525     33600
      3     SAN FRANCISCO  MIDEAST OIL           19434     38397
      4     SAN FRANCISCO  ROYAL CONTAINER        2125     31619
      5     CHICAGO        AMERICAN TRACTOR       5488     97550
      6     CHICAGO        EXMARK                 5300     47000
      7     NEW YORK       ARCON                 48630    126000
      8     NEW YORK       NEXACO                26451     72766
      9     AKRON          FIREMARK               3939    113000
     10     AKRON          GOODSTONE              5791    151263
     11     CINCINNATI     ROCKER AND RAMBLE      6512     52200
     12     CLEVELAND      COMMONWEALTH           2545     39593
     13     CLEVELAND      WIDESPREAD OIL OHIO    2916     21062
```

You can merge these data sets to combine information across levels in the hierarchy. For example, if you need to know the population of the city where each firm is located, merge FIRM and CITY by CITY:

```
PROC SORT DATA=CITY;
   BY CITY;
PROC SORT DATA=FIRM;
   BY CITY;
DATA CF (KEEP=STATE CITY CITYPOP FIRM);
   MERGE CITY FIRM;
   BY CITY;
PROC PRINT;
   TITLE 'DATA SET CF';
RUN;
```

The result is shown in **Output 4.24**.

Output 4.24
SAS Data Set CF

```
                          DATA SET CF

   OBS    STATE    CITY              CITYPOP    FIRM

     1    OHIO     AKRON               679      FIREMARK
     2    OHIO     AKRON               679      GOODSTONE
     3    IL       CHICAGO            6978      AMERICAN TRACTOR
     4    IL       CHICAGO            6978      EXMARK
     5    OHIO     CINCINNATI         1385      ROCKER AND RAMBLE
     6    OHIO     CLEVELAND          2064      COMMONWEALTH
     7    OHIO     CLEVELAND          2064      WIDESPREAD OIL OHIO
     8    CA       LOS ANGELES        7042      PACIFIC OILFIELD
     9    CA       LOS ANGELES        7042      TRAVELERS PETROL.
    10    NY       NEW YORK           9974      ARCON
    11    NY       NEW YORK           9974      NEXACO
    12    CA       SAN FRANCISCO      3109      MIDEAST OIL
    13    CA       SAN FRANCISCO      3109      ROYAL CONTAINER
```

The amount of space you save becomes significant as more and more data are stored. For example, the number of values stored when you have 30 states, 200 cities, and 10,000 firms is

hierarchical sequential file:	30,260
full rectangular file:	70,000
separate files:	40,360

The hierarchical file uses less space, but the data are more difficult to access. You must look through 10,000 firms to collect information on the 30 states. On the other hand, if you store the data in separate data sets, you might have to re-sort intermediate data sets frequently.

Relational Data Model

Using SAS data sets in the ways described in this chapter is similar to working with data sets in a relational data model as implemented in relational data base management systems. Data in a relational model are in rectangular tables and use a JOIN operator very much like the MERGE statement. However, the two systems are not designed for the same purpose: a relational system uses different access methods to handle massive data bases with high transaction rates, whereas SAS uses simple sequential methods to work with rectangular files.

Merge Exercises

Below are some interesting exercises for you to try, illustrating different aspects of the merge operation. Hints for solving some of the exercises are provided at the end of the chapter.

I. Consider the ELECTION and CANDIDAT data sets (shown in **Output 4.25**). ELECTION contains the names of the winners and losers for each presidential election year; CANDIDAT contains the names of the major party candidates, their political parties, and their home states.

Output 4.25
SAS Data Sets ELECTION
and CANDIDAT

```
                    DATA SET ELECTION

        OBS    YEAR     NAME      LOSER

         1     1960    KENNEDY    NIXON
         2     1964    JOHNSON    GOLDWATER
         3     1968    NIXON      HUMPHREY
         4     1972    NIXON      MCGOVERN
         5     1976    CARTER     FORD
         6     1980    REAGAN     CARTER
         7     1984    REAGAN     MONDALE
```

```
                    DATA SET CANDIDAT

        OBS    NAME       PARTY    STATE

         1     NIXON        R      CALIF
         2     GOLDWATER    R      ARIZ
         3     KENNEDY      D      MASS
         4     JOHNSON      D      TEXAS
         5     HUMPHREY     D      MINN
         6     MCGOVERN     D      S.DAK
         7     FORD         R      MICH
         8     CARTER       D      GA
         9     MONDALE      D      MINN
        10     REAGAN       R      CALIF
```

Answer these questions using the two data sets:

1. For each election year, find the party and home state of the loser.
2. For each candidate, find the last election he ran in and if he won.
3. For each candidate, count the number of times he won an election.
4. Find which candidates were both winners and losers.

II. The next four problems are challenges to data management systems and provide material to demonstrate concepts of relational data base management (adapted from examples by Robert T. Teitel).

Data from a transportation survey form the following hierarchy:

The information is stored in four SAS data sets (**Output 4.26**): data set HOUSES contains a unique household id and the owner's name; CARS contains a unique car identifier, and the model, year, and id of the household to which it belongs; PERSONS contains the age and household id of each person; TRIPS has, for each trip, the identifier of the car that was driven, who drove it, and the number of days the trip lasted.

Output 4.26
SAS Data Sets HOUSES,
CARS, PERSONS,
and TRIPS

```
                    DATA SET HOUSES

            OBS    HOUSE    OWNER

             1       1      JOHN SMITH
             2       2      JAMES JONES
             3       3      KEN ANDERS
             4       4      BOB BUNKER
             5       5      ABSENT
```

```
                    DATA SET CARS

        OBS    CAR    MODEL      HOUSE    YEAR

         1      1     OLDS         1      1971
         2      2     CHEVY        1      1981
         3      3     FORD         1      1984
         4      4     TRIUMPH      1      1987
         5      5     BUICK        2      1984
         6      6     VW           2      1985
         7      7     RENAULT      3      1987
         8      8     SIMCA        3      1981
         9      9     FORD         3      1984
```

```
                    DATA SET PERSONS

        OBS    NAME            AGE    HOUSE

         1     JOHN SMITH       27      1
         2     JAMES JONES      52      2
         3     CHARLES SMITH    15      1
         4     JANE SMITH       17      1
         5     JIM JONES        15      2
         6     BRUCE JONES      17      2
         7     ELMER JONES      35      2
         8     CARLA JONES      50      2
         9     KEN ANDERSON     35      3
        10     JOE ANDERSON     26      3
        11     BEN ANDERSON     26      3
        12     ANN ANDERSON     45      3
        13     BOB BUNKER       18      4
        14     HOBO             40      .
```

```
                        DATA SET TRIPS

        OBS     TRIP    CAR    NAME              DAYS

         1       1       2     JANE               .
         2       2       6     JAMES JONES        4
         3       3       5     BRUCE JONES        6
         4       4       5     BRUCE JONES        4
         5       5       7     JOE ANDERSON       4
         6       6       8     JOE ANDERSON       4
         7       7       7     BEN ANDERSON       5
```

1. Produce a crosstabulation counting households in a table of the number of cars in a household by the number of persons in the household over 16. (First, construct a data set that has the number of cars and the number of people over 16 for each household.) The answer should look like **Output 4.27**.

Output 4.27
Crosstabulation That
Counts Households

```
                    TABLE OF CARS BY OVER16

          CARS      OVER16

          FREQUENCY|      1|      2|      4|  TOTAL
          ---------+-------+-------+-------+
                 0 |   2   |   0   |   0   |    2
          ---------+-------+-------+-------+
                 2 |   0   |   0   |   1   |    1
          ---------+-------+-------+-------+
                 3 |   0   |   0   |   1   |    1
          ---------+-------+-------+-------+
                 4 |   0   |   1   |   0   |    1
          ---------+-------+-------+-------+
          TOTAL        2       1       2        5
```

2. Produce a crosstabulation counting trips of at least three days in duration in a table of driver's age by year of the car. The answer should look like **Output 4.28**.

Output 4.28
Crosstabulation That
Counts Trips

```
                    TABLE OF AGE BY YEAR

        AGE       YEAR

        FREQUENCY|  1981|  1984|  1985|  1987|  TOTAL
        ---------+------+------+------+------+
              17 |   0  |   2  |   0  |   0  |    2
        ---------+------+------+------+------+
              26 |   1  |   0  |   0  |   2  |    3
        ---------+------+------+------+------+
              52 |   0  |   0  |   1  |   0  |    1
        ---------+------+------+------+------+
        TOTAL        1      2      1      2        6
```

III. A file contains records that include a person's name, his educational achievement, age, sex, and the names of his father and mother. The file looks like this:

```
MARY                            C    45    F
JOE                             HS   50    M
ALICE      JOE      MARY        C    33    F
JIM        JOE      MARY        HS   32    M
BRUCE      JOE      MARY        EL   12    M
JOHN                            EL   58    M
CARLA                           HS   56    F
WILL       JOHN     CARLA       HS   38    M
BETH       WILL     ALICE       EL   12    F
AL         WILL     ALICE       EL   13    M
```

1. Produce a crosstabulation counting people in a table of mother's education by father's education. The result should look like **Output 4.29**.

Output 4.29
Crosstabulation That
Counts People

```
                    TABLE OF FED BY MED
        FED       MED

        FREQUENCY|        |    C |   HS|  TOTAL
        ---------+--------+--------+--------+
                 |    4 |    0 |    0 |      4
        ---------+--------+--------+--------+
          EL |    0 |    0 |    1 |      1
        ---------+--------+--------+--------+
          HS |    0 |    5 |    0 |      5
        ---------+--------+--------+--------+
        TOTAL       4        5        1       10
```

2. Produce a crosstabulation counting mothers in a table of the age at which they gave birth to their last offspring by the sex of that offspring. The result should look like **Output 4.30**.

Output 4.30
Crosstabulation That
Counts Mothers

```
                    TABLE OF BIRTHAGE BY SEX
        BIRTHAGE      SEX

        FREQUENCY|
        PERCENT  |
        ROW PCT  |
        COL PCT  |      F|      M|  TOTAL
        ---------+--------+--------+
             18 |    0 |    1 |      1
                | 0.00 | 33.33 |  33.33
                | 0.00 | 100.00 |
                | 0.00 | 50.00 |
        ---------+--------+--------+
             21 |    1 |    0 |      1
                | 33.33 | 0.00 |  33.33
                | 100.00 | 0.00 |
                | 100.00 | 0.00 |
        ---------+--------+--------+
             33 |    0 |    1 |      1
                | 0.00 | 33.33 |  33.33
                | 0.00 | 100.00 |
                | 0.00 | 50.00 |
        ---------+--------+--------+
        TOTAL         1        2        3
                    33.33   66.67   100.00
```

IV. From the following list of fathers and sons (**Output 4.31**), how many grandsons are listed? Use SAS software to draw the family tree.

Output 4.31
SAS Data Set TREE

```
                            DATA SET TREE

                  OBS     FATHER       SON

                   1      NOAH         JAPHETH
                   2      HAM          PHUT
                   3      JAPHETH      TIRAS
                   4      HAM          CANAAN
                   5      SALAH        EBER
                   6      HAM          CUSH
                   7      JAPHETH      TUBAL
                   8      NOAH         SHEM
                   9      GOMER        RIPHATH
                  10      SHEM         ARPHAXAD
                  11      CANAAN       ARKITE
                  12      CUSH         RAAMAH
                  13      NOAH         HAM
                  14      SHEM         ASSUR
                  15      MAXRAIN      CASLUHIM
                  16      ARPHAXAD     SALAH
                  17      CANAAN       SINITE
```

V. Suppose that you want future values available for some variable in a long-time series. For example, given data set A (**Output 4.32**), create a data set containing the one-day leads of the variable PRICE.

Output 4.32
SAS Data Set A

```
                            DATA SET A

        OBS     DATE      PRICE    VOLUME    HIGH    LOW

         1      10OCT82    12.4      304     15.2    11.9
         2      20OCT82    12.5      320     15.2    11.9
         3      30OCT82    12.2      290     15.2    11.9
```

Hints for Solving Merge Exercises

Below are hints for solving some of the merge exercises:

II. 1. Use the HOUSES data set to see that every car and person are associated with a household. Count households by accumulating and setting to zero the IN= variables.

2. Combine the data set TRIPS with the data set PERSONS to get age values, subsetting for trips of longer than three days. Then combine the result with the CARS data set to get the model of the car.

III. 1. This is an example of merging a data set with itself twice. First, sort the data set by FATHER, then merge it with itself, changing names as needed. Merge this result with the original data set sorted by MOTHER, with necessary renaming.

2. Merge the data with itself, combining MOTHER with PERSON. Compute the mother's age at the birth of the child by subtracting the person's age from the mother's age. Sort by the new variable and select the last in a BY group to get the observation with the highest age.

V. 1. Combine the data set with itself, but out of sync.

5 Updating and Editing SAS® Data Sets

The last two chapters show you how to change SAS data sets using SET and MERGE statements. Base SAS software also has two methods for updating data sets—the UPDATE statement and the EDITOR procedure. With these methods, you can add records to a data set; correct incorrect values, such as keying errors; update observations with new information; process transactions, like debits and credits; or delete records.

UPDATE or EDITOR?

Use the UPDATE statement when you have several changes to make to a master data set that you can apply all in one job, as when you accumulate updates and apply them to a master file infrequently. If your data set requires constant updating, or if you have only a few transactions to apply to a large data set, use the EDITOR procedure. *

The UPDATE Statement

UPDATE versus MERGE

The UPDATE statement matches observations from two SAS data sets much like in a two-way match merge. The main differences between UPDATE and MERGE are how the two statements handle missing values and how they handle multiple observations in a BY group.

- UPDATE uses only nonmissing values in the transaction data set to update variables in the master file.
- UPDATE only outputs an observation at the end of a BY group after all transactions have been applied.

UPDATE performs the specialized function of updating a master file by applying transactions. Its use has some restrictions:

- UPDATE can operate only on two SAS data sets; MERGE can handle up to fifty.
- UPDATE requires a BY statement; MERGE joins observations one by one when no BY statement appears.
- When you use UPDATE, only one observation in the master file can have each value of the BY variable; MERGE allows duplicate BY values in every data set.

---

* The FSEDIT procedure, available with SAS/FSP software, also updates SAS data sets. FSEDIT is a full-screen procedure that makes updating SAS data sets very easy. Refer to the *SAS/FSP User's Guide, Version 5 Edition* for details on PROC FSEDIT.

The following example combines the two data sets shown in **Output 5.1** first using UPDATE, then using MERGE. Compare the updated data sets from each step; they are shown in **Output 5.2**.

```
DATA JOINUPDT;
   UPDATE OLD NEW;
   BY CITY;
RUN;

DATA JOINMERG;
   MERGE OLD NEW;
   BY CITY;
RUN;
```

Output 5.1
Original Data Sets

```
           THE OLD DATA SET

        CITY      TEMP    HUMID

        ATLANTA    70      40
        CHICAGO    65      20
        DETROIT    63      25
        TULSA      70      15
```

```
           THE NEW DATA SET

        CITY      TEMP    HUMID

        CHICAGO    68      30
        DETROIT     .      35
        TULSA      76      12
        TULSA      77       .
        WAUSAU     65      30
```

Output 5.2
Data Sets Resulting from UPDATE and MERGE

```
          THE JOINUPDT DATA SET

        CITY      TEMP    HUMID

        ATLANTA    70      40
        CHICAGO    68      30
        DETROIT    63      35
        TULSA      77      12
        WAUSAU     65      30
```

```
          THE JOINMERG DATA SET

        CITY      TEMP    HUMID

        ATLANTA    70      40
        CHICAGO    68      30
        DETROIT     .      35
        TULSA      76      12
        TULSA      77       .
        WAUSAU     65      30
```

□ ATLANTA appears only in data set OLD; both UPDATE and MERGE copy the ATLANTA observation without changes to the new data set.

□ UPDATE and MERGE join the CHICAGO observations identically. Values in the new data set come from data set NEW—the data set specified last in the UPDATE and MERGE statements.

□ When building the DETROIT observation, UPDATE uses only the nonmissing value for HUMID from data set NEW; MERGE applies both missing and nonmissing values to the new observation.

□ There are two TULSA observations in data set NEW. UPDATE applies the nonmissing values from the first TULSA observation, then the nonmissing values from the second before outputting an observation to JOIN. MERGE outputs one new observation for each TULSA observation.

□ WAUSAU appears only in data set NEW; a WAUSAU observation is added to both new data sets.

An update application

Suppose you have a master file containing a list of students in a SAS data set named CLASS. **Output 5.3** shows the CLASS data set.

You want to update CLASS with information in your transaction file, a SAS data set named UPDT. The UPDT data set is shown in **Output 5.4**.

Output 5.3
CLASS Data Set before
Update

```
              THE CLASS DATA SET BEFORE UPDATE

     NAME       SEX    AGE    HEIGHT    WEIGHT

     ALFRED      M      14     69.0     112.5
     ALICE       F      13     56.5      84.0
     BARBARA     F      13     65.3      98.0
     CAROL       F      14     62.8     102.5
     HENRY       M      14     63.5     102.5
     JAMES       M      12     57.3      83.0
     JANE        F      12     59.8      84.5
     JANET       F      15     62.5     112.5
     JEFFREY     M      13     62.5      84.0
     JOHN        M      12     59.0     999.5
     JOYCE       F      11     51.3      50.5
     JUDY        F      14     64.3      90.0
     LOUISE      F      12     56.3      77.0
     MARY        F      15     66.5     112.0
     PHILIP      M      16     72.0     150.0
     ROBERT      M      12     64.8     128.0
     RONALD      M      15     67.0     133.0
     THOMAS      M      11     57.5      85.0
     WILLIAM     M      15     66.5     112.0
```

Output 5.4
UPDT Data Set with New
Information on Students

```
                 THE UPDT DATA SET

     NAME       SEX    AGE    HEIGHT    WEIGHT

     DAVID       M      14      70      120.5
     WILLIAM     .              67      120.0
     JOHN        .       .       .       99.5
     ANN         F      13      64       93.0
```

ANN and DAVID are new students joining the class; their observations in UPDT have values for all the variables. JOHN's weight is incorrectly coded in the master file, so values for the BY variable and for WEIGHT appear in the transaction file. WILLIAM has grown one-half inch and gained eight pounds; his observation in UPDT includes values for NAME, HEIGHT, and WEIGHT.

The master file, CLASS, is sorted and uniquely identified by NAME. The transaction file, UPDT, must also be sorted by NAME, although multiple observations with the same NAME may appear. These statements perform the update:

```
PROC SORT DATA=UPDT;
   BY NAME;
RUN;

DATA CLASS2;
   UPDATE CLASS UPDT;
   BY NAME;
RUN;
```

ANN and DAVID are nonmatches. UPDATE interleaves their observations into the master file, leaving CLASS2 sorted by NAME. When an observation with the same NAME appears in both data sets, SAS first brings in the observation from the master file. Then, SAS updates the master using nonmissing values from the transaction record. The updated result is shown in **Output 5.5**.

Output 5.5
Data Set of Student
Information after Update

```
                    THE CLASS2 DATA SET

        NAME       SEX   AGE    HEIGHT    WEIGHT

        ALFRED      M    14      69.0     112.5
        ALICE       F    13      56.5      84.0
        ANN         F    13      64.0      93.0
        BARBARA     F    13      65.3      98.0
        CAROL       F    14      62.8     102.5
        DAVID       M    14      70.0     120.5
        HENRY       M    14      63.5     102.5
        JAMES       M    12      57.3      83.0
        JANE        F    12      59.8      84.5
        JANET       F    15      62.5     112.5
        JEFFREY     M    13      62.5      84.0
        JOHN        M    12      59.0      99.5
        JOYCE       F    11      51.3      50.5
        JUDY        F    14      64.3      90.0
        LOUISE      F    12      56.3      77.0
        MARY        F    15      66.5     112.0
        PHILIP      M    16      72.0     150.0
        ROBERT      M    12      64.8     128.0
        RONALD      M    15      67.0     133.0
        THOMAS      M    11      57.5      85.0
        WILLIAM     M    15      67.0     120.0
```

Multiple Observations in a BY Group

Although several observations from the transaction file can have the same BY value, SAS outputs an observation to the master file only after all transactions are applied. For example, suppose the UPDT file above contains the two observations shown in **Output 5.6** for William, instead of one. UPDATE first changes WILLIAM's height to 67, then his weight to 120.0, before outputting the observation to CLASS2. The resulting observation is the same as before.

Output 5.6
Multiple Records per BY
Value in Transaction File

```
                    MORE OBSERVATIONS FROM UPDT

          NAME      SEX    AGE    HEIGHT    WEIGHT

          WILLIAM    .            67          .
          WILLIAM    .             .        120
```

Updating a Value to Missing

When a student is absent the day weight is updated, you want WEIGHT to be missing in the master file. UPDATE ignores missing values in the transaction file, so how can you change an existing value to missing?

Special missing value

The special missing value underscore, _, updates values to missing. When an underscore appears in the transaction file, UPDATE treats it like a nonmissing value. In the new data set, the value appears as a standard missing value (. for numeric variables or blank for character variables).

When you create the transaction data set, specify _ in a MISSING statement or set values to ._ in assignment statements. For example, these statements create a transaction file to update data set CLASS:

```
DATA TRANS;
   MISSING _;
   INPUT NAME $ SEX $ AGE HEIGHT WEIGHT;
   CARDS;
JOHN . . _ _
RUN;
```

To update CLASS, use these statements as before:

```
DATA CLASS3;
   UPDATE CLASS TRANS;
   BY NAME;
RUN;
```

JOHN's height and weight are missing in CLASS3, which is shown in **Output 5.7.**

```
                        THE CLASS3 DATA SET

            NAME      SEX   AGE   HEIGHT    WEIGHT

            ALFRED     M     14    69.0     112.5
            ALICE      F     13    56.5      84.0
            BARBARA    F     13    65.3      98.0
            CAROL      F     14    62.8     102.5
            HENRY      M     14    63.5     102.5
            JAMES      M     12    57.3      83.0
            JANE       F     12    59.8      84.5
            JANET      F     15    62.5     112.5
            JEFFREY    M     13    62.5      84.0
            JOHN       M     12     .         .
            JOYCE      F     11    51.3      50.5
            JUDY       F     14    64.3      90.0
            LOUISE     F     12    56.3      77.0
            MARY       F     15    66.5     112.0
            PHILIP     M     16    72.0     150.0
            ROBERT     M     12    64.8     128.0
            RONALD     M     15    67.0     133.0
            THOMAS     M     11    57.5      85.0
            WILLIAM    M     15    66.5     112.0
```

Suppose the values to be changed to missing are coded with 999. You can set them equal to the special missing value _ with assignment statements using the special numeric missing value ._.

```
DATA TRANS2;
   INPUT NAME $ HT WT;
   IF HT=999 THEN HT=._;
   IF WT=999 THEN WT=._;
   CARDS;
JOHN 999 999
RUN;
```

After this DATA step has been executed, JOHN's HT and WT values in TRANS2 equal the special missing value _ (see **Output 5.8**). These values change his original height and weight values to missing when the update is done.

```
            DATA SET TRANS2

         NAME     HT    WT

         JOHN     _     _
```

TRANS2 contains only NAME and the variables to be updated. Since all the original variables from the master file appear in the new data set after an update operation, if you do not want to change a variable, it need not appear in the transaction file.

Renaming Variables

The height and weight variables in TRANS2 are called HT and WT—not the same names as the height and weight variables in CLASS. You need to rename these variables for the update.

```
DATA CLASS4;
   UPDATE CLASS TRANS2(RENAME=(HT=HEIGHT WT=WEIGHT));
   BY NAME;
RUN;
```

The CLASS4 data set, updated with renamed variables, is shown in **Output 5.9.**

Output 5.9
A Data Set Updated after Renaming Variables

```
                      THE CLASS4 DATA SET

          NAME       SEX   AGE   HEIGHT   WEIGHT

          ALFRED      M    14    69.0     112.5
          ALICE       F    13    56.5      84.0
          BARBARA     F    13    65.3      98.0
          CAROL       F    14    62.8     102.5
          HENRY       M    14    63.5     102.5
          JAMES       M    12    57.3      83.0
          JANE        F    12    59.8      84.5
          JANET       F    15    62.5     112.5
          JEFFREY     M    13    62.5      84.0
          JOHN        M    12     .         .
          JOYCE       F    11    51.3      50.5
          JUDY        F    14    64.3      90.0
          LOUISE      F    12    56.3      77.0
          MARY        F    15    66.5     112.0
          PHILIP      M    16    72.0     150.0
          ROBERT      M    12    64.8     128.0
          RONALD      M    15    67.0     133.0
          THOMAS      M    11    57.5      85.0
          WILLIAM     M    15    66.5     112.0
```

RETAIN Features

The values of all the variables in master and transaction data sets are retained during the processing of a BY value and are reset to missing at the beginning of a new BY value. During the processing of a BY group, these variables keep the values they have for the first observation until the value is either updated or changed with an assignment statement. Listing these variables in a RETAIN statement or using them in sum statements has no effect; a RETAIN statement is ignored for variables in the master and transaction data sets.

Any variables not in either of the data sets but created within the DATA step, are set to missing each time SAS reads a new observation—even if the BY value has not changed. To retain the values of these variables both within a BY group and when the BY value changes, include their names in a RETAIN or sum statement.

An example

To understand how values are retained in an update operation, consider this example. Data set MASTER contains the variables ID, NAME, N (number of tests), and AVERAGE; and data set TRANSACT includes ID and GRADE. The DATA step below uses MASTER and TRANSACT to create the updated data set NEWMASTR. Variables NEWGRADE and TOTALP are created during processing. Because the two data sets have only the BY variable, ID, in common, programming statements are used to change a student's AVERAGE.

Refer to the step-by-step explanation that follows for a detailed
description of the processing of this DATA step. The MASTER and
TRANSACT data sets are shown in **Output 5.10**. NEWMASTR is
shown in **Output 5.11**.

```
DATA NEWMASTR (DROP=TOTALP);
    UPDATE MASTER TRANSACT(IN=NEWGRADE);
    BY ID;
    IF NEWGRADE THEN DO;
        TOTALP=SUM(N*AVERAGE,GRADE);
        N+1;
        AVERAGE=TOTALP/N;
        END;
RUN;
```

Output 5.10
Original Data Sets with
Grade Information

```
                      THE MASTER DATA SET

                 ID    NAME    AVERAGE    N
                 1     ANN       90       4
                 2     BOB       70       4
                 3     JOE       84       4
```

```
                     THE TRANSACT DATA SET

                      ID    GRADE
                      1      76
                      1      84
                      3       0
                      4      60
```

Output 5.11
Updated Data Set with
Grade Information

```
                      THE NEWMASTR DATA SET

             ID    NAME    AVERAGE    N    GRADE
             1     ANN     86.6667    6      84
             2     BOB     70.0000    4       .
             3     JOE     67.2000    5       0
             4             60.0000    1      60
```

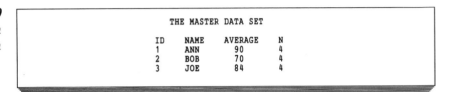

1. ready for first observation, all variables set to missing

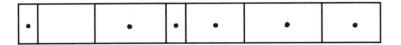

2. lowest ID value? observation from MASTER, ID=1

3. matching ID from TRANSACT? Yes, bring in observation, set NEWGRADE

| 1 | ANN | 90 | 4 | 76 | 1 | . |

4. IF statement true? Yes, calculate TOTALP

| 1 | ANN | 90 | 4 | 76 | 1 | 436 |

5. increment N

| 1 | ANN | 90 | 5 | 76 | 1 | 436 |

6. compute AVERAGE

| 1 | ANN | 87.2 | 5 | 76 | 1 | 436 |

7. more observations in BY group? Yes, reset NEWGRADE and TOTALP to missing; retain other variables

| 1 | ANN | 87.2 | 5 | 76 | • | • |

8. new observation in BY group ID=1, set NEWGRADE

| 1 | ANN | 87.2 | 5 | 84 | 1 | • |

9. IF statement true? Yes, calculate TOTALP

| 1 | ANN | 87.2 | 5 | 84 | 1 | 520 |

10. increment N

| 1 | ANN | 87.2 | 6 | 84 | 1 | 520 |

11. compute AVERAGE

1	ANN	86.6667	6	84	1	520

12. more observations in BY group? No, output observation, dropping TOTALP

Output ⟶

1	ANN	86.6667	6	84	1	~~520~~

13. set variables to missing

.		.	.	.	.	.

14. next ID? observation from MASTER, ID=2

2	BOB	70	4	.	.	.

15. matching ID from TRANSACT? No, output observation, dropping TOTALP

Output ⟶

2	BOB	70	4	.	.	✕

16. set variables to missing

.		.	.	.	.	.

17. next ID? observation from MASTER, ID=3

3	JOE	84	4	.	.	.

18. matching ID from TRANSACT? Yes, set NEWGRADE

3	JOE	84	4	Ø	I	•

19. IF statement true? Yes, calculate TOTALP

3	JOE	84	4	Ø	I	336

20. increment N

3	JOE	84	5	Ø	I	336

21. compute AVERAGE

3	JOE	67.2	5	Ø	I	336

22. more observations in BY group? No, output observation, dropping TOTALP

Output ⟶

3	JOE	67.2	5	Ø	I	~~336~~

23. set variables to missing

•		•	•	•	•	•

24. next ID? observation from TRANSACT, ID=4, set NEWGRADE

4		•	•	60	I	•

25. IF statement true? Yes, compute TOTALP

4		•	• 60	1	60

26. increment N

4		•	1 60	1	60

27. compute AVERAGE

4	60	1 60	1	60

28. no more observations; output observation, dropping TOTALP.

Output ⟶

4	60	1 60	1	✕✕

Another example

Programming statements can also be used to update bank checking accounts. To change a dollar balance in a master account, you must add deposits and subtract the amounts of any checks written.

Consider the data sets CURRENT and DAILY. CURRENT contains account numbers and current balances. DAILY contains daily deposits and withdrawals. The DAILY data set of bank transactions is sorted and applied daily to the master accounts. The two data sets are shown in **Output 5.12**.

Output 5.12
Master and Transaction
Banking Data Sets

```
                    THE CURRENT DATA SET

            ACCT        BALANCE

           2152617      1203.35
           3355912       342.13
           4102477       200.34
           6999249      9823.45
```

```
                        THE DAILY DATA SET

                  ACCT        TYPE       AMOUNT

                  3355912     DEBIT       23.12
                  4102477     CREDIT     110.00
                  4102477     DEBIT        1.23
                  5023541     CREDIT     100.00
```

CURRENT and DAILY have different sets of variables (except for the BY variable, ACCT), so no direct updating is performed. However, programming statements check the value of TYPE to see if a credit is to be added or a debit to be subtracted from BALANCE:

```
PROC SORT DATA=DAILY;
   BY ACCT;
RUN;
DATA CURRENT2;
   UPDATE CURRENT DAILY (IN=INDAILY);
   BY ACCT;
   IF TYPE='CREDIT' THEN BALANCE+AMOUNT;
   ELSE IF TYPE='DEBIT' THEN BALANCE+ -AMOUNT;
   ELSE IF INDAILY THEN DO;
      PUT 'ERROR: AN INVALID TYPE HAS BEEN SPECIFIED.';
      PUT '       THE AMOUNT WILL NOT BE ADDED.';
      PUT _ALL_;
      END;
   KEEP ACCT BALANCE;
RUN;
```

Since BALANCE is a variable in data set CURRENT, its value is retained within each BY group and set to missing at the beginning of each new BY group; the retain implied by the sum statement is ignored. Thus, BALANCE is missing if you open a new account. For example, account number 5023541 occurs only in DAILY; it is copied to CURRENT2. The new data set is shown in **Output 5.13**.

Output 5.13
Banking Data after Update

```
                       THE CURRENT2 DATA SET

                     ACCT        BALANCE

                   2152617      1203.35
                   3355912       319.01
                   4102477       309.11
                   5023541       100.00
                   6999249      9823.45
```

When an account has no transaction (no matching ACCT in the transaction file), TYPE is missing and BALANCE in the master file is not changed.

Deleting Observations

How do you delete records from the master file? Since UPDATE includes no automatic feature for deleting records, you must use programming statements.

The statements in the next DATA step tell SAS to delete a record and print a message in the log whenever TYPE='DELETE'. The step uses the files MAY19 and TODAY (see **Output 5.14**) to create the data set MAY20 (see **Output 5.15**).

```
DATA MAY20;
   UPDATE MAY19 TODAY (IN=INTODAY);
   BY ACCT;
   IF TYPE='CREDIT' THEN BALANCE+AMOUNT;
   ELSE IF TYPE='DEBIT' THEN BALANCE+ -AMOUNT;
   ELSE IF TYPE='DELETE' THEN DO;
      PUT 'DELETED ' ACCT= BALANCE= /;
      DELETE;
      END;
   ELSE IF INTODAY THEN DO;
      PUT 'ERROR: AN INVALID TYPE HAS BEEN SPECIFIED.';
      PUT '        THE AMOUNT WILL NOT BE ADDED.';
      PUT _ALL_;
      END;
   KEEP ACCT BALANCE;
RUN;
```

The DATA step prints the following message in the SAS log:

```
DELETED ACCT=5999999 BALANCE=671.89
```

Output 5.14
Banking Data before Update

```
          THE MAY19 DATA SET

            ACCT      BALANCE

          2152617     1203.35
          3355912      342.13
          4102477      200.34
          5999999      671.89
          6999249     9823.45
```

```
          THE TODAY DATA SET

            ACCT      TYPE      AMOUNT

          3355912     DEBIT      23.12
          4102477     CREDIT    110.00
          4102477     DEBIT       1.23
          5023541     CREDIT    100.00
          5999999     DELETE        .
```

Output 5.15
Banking Data after Update to Delete a Record

```
          THE MAY20 DATA SET

            ACCT      BALANCE

          2152617     1203.35
          3355912      319.01
          4102477      309.11
          5023541      100.00
          6999249     9823.45
```

Adding Other Features

You can add other features to the update. For example,

```
IF BALANCE<0 THEN PUT 'OVERDRAWN' ACCOUNT= BALANCE=;
```

prints a message for overdrawn accounts. To log inactive accounts, you can sum the transactions for each account during a month and record the date of the last transaction. Suppose that LASTDATE, the date of the last transaction, and NTRANS, the number of transactions made for an account at the last update, are variables in CURRENT. These statements identify accounts with no transactions during the last year:

```
DATA ENDOFYR;
   UPDATE CURRENT DAILY(IN=D);
   BY ACCT;
   IF D THEN LASTDATE=TODAY( );
   IF TODAY( )-LASTDATE>365
      THEN PUT 'INACTIVE ' ACCT= LASTDATE= DATE7.;
   NTRANS+D;
RUN;
```

Multiple output data sets

To put observations with balances less than zero in a data set OVERDRAW and accounts to be closed in a data set CLOSEOUT, use these statements:

```
DATA OVERDRAW CLOSEOUT;
   UPDATE CURRENT DAILY(IN=D);
   BY ACCT;
   IF TYPE='CREDIT' THEN BALANCE+AMOUNT;
   ELSE IF TYPE='DEBIT' THEN BALANCE+ -AMOUNT;
   ELSE IF TYPE='DELETE' THEN DO;
      OUTPUT CLOSEOUT;
      DELETE;
      END;
   ELSE IF D THEN DO;
      PUT 'ERROR: AN INVALID TYPE HAS BEEN SPECIFIED.';
      PUT '       THE AMOUNT WILL NOT BE ADDED.';
      PUT _ALL_;
      END;
   IF LAST.ACCT AND BALANCE<0 THEN OUTPUT OVERDRAW;
RUN;
```

Renaming the Latest Master File

The main advantage to using UPDATE is that your original master file remains available as a backup. However, if you give the same name to the new and old master files when you perform the update, you no longer have a backup.

```
DATA MASTER;
   UPDATE MASTER TRANSACT;
   BY ID;
RUN;
```

If a SAS syntax error or a system abend occurs in this program, the original MASTER data set is not replaced. However, if the job contains programming errors or if there are errors in the transactions, SAS may create an incorrect new master. If you want your current master file always to have the same name, you can use the SAS procedure DATASETS to rename the latest version. (See Chapter 7, "Managing SAS Data Libraries," for more about the DATASETS procedure.)

The EDITOR Procedure

UPDATE is not a very efficient way to change one observation in a data set containing thousands since it reads the entire file to produce a copy. The EDITOR procedure, however, allows you to go directly to an observation and change it in place.*

PROC EDITOR uses direct-access methods. If you know the observation number of the record you want to change, the direct-access capability allows EDITOR to go directly to that observation without reading all the observations before it.

EDITOR is typically used for interactive processing but can also be used for batch processing. For an example using EDITOR in a batch program, refer to the section **EDITOR in Batch** later in this chapter.

EDITOR Limitations

Differences in the updating capabilities of UPDATE and EDITOR include the following:

□ EDITOR edits the SAS data set in place; it makes no copy of the data set.
□ EDITOR adds new observations to the end of the data set; they cannot be inserted in the middle.
□ EDITOR keeps deleted observations in the data set with all variable values missing.
□ EDITOR does not allow you to use new variables.
□ EDITOR does not allow you to change the type or length of a variable.
□ EDITOR does not access tape data sets; your data set must be on disk.

The main advantage to using EDITOR is that you can update your data sets directly and in place. The disadvantage is that you have no backup. Once you make a change, you cannot recover previous values unless you have your own backup.

Interactive Editing

Suppose you want to change JOHN Q. SMITH's phone number in your SAS data set to 814-382-9919. First, begin an interactive EDITOR session by entering the PROC statement, for example,

```
PROC EDITOR DATA=MAILDATA;
```

EDITOR then prompts you for commands to list, replace, find, or add observations. After you enter a command, EDITOR performs it and prompts for more.

---

* PROC EDITOR is most useful for batch processing or for editing interactively if you do not have a full-screen terminal. If you use a full-screen terminal and your computing installation licenses SAS/FSP software, PROC FSEDIT is the most convenient way of editing a SAS data set.

You issue a FIND command to find John's observation number:

```
FIND 1,LAST NAME='JOHN Q. SMITH';
```

EDITOR responds with this message:

```
NOTE: FOUND AT OBS 56374
```

Now tell SAS to replace the phone number:

```
REPLACE 56374 PHONE=8143829919;
```

Your data set now contains the corrected phone number for JOHN Q. SMITH.

Example

An example earlier in this chapter uses UPDATE to make changes to the CLASS data set. You can also use EDITOR to make changes:

□ Add ANN and DAVID to the class.
□ Change William's height to 67 and his weight to 120.0.
□ Change Judy's name to Judith.
□ Change John's weight to 106.5.
□ Delete JANET.
□ Locate any observations where HEIGHT=72.0 and delete.
□ Search for observations in which NAME=CAROL and SEX=F.
□ Search for observations in which NAME=CAROL and SEX=M.

Output 5.16 shows an interactive session using EDITOR to edit the CLASS data set, making the changes listed above.

Output 5.16
An Interactive PROC
EDITOR Session

```
  30?
proc editor data=class;
NOTE: WELCOME TO THE EDITOR PROCEDURE. BEGIN ENTERING COMMANDS.
  31>
add name=ann sex=f age=13 height=64 weight=93.0;
  32>
list;
20 NAME=ANN SEX=F AGE=13 HEIGHT=64 WEIGHT=93;
  33>
add name=david sex=m age=14 height=70 weight=120.5;
  34>
list;
21 NAME=DAVID SEX=M AGE=14 HEIGHT=70 WEIGHT=120.5;
  35>
find 1,last name=william;
NOTE: FOUND AT OBS 19.
  36>
list;
19 NAME=WILLIAM SEX=M AGE=15 HEIGHT=66.5 WEIGHT=112;
  37>
replace 19 height=67 weight=120;
  38>
list;
19 NAME=WILLIAM SEX=M AGE=15 HEIGHT=67 WEIGHT=120;
  39>
verify on;
  40>
find 1,last name=judy;
NOTE: FOUND AT OBS 12.
  41>
replace name=judith;
```

(continued on next page)

(continued from previous page)

```
12 NAME=JUDY;
12 NAME=JUDITH;
 42>
find 1,last name=john;
NOTE: FOUND AT OBS 10.
 43>
replace weight 106.5;
 43 replace weight 106.5;
                 -----
                   1
ERROR 1: SYNTAX ERROR: EXPECTING EQUALS (=).
 44>
replace weight=106.5;
10 WEIGHT=999.5;
10 WEIGHT=106.5;
 45>
find 1,last name=janet;
NOTE: FOUND AT OBS 8.
 46>
list;
8 NAME=JANET SEX=F AGE=15 HEIGHT=62.5 WEIGHT=112.5;
 47>
delete;
 48>
name height;
 49>
locate 1,last 72.0;
NOTE: FOUND AT OBS 15.
 50>
list;
15 NAME=PHILIP SEX=M AGE=16 HEIGHT=72 WEIGHT=150;
 51>
delete;
 52>
string name sex;
 53>
search 1,last carol f;
NOTE: FOUND AT OBS 4.
 54>
list;
4 NAME=CAROL SEX=F AGE=14 HEIGHT=62.8 WEIGHT=102.5;
 55>
search 1,last carol m;
NOTE: NOT FOUND. OBS=21.
 56>
end;
NOTE: EXITING FROM THE EDITOR PROCEDURE.

 57?
proc print data=class;
 58>
title 'CLASS DATA SET AFTER INTERACTIVE EDIT';
 59>
run;
```

```
              CLASS DATA SET AFTER INTERACTIVE EDIT

        OBS    NAME      SEX    AGE    HEIGHT    WEIGHT
          1    ALFRED     M      14     69.0      112.5
          2    ALICE      F      13     56.5       84.0
          3    BARBARA    F      13     65.3       98.0
          4    CAROL      F      14     62.8      102.5
          5    HENRY      M      14     63.5      102.5
          6    JAMES      M      12     57.3       83.0
          7    JANE       F      12     59.8       84.5
          8                       .       .          .
          9    JEFFREY    M      13     62.5       84.0
         10    JOHN       M      12     59.0      106.5
         11    JOYCE      F      11     51.3       50.5
         12    JUDITH     F      14     64.3       90.0
         13    LOUISE     F      12     56.3       77.0
         14    MARY       F      15     66.5      112.0
         15                       .       .          .
         16    ROBERT     M      12     64.8      128.0
         17    RONALD     M      15     67.0      133.0
         18    THOMAS     M      11     57.5       85.0
         19    WILLIAM    M      15     67.0      120.0
         20    ANN        F      13     64.0       93.0
         21    DAVID      M      14     70.0      120.5
```

```
 60?
```

EDITOR in Batch   You can also use the EDITOR procedure in a batch job. In batch, the log shows the result of each command before the command itself is printed. **Output 5.17** shows the SAS log from a batch EDITOR program.

Notice that in the batch job the VERIFY (or VER) option is used on each FIND command. This option is activated if the target of a FIND, LOCATE, or SEARCH command is not found, in other words, when no match is found by a searching command. The VERIFY option causes SAS to stop executing change commands until a VERIFY RESET command executes. This protects you from inadvertently changing observations when SAS doesn't find the observation you want to change.

For example, suppose you execute this FIND command:

```
FIND 1,LAST NAME=DONALD;
```

When the FIND command doesn't find an observation with the specified value, it stops at the last observation in the data set. Thus, if the data set does not include an observation where NAME=DONALD, the EDITOR's pointer stops on the last observation in the data set. If the next command is one of the changing commands, for example

```
DELETE;
```

then the last observation is deleted from the data set because the EDITOR's pointer is positioned there. However, if you add the VERIFY option to the FIND command

```
FIND VER 1,LAST NAME=DONALD;
DELETE;
```

the DELETE command is not executed when there is no match for the observation. In order to resume execution of changing commands, use the VERIFY statement with the RESET specification after the change command:

```
FIND VER 1,LAST NAME=DONALD;
DELETE;
VERIFY RESET;
```

Output 5.17
A Batch PROC EDITOR
Program

```
NOTE: WELCOME TO THE EDITOR PROCEDURE. BEGIN ENTERING COMMANDS.
33          PROC EDITOR DATA=CLASS;
34          RUN;
35
36          VERIFY ON;
37
38          ADD NAME=ANN SEX=F AGE=13 HEIGHT=64 WEIGHT=93.0;
20 NAME=ANN SEX=F AGE=13 HEIGHT=64 WEIGHT=93;
39          LIST;
40
41          ADD NAME=DAVID SEX=M AGE=14 HEIGHT=70 WEIGHT=120.5;
21 NAME=DAVID SEX=M AGE=14 HEIGHT=70 WEIGHT=120.5;
42          LIST;
43
```

(continued on next page)

```
(continued from previous page)
NOTE: FOUND AT OBS 19.
44          FIND VER 1,LAST NAME=WILLIAM;
19 NAME=WILLIAM SEX=M AGE=15 HEIGHT=66.5 WEIGHT=112;
45          LIST;
19 HEIGHT=66.5 WEIGHT=112;
19 HEIGHT=67 WEIGHT=120;
46          REPLACE HEIGHT=67 WEIGHT=120;
47          VERIFY RESET;
19 NAME=WILLIAM SEX=M AGE=15 HEIGHT=67 WEIGHT=120;
48          LIST;
49
NOTE: FOUND AT OBS 12.
50          FIND VER 1,LAST NAME=JUDY;
12 NAME=JUDY SEX=F AGE=14 HEIGHT=64.3 WEIGHT=90;
51          LIST;
12 NAME=JUDY;
```

```
            SAS(R) LOG   OS SAS 5.16        MVS/XA JOB CH5E14   STEP SAS

12 NAME=JUDITH;
52          REPLACE NAME=JUDITH;
53          VERIFY RESET;
12 NAME=JUDITH SEX=F AGE=14 HEIGHT=64.3 WEIGHT=90;
54          LIST;
55
NOTE: FOUND AT OBS 10.
56          FIND VER 1,LAST NAME=JOHN;
10 NAME=JOHN SEX=M AGE=12 HEIGHT=59 WEIGHT=999.5;
57          LIST;
10 WEIGHT=999.5;
10 WEIGHT=106.5;
58          REPLACE WEIGHT=106.5;
59          VERIFY RESET;
10 NAME=JOHN SEX=M AGE=12 HEIGHT=59 WEIGHT=106.5;
60          LIST;
61
NOTE: FOUND AT OBS 8.
62          FIND VER 1,LAST NAME=JANET;
8 NAME=JANET SEX=F AGE=15 HEIGHT=62.5 WEIGHT=112.5;
63          LIST;
64          DELETE;
65          VERIFY RESET;
8 NAME= SEX= AGE=. HEIGHT=. WEIGHT=.;
66          LIST;
67
68          NAME HEIGHT;
NOTE: FOUND AT OBS 15.
69          LOCATE 1,LAST 72.0;
70          DELETE;
71          VERIFY RESET;
15 NAME= SEX= AGE=. HEIGHT=. WEIGHT=.;
72          LIST;
73
74          STRING NAME SEX;
NOTE: FOUND AT OBS 4.
75          SEARCH VER 1,LAST CAROL F;
4 NAME=CAROL SEX=F AGE=14 HEIGHT=62.8 WEIGHT=102.5;
76          LIST;
77
NOTE: NOT FOUND. OBS=21.
78          SEARCH VER 1,LAST CAROL M;
ERROR: NO CHANGES MADE BECAUSE NOGO SWITCH IS SET.
ERROR: NO CHANGES MADE BECAUSE NOGO SWITCH IS SET.
79          DELETE;
80
NOTE: EXITING FROM THE EDITOR PROCEDURE.
81          END;
NOTE: THE PROCEDURE EDITOR USED 0.18 SECONDS AND 184K.
```

```
82
83          PROC PRINT DATA=CLASS;
84          TITLE 'CLASS DATA SET AFTER BATCH EDIT';
85          RUN;
NOTE: THE PROCEDURE PRINT USED 0.09 SECONDS AND 212K
      AND PRINTED PAGE 1.

NOTE: SAS USED 212K MEMORY.
```

```
            SAS(R) LOG   OS SAS 5.16          MVS/XA JOB CH5E14   STEP SAS

ERROR: ERRORS ON PAGES 2.
ERROR: ERRORS ON PAGES 2.

NOTE: SAS INSTITUTE INC.
      SAS CIRCLE
      PO BOX 8000
      CARY, N.C. 27511-8000
```

```
                    CLASS DATA SET AFTER BATCH EDIT

        OBS    NAME      SEX   AGE   HEIGHT   WEIGHT

         1    ALFRED      M    14     69.0    112.5
         2    ALICE       F    13     56.5     84.0
         3    BARBARA     F    13     65.3     98.0
         4    CAROL       F    14     62.8    102.5
         5    HENRY       M    14     63.5    102.5
         6    JAMES       M    12     57.3     83.0
         7    JANE        F    12     59.8     84.5
         8                      .       .        .
         9    JEFFREY     M    13     62.5     84.0
        10    JOHN        M    12     59.0    106.5
        11    JOYCE       F    11     51.3     50.5
        12    JUDITH      F    14     64.3     90.0
        13    LOUISE      F    12     56.3     77.0
        14    MARY        F    15     66.5    112.0
        15                      .       .        .
        16    ROBERT      M    12     64.8    128.0
        17    RONALD      M    15     67.0    133.0
        18    THOMAS      M    11     57.5     85.0
        19    WILLIAM     M    15     67.0    120.0
        20    ANN         F    13     64.0     93.0
        21    DAVID       M    14     70.0    120.5
```

Some UPDATE Applications

In each example below, change the values of LOCATION in data set A for observations with certain ID values.

1. For all IDs between 1200 and 2000, change the LOCATION value to 5.
2. For a large set of IDs, change LOCATION's values.
3. For three IDs (you know the observation numbers) change the LOCATION value.

In each example, one method for updating data set A is better.

1. To make many changes that follow an easily stated pattern, create a new data set to replace A:

```
DATA B;
   SET A;
   IF 1200<=ID<=2000 THEN LOCATION=5;
RUN;
```

2. Create data set B containing the correct LOCATION value for each ID to be changed. Sort A and B by ID and then use UPDATE:

```
DATA C;
   UPDATE A B;
   BY ID;
RUN;
```

3. Edit the data set in place:

```
PROC EDITOR DATA=A;
REP 1205 LOCATION=4;
REP 1237, 1255 LOCATION=5;
END;
```

6 Writing Reports

A report is a useful summary of the information in a data file. When you begin to write a report, you may have one of these goals in mind:

□ to present information in an easy-to-read form, with a minimum of programming effort
□ to display information in detail that meets exact formatting specifications without regard to the time and effort required to do the programming.

The SAS System has features that help you meet either of these two goals. This chapter introduces you to report writing with SAS software with examples of some of the most commonly used SAS tools for writing reports.

□ PROC PRINT gives you well-structured, nicely formatted reports that require few user specifications.
□ PROC TABULATE produces tables of descriptive statistics in the form that you specify.
□ The DATA step gives you all the flexibility of programming statements to create customized reports that meet exact specifications. The FILE and PUT statements are the keys to DATA step report writing. Combined with the other DATA step programming tools, such as SAS functions, heading subroutines, and BY-group processing, you can design any report you need.
□ PROC FORMS allows you to print SAS data set information on prepared forms, such as checks or mailing labels.
□ Certain SAS system options are especially useful when writing reports, whether you use a SAS procedure or the DATA step to produce the report.

For detailed descriptions of SAS features discussed in this chapter and for information on other SAS report-writing facilities, refer to the *SAS User's Guide: Basics, Version 5 Edition.*

The PRINT Procedure

Use the PRINT procedure when your report is to be a listing of all the observations and some or all of the variables in a SAS data set, and when your goal is to produce a readable report with little effort.

The statement

```
PROC PRINT DATA=SASdataset;
```

produces a listing of all the observations and all the variables in a SAS data set. The headings printed are the variable names, and the values of the variables are centered under each heading. In addition, you can use these features to enhance the report that PROC PRINT produces:

□ A BY statement lets you separate groups.
□ PROC PRINT uses the format associated with each variable that it prints; a FORMAT statement assigns new formats.
□ The LABEL and SPLIT= options for PROC PRINT tell SAS to use labels instead of variable names as column headings. The DOUBLE option causes your report to be double-spaced.
□ Up to ten TITLE statements and ten FOOTNOTE statements can be used with the procedure.
□ A SUM statement lets you specify variables you want totaled.
□ A PAGEBY statement lets you start a new page for a new BY group.
□ When you have more than one BY variable, a SUMBY statement controls the level of subgrouping for which totals are calculated.

A Simple Example Suny Stereo Inc. is a chain that sells various stereo products at six stores in three North Carolina cities. The company's business department maintains a data file that contains monthly sales figures for each product in each store. The data file has the following form:

```
23515.21 28219.53 21531.90 1 1 1
11223.22 12122.33 15323.23 1 1 3
25211.09 31233.15 21523.51 1 1 4
21821.38 20829.53 20822.23 2 3 6
19321.55 18417.52 21562.41 2 4 1
24217.14 21015.27 19218.33 2 4 2
29816.00 31233.19 26984.51 1 2 4
22578.63 24548.37 25618.23 3 6 6
21926.00 22905.00 24936.86 1 2 5
28196.59 23590.06 23215.10 1 2 6
15321.55 12318.52 21512.31 2 3 1
23218.13 21015.28 15212.33 2 3 2
12157.12 15378.58 13582.33 2 4 3
31072.68 31243.90 32945.31 2 4 4
25533.31 22311.09 28121.01 3 5 5
22582.13 23532.38 25112.23 3 5 6
24672.50 19143.00 16588.09 3 6 1
23476.51 24981.85 20611.72 3 6 2
30548.12 32847.22 29430.45 2 4 5
21726.47 20720.93 20722.83 2 4 6
23182.59 15133.09 11522.95 3 5 1
```

```
23381.51 23521.25 20111.82 3 5 2
15111.38 15335.89 12252.22 3 5 3
33135.38 31328.31 30111.82 3 5 4
21521.00 22505.90 23531.21 1 1 5
22151.55 23559.01 23215.19 1 1 6
24519.21 27210.54 21546.00 1 2 1
28349.28 24318.06 29783.49 1 2 2
12158.12 15382.52 13522.33 2 3 3
31082.12 31233.50 32535.31 2 3 4
30532.12 32238.22 25339.35 2 3 5
16283.82 18122.33 19323.83 1 2 3
22335.22 23312.01 25823.35 1 1 2
19161.47 19445.70 18892.28 3 6 3
34145.37 31427.36 30661.78 3 6 4
25934.46 28316.00 27186.06 3 6 5
```

PROC PRINT can produce the report only if the data are in the form of a SAS data set. These statements read the data from an external file on disk and create a SAS data set named REPORT:

```
DATA REPORT;
   INFILE SALES;
   INPUT (JAN FEB MAR) (9.2) CITY 2. STORE 2. PRODUCT 2.;
   YTD=SUM(JAN,FEB,MAR);
RUN;
```

To produce an ordered listing of the data in REPORT, first sort the data set by STORE and PRODUCT within STORE. Then invoke the PRINT procedure in its simplest form:

```
PROC SORT DATA=REPORT;
   BY STORE PRODUCT;
RUN;
PROC PRINT DATA=REPORT;
RUN;
```

The results of the PROC PRINT step are shown in **Output 6.1.** Notice that the values of the variables JAN, FEB, MAR, and YTD have only one decimal place in the PRINT output. This is because no formats were assigned to these variables. When the PRINT procedure has unformatted numeric values to print, it chooses the most efficient way of printing those values. Sometimes this results in rounding of numeric values.

```
                                        SAS

   OBS      JAN        FEB        MAR      CITY    STORE    PRODUCT      YTD

     1    23515.2    28219.5    21531.9     1        1         1       73266.6
     2    22335.2    23312.0    25823.3     1        1         2       71470.6
     3    11223.2    12122.3    15323.2     1        1         3       38668.8
     4    25211.1    31233.1    21523.5     1        1         4       77967.7
     5    21521.0    22505.9    23531.2     1        1         5       67558.1
     6    22151.5    23559.0    23215.2     1        1         6       68925.7
     7    24519.2    27210.5    21546.0     1        2         1       73275.7
     8    28349.3    24318.1    29783.5     1        2         2       82450.8
     9    16283.8    18122.3    19323.8     1        2         3       53730.0
    10    29816.0    31233.2    26984.5     1        2         4       88033.7
    11    21926.0    22905.0    24936.9     1        2         5       69767.9
    12    28196.6    23590.1    23215.1     1        2         6       75001.7
    13    15321.5    12318.5    21512.3     2        3         1       49152.4
    14    23218.1    21015.3    15212.3     2        3         2       59445.7
    15    12158.1    15382.5    13522.3     2        3         3       41063.0
    16    31082.1    31233.5    32535.3     2        3         4       94850.9
    17    30532.1    32238.2    25339.3     2        3         5       88109.7
    18    21821.4    20829.5    20822.2     2        3         6       63473.1
    19    19321.5    18417.5    21562.4     2        4         1       59301.5
    20    24217.1    21015.3    19218.3     2        4         2       64450.7
    21    12157.1    15378.6    13582.3     2        4         3       41118.0
    22    31072.7    31243.9    32945.3     2        4         4       95261.9
    23    30548.1    32847.2    29430.4     2        4         5       92825.8
    24    21726.5    20720.9    20722.8     2        4         6       63170.2
    25    23182.6    15133.1    11522.9     3        5         1       49838.6
    26    23381.5    23521.3    20111.8     3        5         2       67014.6
    27    15111.4    15335.9    12252.2     3        5         3       42699.5
    28    33135.4    31328.3    30111.8     3        5         4       94575.5
    29    25533.3    22311.1    28121.0     3        5         5       75965.4
    30    22582.1    23532.4    25112.2     3        5         6       71226.7
    31    24672.5    19143.0    16588.1     3        6         1       60403.6
    32    23476.5    24981.8    20611.7     3        6         2       69070.1
    33    19161.5    19445.7    18892.3     3        6         3       57499.4
    34    34145.4    31427.4    30661.8     3        6         4       96234.5
    35    25934.5    28316.0    27186.1     3        6         5       81436.5
    36    22578.6    24548.4    25618.2     3        6         6       72745.2
```

If you do not want PRINT to round numeric values, use a FORMAT statement to assign formats directly. For example, when a FORMAT statement is added to the DATA step that creates the REPORT data set, the values are no longer rounded by PROC PRINT, as shown in **Output 6.2.**

```
DATA REPORT;
   INFILE SALES;
   INPUT (JAN FEB MAR) (9.2) CITY 2. STORE 2. PRODUCT 2.;
   FORMAT JAN FEB MAR YTD 12.2;
   YTD=SUM(JAN,FEB,MAR);
RUN;
PROC SORT DATA=REPORT;
   BY STORE PRODUCT;
RUN;
PROC PRINT DATA=REPORT;
RUN;
```

Output 6.2
Same Data Set but Some
Values Formatted

```
                                     SAS

 OBS      JAN        FEB        MAR     CITY   STORE   PRODUCT     YTD

   1   23515.21   28219.53   21531.90    1       1        1     73266.64
   2   22335.22   23312.01   25823.35    1       1        2     71470.58
   3   11223.22   12122.33   15323.23    1       1        3     38668.78
   4   25211.09   31233.15   21523.51    1       1        4     77967.75
   5   21521.00   22505.90   23531.21    1       1        5     67558.11
   6   22151.55   23559.01   23215.19    1       1        6     68925.75
   7   24519.21   27210.54   21546.00    1       2        1     73275.75
   8   28349.28   24318.06   29783.49    1       2        2     82450.83
   9   16283.82   18122.33   19323.83    1       2        3     53729.98
  10   29816.00   31233.19   26984.51    1       2        4     88033.70
  11   21926.00   22905.00   24936.86    1       2        5     69767.86
  12   28196.59   23590.06   23215.10    1       2        6     75001.75
  13   15321.55   12318.52   21512.31    2       3        1     49152.38
  14   23218.13   21015.28   15212.33    2       3        2     59445.74
  15   12158.12   15382.52   13522.33    2       3        3     41062.97
  16   31082.12   31233.50   32535.31    2       3        4     94850.93
  17   30532.12   32238.22   25339.35    2       3        5     88109.69
  18   21821.38   20829.53   20822.23    2       3        6     63473.14
  19   19321.55   18417.52   21562.41    2       4        1     59301.48
  20   24217.14   21015.27   19218.33    2       4        2     64450.74
  21   12157.12   15378.58   13582.33    2       4        3     41118.03
  22   31072.68   31243.90   32945.31    2       4        4     95261.89
  23   30548.12   32847.22   29430.45    2       4        5     92825.79
  24   21726.47   20720.93   20722.83    2       4        6     63170.23
  25   23182.59   15133.09   11522.95    3       5        1     49838.63
  26   23381.51   23521.25   20111.82    3       5        2     67014.58
  27   15111.38   15335.89   12252.22    3       5        3     42699.49
  28   33135.38   31328.31   30111.82    3       5        4     94575.51
  29   25533.31   22311.09   28121.01    3       5        5     75965.41
  30   22582.13   23532.38   25112.23    3       5        6     71226.74
  31   24672.50   19143.00   16588.09    3       6        1     60403.59
  32   23476.51   24981.85   20611.72    3       6        2     69070.08
  33   19161.47   19445.70   18892.28    3       6        3     57499.45
  34   34145.37   31427.36   30661.78    3       6        4     96234.51
  35   25934.46   28316.00   27186.06    3       6        5     81436.52
  36   22578.63   24548.37   25618.23    3       6        6     72745.23
```

There are two ways to use a FORMAT statement to assign a format:

☐ in the DATA step that creates the data set, as in the example above
☐ in a DATA or PROC step that reads a data set.

Assigning a format when the data set is created causes the format to be associated with the variable permanently. Thus, each time the data set is processed, the format is used to output the variable's values, unless you override it with another FORMAT statement.* If a format is assigned when the data set is read, for example, in a PRINT step, the format is not permanently associated with the variable. If you know that you always want to print a variable using a particular format, it is most convenient to specify the FORMAT statement one time, when the data set is created.

---

* You can specify SAS formats or user-written formats in the FORMAT statement. When you create a permanent SAS data set and assign user-written formats to any of its variables, be sure you also store the formats permanently. Serious complications arise if you do not save the format of a permanent data set variable. Directions for storing user-written formats are different for each operating system. See the description of the FORMAT procedure for the directions appropriate to your operating environment.

Refining the Report Give this report added impact using procedure options and information statements. You can also add an OPTIONS statement to set the width of the printout to 72 print positions. (Then you can print the output on 8-1/2x11 paper for distribution to each store.)

```
OPTIONS LS=72;
PROC PRINT DATA=REPORT SPLIT='*';
   BY STORE;
   ID PRODUCT;
   VAR JAN FEB MAR YTD;
   LABEL YTD='YEAR TO*  DATE';
RUN;
```

□ The SPLIT= option in the PROC statement tells SAS that variable labels should be broken (split) where asterisks appear.
□ The BY statement separates each STORE from other stores in the report.
□ The ID statement specifies a variable whose values should identify lines in the report, rather than the observation number OBS.
□ The VAR statement lists the variables you want printed. Variables are printed from left to right in the order listed in the VAR statement.
□ The LABEL statement specifies labels for variables, so the labels are printed rather than variable names.

The new report is shown in **Output 6.3.**

Output 6.3
Report with Variable
Label and BY Groups

```
                              SAS
------------------------------ STORE=1 ------------------------------

     PRODUCT      JAN         FEB         MAR       YEAR TO
                                                     DATE

        1      23515.21    28219.53    21531.90    73266.64
        2      22335.22    23312.01    25823.35    71470.58
        3      11223.22    12122.33    15323.23    38668.78
        4      25211.09    31233.15    21523.51    77967.75
        5      21521.00    22505.90    23531.21    67558.11
        6      22151.55    23559.01    23215.19    68925.75


------------------------------ STORE=2 ------------------------------

     PRODUCT      JAN         FEB         MAR       YEAR TO
                                                     DATE

        1      24519.21    27210.54    21546.00    73275.75
        2      28349.28    24318.06    29783.49    82450.83
        3      16283.82    18122.33    19323.83    53729.98
        4      29816.00    31233.19    26984.51    88033.70
        5      21926.00    22905.00    24936.86    69767.86
        6      28196.59    23590.06    23215.10    75001.75
```

```
------------------------ STORE=3 ---------------------------

        PRODUCT      JAN        FEB        MAR      YEAR TO
                                                     DATE

           1       15321.55   12318.52   21512.31   49152.38
           2       23218.13   21015.28   15212.33   59445.74
           3       12158.12   15382.52   13522.33   41062.97
           4       31082.12   31233.50   32535.31   94850.93
           5       30532.12   32238.22   25339.35   88109.69
           6       21821.38   20829.53   20822.23   63473.14


------------------------ STORE=4 ---------------------------

        PRODUCT      JAN        FEB        MAR      YEAR TO
                                                     DATE

           1       19321.55   18417.52   21562.41   59301.48
           2       24217.14   21015.27   19218.33   64450.74
           3       12157.12   15378.58   13582.33   41118.03
           4       31072.68   31243.90   32945.31   95261.89
           5       30548.12   32847.22   29430.45   92825.79
           6       21726.47   20720.93   20722.83   63170.23
```

```
                             SAS
------------------------ STORE=5 ---------------------------

        PRODUCT      JAN        FEB        MAR      YEAR TO
                                                     DATE

           1       23182.59   15133.09   11522.95   49838.63
           2       23381.51   23521.25   20111.82   67014.58
           3       15111.38   15335.89   12252.22   42699.49
           4       33135.38   31328.31   30111.82   94575.51
           5       25533.31   22311.09   28121.01   75965.41
           6       22582.13   23532.38   25112.23   71226.74


------------------------ STORE=6 ---------------------------

        PRODUCT      JAN        FEB        MAR      YEAR TO
                                                     DATE

           1       24672.50   19143.00   16588.09   60403.59
           2       23476.51   24981.85   20611.72   69070.08
           3       19161.47   19445.70   18892.28   57499.45
           4       34145.37   31427.36   30661.78   96234.51
           5       25934.46   28316.00   27186.06   81436.52
           6       22578.63   24548.37   25618.23   72745.23
```

Titles for the report

Use TITLE statements to give headings to your report:

```
TITLE1 'FIRST QUARTER SALES REPORT FOR SUNY STEREO INC.';
TITLE2 'IN DOLLARS BY STORE';
```

Footnotes for the report

You might want to use footnotes as well as titles, or instead of titles. Use FOOTNOTE statements with the procedure to add text at the bottom of each page, for example,

```
FOOTNOTE 'CONFIDENTIAL INFORMATION FOR MANAGERS ONLY';
```

Value labels

In an earlier example, a FORMAT statement was added to the DATA step creating the REPORT data set to specify a format for the JAN,

FEB, MAR, and YTD variables. FORMAT statements can also be used in PROC steps to assign formats on a temporary basis. You can specify SAS formats, or you can specify formats you have created with the FORMAT procedure.

You can improve the readability of the sales report by printing the values of STORE and PRODUCT with formats. However, there are no SAS formats appropriate for these variables, so you need to create formats. The statements below define more meaningful labels for printing the values of STORE and PRODUCT:

```
PROC FORMAT;
   VALUE SCODE 1='MURPHY ST.'
               2='APPLETON ST.'
               3='MARKET SQ.'
               4='CARSON MALL'
               5='MAIN ST.'
               6='SALEM BLVD.';
   VALUE PCODE 1='AMPLIFIERS'
               2='RECEIVERS'
               3='TURNTABLES'
               4='TAPE DECKS'
               5='SPEAKERS'
               6='OTHER AUDIO';
RUN;
```

Now use a FORMAT statement with the procedure to associate the formats defined above with the variables STORE and PRODUCT:

```
PROC PRINT DATA=REPORT SPLIT='*';
   BY STORE;
   ID PRODUCT;
   VAR JAN FEB MAR YTD;
   FORMAT STORE SCODE. PRODUCT PCODE.;
   LABEL YTD='YEAR TO*  DATE';
   TITLE1 'FIRST QUARTER SALES REPORT FOR SUNY STEREO INC.';
   TITLE2 'IN DOLLARS BY STORE';
RUN;
```

The report produced by this program is shown in **Output 6.4.**

Output 6.4
Report with Titles and
User Formats Added

```
                    FIRST QUARTER SALES REPORT FOR SUNY STEREO INC.
                                  IN DOLLARS BY STORE
--------------------------------- STORE=MURPHY ST. -------------------------------

        PRODUCT         JAN         FEB         MAR       YEAR TO
                                                            DATE

        AMPLIFIERS    23515.21    28219.53    21531.90    73266.64
        RECEIVERS     22335.22    23312.01    25823.35    71470.58
        TURNTABLES    11223.22    12122.33    15323.23    38668.78
        TAPE DECKS    25211.09    31233.15    21523.51    77967.75
        SPEAKERS      21521.00    22505.90    23531.21    67558.11
        OTHER AUDIO   22151.55    23559.01    23215.19    68925.75


--------------------------------- STORE=APPLETON ST. -----------------------------

        PRODUCT         JAN         FEB         MAR       YEAR TO
                                                            DATE

        AMPLIFIERS    24519.21    27210.54    21546.00    73275.75
        RECEIVERS     28349.28    24318.06    29783.49    82450.83
        TURNTABLES    16283.82    18122.33    19323.83    53729.98
        TAPE DECKS    29816.00    31233.19    26984.51    88033.70
        SPEAKERS      21926.00    22905.00    24936.86    69767.86
        OTHER AUDIO   28196.59    23590.06    23215.10    75001.75


--------------------------------- STORE=MARKET SQ. -------------------------------

        PRODUCT         JAN         FEB         MAR       YEAR TO
                                                            DATE

        AMPLIFIERS    15321.55    12318.52    21512.31    49152.38
        RECEIVERS     23218.13    21015.28    15212.33    59445.74
        TURNTABLES    12158.12    15382.52    13522.33    41062.97
        TAPE DECKS    31082.12    31233.50    32535.31    94850.93
        SPEAKERS      30532.12    32238.22    25339.35    88109.69
        OTHER AUDIO   21821.38    20829.53    20822.23    63473.14


--------------------------------- STORE=CARSON MALL ------------------------------

        PRODUCT         JAN         FEB         MAR       YEAR TO
                                                            DATE

        AMPLIFIERS    19321.55    18417.52    21562.41    59301.48
        RECEIVERS     24217.14    21015.27    19218.33    64450.74
        TURNTABLES    12157.12    15378.58    13582.33    41118.03
        TAPE DECKS    31072.68    31243.90    32945.31    95261.89
        SPEAKERS      30548.12    32847.22    29430.45    92825.79
        OTHER AUDIO   21726.47    20720.93    20722.83    63170.23
```

```
                    FIRST QUARTER SALES REPORT FOR SUNY STEREO INC.
                                  IN DOLLARS BY STORE
--------------------------------- STORE=MAIN ST. ---------------------------------

        PRODUCT         JAN         FEB         MAR       YEAR TO
                                                            DATE

        AMPLIFIERS    23182.59    15133.09    11522.95    49838.63
        RECEIVERS     23381.51    23521.25    20111.82    67014.58
        TURNTABLES    15111.38    15335.89    12252.22    42699.49
        TAPE DECKS    33135.38    31328.31    30111.82    94575.51
        SPEAKERS      25533.31    22311.09    28121.01    75965.41
        OTHER AUDIO   22582.13    23532.38    25112.23    71226.74


--------------------------------- STORE=SALEM BLVD. ------------------------------

        PRODUCT         JAN         FEB         MAR       YEAR TO
                                                            DATE

        AMPLIFIERS    24672.50    19143.00    16588.09    60403.59
        RECEIVERS     23476.51    24981.85    20611.72    69070.08
        TURNTABLES    19161.47    19445.70    18892.28    57499.45
        TAPE DECKS    34145.37    31427.36    30661.78    96234.51
        SPEAKERS      25934.46    28316.00    27186.06    81436.52
        OTHER AUDIO   22578.63    24548.37    25618.23    72745.23
```

Column totals

Column totals would be useful on this sales report. A SUM statement with PROC PRINT tells SAS which variables to total. The statements below produce a report with monthly totals for each STORE and for all stores at the end of the report. The revised report is shown in **Output 6.5.**

```
PROC PRINT DATA=REPORT SPLIT='*';
   BY STORE;
   ID PRODUCT;
   VAR JAN FEB MAR YTD;
   SUM JAN FEB MAR YTD;
   FORMAT STORE SCODE. PRODUCT PCODE.;
   LABEL YTD='YEAR TO*  DATE';
   TITLE1 'FIRST QUARTER SALES REPORT FOR SUNY STEREO INC.';
   TITLE2 'IN DOLLARS BY STORE';
RUN;
```

Output 6.5
Sales Report Including
Sums

```
            FIRST QUARTER SALES REPORT FOR SUNY STEREO INC.
                        IN DOLLARS BY STORE
------------------------------ STORE=MURPHY ST. -------------------------------

       PRODUCT          JAN         FEB         MAR      YEAR TO
                                                           DATE

       AMPLIFIERS    23515.21    28219.53    21531.90    73266.64
       RECEIVERS     22335.22    23312.01    25823.35    71470.58
       TURNTABLES    11223.22    12122.33    15323.23    38668.78
       TAPE DECKS    25211.09    31233.15    21523.51    77967.75
       SPEAKERS      21521.00    22505.90    23531.21    67558.11
       OTHER AUDIO   22151.55    23559.01    23215.19    68925.75
                    ---------   ---------   ---------   ---------
          STORE    125957.29   140951.93   130948.39   397857.61


------------------------------ STORE=APPLETON ST. -----------------------------

       PRODUCT          JAN         FEB         MAR      YEAR TO
                                                           DATE

       AMPLIFIERS    24519.21    27210.54    21546.00    73275.75
       RECEIVERS     28349.28    24318.06    29783.49    82450.83
       TURNTABLES    16283.82    18122.33    19323.83    53729.98
       TAPE DECKS    29816.00    31233.19    26984.51    88033.70
       SPEAKERS      21926.00    22905.00    24936.86    69767.86
       OTHER AUDIO   28196.59    23590.06    23215.10    75001.75
                    ---------   ---------   ---------   ---------
          STORE    149090.90   147379.18   145789.79   442259.87


------------------------------ STORE=MARKET SQ. -------------------------------

       PRODUCT          JAN         FEB         MAR      YEAR TO
                                                           DATE

       AMPLIFIERS    15321.55    12318.52    21512.31    49152.38
       RECEIVERS     23218.13    21015.28    15212.33    59445.74
       TURNTABLES    12158.12    15382.52    13522.33    41062.97
       TAPE DECKS    31082.12    31233.50    32535.31    94850.93
       SPEAKERS      30532.12    32238.22    25339.35    88109.69
       OTHER AUDIO   21821.38    20829.53    20822.23    63473.14
                    ---------   ---------   ---------   ---------
          STORE    134133.42   133017.57   128943.86   396094.85
```

```
                      FIRST QUARTER SALES REPORT FOR SUNY STEREO INC.
                                   IN DOLLARS BY STORE
     ------------------------------ STORE=CARSON MALL ------------------------------

         PRODUCT            JAN            FEB            MAR        YEAR TO
                                                                       DATE

         AMPLIFIERS       19321.55       18417.52       21562.41      59301.48
         RECEIVERS        24217.14       21015.27       19218.33      64450.74
         TURNTABLES       12157.12       15378.58       13582.33      41118.03
         TAPE DECKS       31072.68       31243.90       32945.31      95261.89
         SPEAKERS         30548.12       32847.22       29430.45      92825.79
         OTHER AUDIO      21726.47       20720.93       20722.83      63170.23
                         ----------     ----------     ----------    ----------
            STORE        139043.08      139623.42      137461.66     416128.16


     ------------------------------ STORE=MAIN ST. ------------------------------

         PRODUCT            JAN            FEB            MAR        YEAR TO
                                                                       DATE

         AMPLIFIERS       23182.59       15133.09       11522.95      49838.63
         RECEIVERS        23381.51       23521.25       20111.82      67014.58
         TURNTABLES       15111.38       15335.89       12252.22      42699.49
         TAPE DECKS       33135.38       31328.31       30111.82      94575.51
         SPEAKERS         25533.31       22311.09       28121.01      75965.41
         OTHER AUDIO      22582.13       23532.38       25112.23      71226.74
                         ----------     ----------     ----------    ----------
            STORE        142926.30      131162.01      127232.05     401320.36


     ------------------------------ STORE=SALEM BLVD. ------------------------------

         PRODUCT            JAN            FEB            MAR        YEAR TO
                                                                       DATE

         AMPLIFIERS       24672.50       19143.00       16588.09      60403.59
         RECEIVERS        23476.51       24981.85       20611.72      69070.08
         TURNTABLES       19161.47       19445.70       18892.28      57499.45
         TAPE DECKS       34145.37       31427.36       30661.78      96234.51
         SPEAKERS         25934.46       28316.00       27186.06      81436.52
         OTHER AUDIO      22578.63       24548.37       25618.23      72745.23
                         ----------     ----------     ----------    ----------
            STORE        149968.94      147862.28      139558.16     437389.38
                         ==========     ==========     ==========    ==========
                         841119.93      839996.39      809933.91    2491050.23
```

Combining Data Sets to Write Reports

Suppose you want to add other information to the report. For example, say you want to show the average sales for each month so that each store's manager can see which products fall below the average. Use a SAS procedure to calculate the means and output them to a SAS data set. Then, combine the information in the summary data set with the original sales data.

PROC SUMMARY automatically produces a SAS data set containing summary statistics for subgroups and does not require you to sort the data set used as input. The following SUMMARY step produces data set NEW containing the average sales for each month. Because SUMMARY does not produce printed output, a PROC PRINT step is added to show SUMMARY's output data set (see **Output 6.6**).

```
PROC SUMMARY DATA=REPORT;
   CLASS STORE;
   VAR JAN FEB MAR YTD;
   OUTPUT OUT=OUTDATA MEAN=JAN FEB MAR YTD;
RUN;
PROC PRINT DATA=OUTDATA;
   TITLE 'THE OUTDATA DATA SET';
RUN;
```

```
                              THE OUTDATA DATA SET

  OBS    STORE    _TYPE_    _FREQ_      JAN          FEB          MAR          YTD

   1       .         0        36      23364.44     23333.23     22498.16     69195.84
   2       1         1         6      20992.88     23491.99     21824.73     66309.60
   3       2         1         6      24848.48     24563.20     24298.30     73709.98
   4       3         1         6      22355.57     22169.59     21490.64     66015.81
   5       4         1         6      23173.85     23270.57     22910.28     69354.69
   6       5         1         6      23821.05     21860.33     21205.34     66886.73
   7       6         1         6      24994.82     24643.71     23259.69     72898.23
```

Now, to combine the sales averages from OUTDATA with the
REPORT data set, interleave REPORT and OUTDATA with a SET
statement and BY STORE statement:

```
DATA FINAL;
   SET REPORT OUTDATA(IN=INO);
   BY STORE;
   IF _TYPE_=0 THEN DELETE;
   IF INO THEN PRODUCT=7;
RUN;
```

Define an additional label for the new value of the PRODUCT
variable:

```
PROC FORMAT;
   VALUE PCODE 1='AMPLIFIERS'
               2='RECEIVERS'
               3='TURNTABLES'
               4='TAPE DECKS'
               5='SPEAKERS'
               6='OTHER AUDIO'
               7='  AVERAGE SALES';
   RUN;
```

Print the expanded report, using the COMMA. format for the
numeric variables and adding another title:

```
PROC PRINT DATA=FINAL SPLIT='*';
   BY STORE;
   ID PRODUCT;
   VAR JAN FEB MAR YTD;
   FORMAT STORE SCODE. PRODUCT PCODE. JAN FEB MAR YTD COMMA12.2;
   LABEL YTD='YEAR TO*  DATE';
   TITLE1 'FIRST QUARTER SALES REPORT FOR SUNY STEREO INC.';
   TITLE2 'IN DOLLARS BY STORE';
   TITLE3 'INCLUDES AVERAGE SALES FOR THE MONTH';
RUN;
```

The report from this program is shown in **Output 6.7.**

Output 6.7
Report Resulting from
Combined Data Sets

```
              FIRST QUARTER SALES REPORT FOR SUNY STEREO INC.
                        IN DOLLARS BY STORE
                INCLUDES AVERAGE SALES FOR THE MONTH

----------------------------- STORE=MURPHY ST. -----------------------------

       PRODUCT          JAN         FEB         MAR        YEAR TO
                                                            DATE

    AMPLIFIERS       23,515.21   28,219.53   21,531.90   73,266.64
    RECEIVERS        22,335.22   23,312.01   25,823.35   71,470.58
    TURNTABLES       11,223.22   12,122.33   15,323.23   38,668.78
    TAPE DECKS       25,211.09   31,233.15   21,523.51   77,967.75
    SPEAKERS         21,521.00   22,505.90   23,531.21   67,558.11
    OTHER AUDIO      22,151.55   23,559.01   23,215.19   68,925.75
      AVERAGE SALES  20,992.88   23,491.99   21,824.73   66,309.60


----------------------------- STORE=APPLETON ST. ----------------------------

       PRODUCT          JAN         FEB         MAR        YEAR TO
                                                            DATE

    AMPLIFIERS       24,519.21   27,210.54   21,546.00   73,275.75
    RECEIVERS        28,349.28   24,318.06   29,783.49   82,450.83
    TURNTABLES       16,283.82   18,122.33   19,323.83   53,729.98
    TAPE DECKS       29,816.00   31,233.19   26,984.51   88,033.70
    SPEAKERS         21,926.00   22,905.00   24,936.86   69,767.86
    OTHER AUDIO      28,196.59   23,590.06   23,215.10   75,001.75
      AVERAGE SALES  24,848.48   24,563.20   24,298.30   73,709.98


----------------------------- STORE=MARKET SQ. -----------------------------

       PRODUCT          JAN         FEB         MAR        YEAR TO
                                                            DATE

    AMPLIFIERS       15,321.55   12,318.52   21,512.31   49,152.38
    RECEIVERS        23,218.13   21,015.28   15,212.33   59,445.74
    TURNTABLES       12,158.12   15,382.52   13,522.33   41,062.97
    TAPE DECKS       31,082.12   31,233.50   32,535.31   94,850.93
    SPEAKERS         30,532.12   32,238.22   25,339.35   88,109.69
    OTHER AUDIO      21,821.38   20,829.53   20,822.23   63,473.14
      AVERAGE SALES  22,355.57   22,169.59   21,490.64   66,015.81


----------------------------- STORE=CARSON MALL ----------------------------

       PRODUCT          JAN         FEB         MAR        YEAR TO
                                                            DATE

    AMPLIFIERS       19,321.55   18,417.52   21,562.41   59,301.48
    RECEIVERS        24,217.14   21,015.27   19,218.33   64,450.74
    TURNTABLES       12,157.12   15,378.58   13,582.33   41,118.03
    TAPE DECKS       31,072.68   31,243.90   32,945.31   95,261.89
    SPEAKERS         30,548.12   32,847.22   29,430.45   92,825.79
    OTHER AUDIO      21,726.47   20,720.93   20,722.83   63,170.23
      AVERAGE SALES  23,173.85   23,270.57   22,910.28   69,354.69
```

```
              FIRST QUARTER SALES REPORT FOR SUNY STEREO INC.
                        IN DOLLARS BY STORE
                INCLUDES AVERAGE SALES FOR THE MONTH

----------------------------- STORE=MAIN ST. -----------------------------

       PRODUCT          JAN         FEB         MAR        YEAR TO
                                                            DATE

    AMPLIFIERS       23,182.59   15,133.09   11,522.95   49,838.63
    RECEIVERS        23,381.51   23,521.25   20,111.82   67,014.58
    TURNTABLES       15,111.38   15,335.89   12,252.22   42,699.49
    TAPE DECKS       33,135.38   31,328.31   30,111.82   94,575.51
    SPEAKERS         25,533.31   22,311.09   28,121.01   75,965.41
    OTHER AUDIO      22,582.13   23,532.38   25,112.23   71,226.74
      AVERAGE SALES  23,821.05   21,860.33   21,205.34   66,886.73
```

(continued on next page)

(continued from previous page)

```
----------------------------- STORE=SALEM BLVD. -----------------------------

     PRODUCT          JAN          FEB          MAR       YEAR TO
                                                            DATE

   AMPLIFIERS      24,672.50    19,143.00    16,588.09    60,403.59
   RECEIVERS       23,476.51    24,981.85    20,611.72    69,070.08
   TURNTABLES      19,161.47    19,445.70    18,892.28    57,499.45
   TAPE DECKS      34,145.37    31,427.36    30,661.78    96,234.51
   SPEAKERS        25,934.46    28,316.00    27,186.06    81,436.52
   OTHER AUDIO     22,578.63    24,548.37    25,618.23    72,745.23
      AVERAGE SALES 24,994.82   24,643.71    23,259.69    72,898.23
```

BY-Group Totals

The PRINT procedure includes two statements that allow you to produce reports emphasizing BY groups. The SUMBY statement specifies the level of subgrouping for which sums should be calculated. Without SUMBY, the PRINT procedure calculates sums for each BY group having more than one observation. The PAGEBY statement tells SAS that the report should begin a new page for specified BY groups.

To refine the sales report even more, take advantage of SUMBY and PAGEBY. You can produce a report showing the sales totals by CITY, combining the sales of both stores in each city, using SUMBY. When you use PAGEBY, the report begins on a new page for each city.

First, create labels for the CITY values:

```
PROC FORMAT;
   VALUE CCODE 1='RALEIGH NC'
               2='CHARLOTTE NC'
               3='WINSTON-SALEM NC';
RUN;
```

Next, sort the data by CITY and STORE within CITY:

```
PROC SORT DATA=REPORT OUT=SORTED;
   BY CITY STORE;
RUN;
```

Finally, add SUMBY and PAGEBY statements to the PRINT step. The output from this program is shown in **Output 6.8.**

```
PROC PRINT DATA=SORTED SPLIT='*';
   BY CITY STORE;
   ID PRODUCT;
   VAR JAN FEB MAR YTD;
   SUM JAN FEB MAR YTD;
   SUMBY CITY;
   PAGEBY CITY;
   FORMAT CITY CCODE. STORE SCODE. PRODUCT PCODE.
          JAN FEB MAR YTD COMMA12.2;
   LABEL YTD='YEAR TO*  DATE';
   TITLE1 'FIRST QUARTER SALES REPORT FOR SUNY STEREO INC.';
   TITLE2 'IN DOLLARS BY CITY AND STORE';
RUN;
```

Output 6.8
Report Produced Using
PAGEBY and SUMBY

```
                 FIRST QUARTER SALES REPORT FOR SUNY STEREO INC.
                           IN DOLLARS BY CITY AND STORE

---------------------- CITY=RALEIGH NC STORE=MURPHY ST. ----------------------

        PRODUCT        JAN           FEB           MAR        YEAR TO
                                                              DATE

        AMPLIFIERS   23,515.21     28,219.53     21,531.90    73,266.64
        RECEIVERS    22,335.22     23,312.01     25,823.35    71,470.58
        TURNTABLES   11,223.22     12,122.33     15,323.23    38,668.78
        TAPE DECKS   25,211.09     31,233.15     21,523.51    77,967.75
        SPEAKERS     21,521.00     22,505.90     23,531.21    67,558.11
        OTHER AUDIO  22,151.55     23,559.01     23,215.19    68,925.75


---------------------- CITY=RALEIGH NC STORE=APPLETON ST. ----------------------

        PRODUCT        JAN           FEB           MAR        YEAR TO
                                                              DATE

        AMPLIFIERS   24,519.21     27,210.54     21,546.00    73,275.75
        RECEIVERS    28,349.28     24,318.06     29,783.49    82,450.83
        TURNTABLES   16,283.82     18,122.33     19,323.83    53,729.98
        TAPE DECKS   29,816.00     31,233.19     26,984.51    88,033.70
        SPEAKERS     21,926.00     22,905.00     24,936.86    69,767.86
        OTHER AUDIO  28,196.59     23,590.06     23,215.10    75,001.75
                     ----------    ----------    ----------   ----------
           CITY     275,048.19    288,331.11    276,738.18   840,117.48
```

```
                 FIRST QUARTER SALES REPORT FOR SUNY STEREO INC.
                           IN DOLLARS BY CITY AND STORE

---------------------- CITY=CHARLOTTE NC STORE=MARKET SQ. ----------------------

        PRODUCT        JAN           FEB           MAR        YEAR TO
                                                              DATE

        AMPLIFIERS   15,321.55     12,318.52     21,512.31    49,152.38
        RECEIVERS    23,218.13     21,015.28     15,212.33    59,445.74
        TURNTABLES   12,158.12     15,382.52     13,522.33    41,062.97
        TAPE DECKS   31,082.12     31,233.50     32,535.31    94,850.93
        SPEAKERS     30,532.12     32,238.22     25,339.35    88,109.69
        OTHER AUDIO  21,821.38     20,829.53     20,822.23    63,473.14

---------------------- CITY=CHARLOTTE NC STORE=CARSON MALL ----------------------

        PRODUCT        JAN           FEB           MAR        YEAR TO
                                                              DATE

        AMPLIFIERS   19,321.55     18,417.52     21,562.41    59,301.48
        RECEIVERS    24,217.14     21,015.27     19,218.33    64,450.74
        TURNTABLES   12,157.12     15,378.58     13,582.33    41,118.03
        TAPE DECKS   31,072.68     31,243.90     32,945.31    95,261.89
        SPEAKERS     30,548.12     32,847.22     29,430.45    92,825.79
        OTHER AUDIO  21,726.47     20,720.93     20,722.83    63,170.23
                     ----------    ----------    ----------   ----------
           CITY     273,176.50    272,640.99    266,405.52   812,223.01
```

```
                   FIRST QUARTER SALES REPORT FOR SUNY STEREO INC.
                            IN DOLLARS BY CITY AND STORE
     --------------------- CITY=WINSTON-SALEM NC STORE=MAIN ST. ---------------------

        PRODUCT          JAN           FEB           MAR         YEAR TO
                                                                  DATE

        AMPLIFIERS    23,182.59     15,133.09     11,522.95     49,838.63
        RECEIVERS     23,381.51     23,521.25     20,111.82     67,014.58
        TURNTABLES    15,111.38     15,335.89     12,252.22     42,699.49
        TAPE DECKS    33,135.38     31,328.31     30,111.82     94,575.51
        SPEAKERS      25,533.31     22,311.09     28,121.01     75,965.41
        OTHER AUDIO   22,582.13     23,532.38     25,112.23     71,226.74


     -------------------- CITY=WINSTON-SALEM NC STORE=SALEM BLVD. --------------------

        PRODUCT          JAN           FEB           MAR         YEAR TO
                                                                  DATE

        AMPLIFIERS    24,672.50     19,143.00     16,588.09     60,403.59
        RECEIVERS     23,476.51     24,981.85     20,611.72     69,070.08
        TURNTABLES    19,161.47     19,445.70     18,892.28     57,499.45
        TAPE DECKS    34,145.37     31,427.36     30,661.78     96,234.51
        SPEAKERS      25,934.46     28,316.00     27,186.06     81,436.52
        OTHER AUDIO   22,578.63     24,548.37     25,618.23     72,745.23
        -----------   ----------    ----------    ----------    -----------
        CITY         292,895.24    279,024.29    266,790.21    838,709.74
                     ==========    ==========    ==========    ============
                     841,119.93    839,996.39    809,933.91    2,491,050.23
```

The TABULATE Procedure

TABULATE is a powerful procedure that combines the report-generating capabilities of PROC PRINT with the statistical capabilities of the MEANS, SUMMARY, and FREQ procedures. You can use PROC TABULATE to calculate descriptive statistics from an input data set and display the results in a detailed table. You can format the table in three dimensions: column dimension, row dimension, and page dimension. Any table can have multiple classification variables. And, unlike PROC PRINT, TABULATE can supply both row and column totals with the use of the special class variable ALL.

This section introduces some TABULATE features with two examples using the REPORT data set.

Earlier in this chapter, PROC PRINT was used to create a report in which sales figures (variables JAN, FEB, MAR, and YTD) were summed for all PRODUCTs for each STORE and all STOREs (see **Output 6.5**). You can use PROC TABULATE to generate the same results in table format:

```
    PROC TABULATE DATA=REPORT;
       CLASS STORE PRODUCT;
       VAR JAN FEB MAR YTD;
       TABLE STORE*(PRODUCT ALL) ALL,JAN FEB MAR YTD;
       TITLE 'TABULATE OUTPUT TO COMPARE TO PROC PRINT OUTPUT 6.5';
    RUN;
```

In this example, the procedure creates a table in which

□ STORE and PRODUCT are class variables. The resulting table has rows for each PRODUCT in each STORE:

```
TABLE STORE*(PRODUCT
```

ALL PRODUCTs in each STORE:

```
TABLE STORE*(PRODUCT ALL)
```

and ALL PRODUCTs in ALL STOREs:

```
TABLE STORE*(PRODUCT ALL) ALL
```

□ the sales figures JAN, FEB, MAR, and YTD are analysis variables. The columns of the table are the analysis variables:

```
TABLE STORE*(PRODUCT ALL) ALL,JAN FEB MAR YTD;
```

□ each cell in the table contains the default statistic SUM because a VAR statement is specified and no other statistic is requested in the TABLE statement.

The table is shown in **Output 6.9**. The information is the same as that in **Output 6.5** from PROC PRINT, but the format is different.

Output 6.9
Report Produced with
PROC TABULATE

```
             TABULATE OUTPUT TO COMPARE TO PROC PRINT OUTPUT 6.5

      ---------------------------------------------------------------------
      |                  |     JAN   |    FEB    |    MAR    |    YTD     |
      |                  |-----------+-----------+-----------+------------|
      |                  |     SUM   |    SUM    |    SUM    |    SUM     |
      |--------+---------+-----------+-----------+-----------+------------|
      |STORE   |PRODUCT  |           |           |           |            |
      |--------+---------|           |           |           |            |
      |1       |1        |   23515.21|   28219.53|   21531.90|    73266.64|
      |        |---------+-----------+-----------+-----------+------------|
      |        |2        |   22335.22|   23312.01|   25823.35|    71470.58|
      |        |---------+-----------+-----------+-----------+------------|
      |        |3        |   11223.22|   12122.33|   15323.23|    38668.78|
      |        |---------+-----------+-----------+-----------+------------|
      |        |4        |   25211.09|   31233.15|   21523.51|    77967.75|
      |        |---------+-----------+-----------+-----------+------------|
      |        |5        |   21521.00|   22505.90|   23531.21|    67558.11|
      |        |---------+-----------+-----------+-----------+------------|
      |        |6        |   22151.55|   23559.01|   23215.19|    68925.75|
      |        |---------+-----------+-----------+-----------+------------|
      |        |ALL      |  125957.29|  140951.93|  130948.39|   397857.61|
      |--------+---------+-----------+-----------+-----------+------------|
```

(continued on next page)

(continued from previous page)

2	PRODUCT				
	1	24519.21	27210.54	21546.00	73275.75
	2	28349.28	24318.06	29783.49	82450.83
	3	16283.82	18122.33	19323.83	53729.98
	4	29816.00	31233.19	26984.51	88033.70
	5	21926.00	22905.00	24936.86	69767.86
	6	28196.59	23590.06	23215.10	75001.75
	ALL	149090.90	147379.18	145789.79	442259.87
3	PRODUCT				
	1	15321.55	12318.52	21512.31	49152.38
	2	23218.13	21015.28	15212.33	59445.74
	3	12158.12	15382.52	13522.33	41062.97
	4	31082.12	31233.50	32535.31	94850.93
	5	30532.12	32238.22	25339.35	88109.69
	6	21821.38	20829.53	20822.23	63473.14
	ALL	134133.42	133017.57	128943.86	396094.85

(CONTINUED)

TABULATE OUTPUT TO COMPARE TO PROC PRINT OUTPUT 6.5

		JAN	FEB	MAR	YTD
		SUM	SUM	SUM	SUM
STORE	PRODUCT				
4	1	19321.55	18417.52	21562.41	59301.48
	2	24217.14	21015.27	19218.33	64450.74
	3	12157.12	15378.58	13582.33	41118.03
	4	31072.68	31243.90	32945.31	95261.89
	5	30548.12	32847.22	29430.45	92825.79
	6	21726.47	20720.93	20722.83	63170.23
	ALL	139043.08	139623.42	137461.66	416128.16
5	PRODUCT				
	1	23182.59	15133.09	11522.95	49838.63
	2	23381.51	23521.25	20111.82	67014.58
	3	15111.38	15335.89	12252.22	42699.49
	4	33135.38	31328.31	30111.82	94575.51
	5	25533.31	22311.09	28121.01	75965.41
	6	22582.13	23532.38	25112.23	71226.74
	ALL	142926.30	131162.01	127232.05	401320.36

```
|6      |PRODUCT |          |          |          |          |
|       |--------|          |          |          |          |
|       |1       | 24672.50|  19143.00|  16588.09|  60403.59|
|       |--------+----------+----------+----------+----------|
|       |2       | 23476.51|  24981.85|  20611.72|  69070.08|
|       |--------+----------+----------+----------+----------|
|       |3       | 19161.47|  19445.70|  18892.28|  57499.45|
|       |--------+----------+----------+----------+----------|
|       |4       | 34145.37|  31427.36|  30661.78|  96234.51|
|       |--------+----------+----------+----------+----------|
|       |5       | 25934.46|  28316.00|  27186.06|  81436.52|
|       |--------+----------+----------+----------+----------|
|       |6       | 22578.63|  24548.37|  25618.23|  72745.23|
|       |--------+----------+----------+----------+----------|
|       |ALL     |149968.94| 147862.28| 139558.16| 437389.38|
----------------------------------------------------------------

(CONTINUED)
```

```
            TABULATE OUTPUT TO COMPARE TO PROC PRINT OUTPUT 6.5
--------------------------------------------------------------------
|          |     JAN   |    FEB    |    MAR    |    YTD    |
|          |-----------+-----------+-----------+-----------|
|          |     SUM   |    SUM    |    SUM    |    SUM    |
|----------+-----------+-----------+-----------+-----------|
|ALL       |  841119.93|  839996.39|  809933.91| 2491050.23|
--------------------------------------------------------------------
```

By adding format specifications and labels to the TABULATE step, you can make the table more readable. Formats for cell values are specified in this form:

```
variable or statistic*F=format
```

Specify row and column labels for any variable or statistic in the table in this form:

```
variable or statistic='label'
```

The second TABULATE example, shown below, adds cell value formats and variable and statistic labels. The resulting table is shown in **Output 6.10.**

```
PROC FORMAT;
   VALUE SCODE 1='MURPHY ST.'
               2='APPLETON ST.'
               3='MARKET SQ.'
               4='CARSON MALL'
               5='MAIN ST.'
               6='SALEM BLVD.';
```

```
                    VALUE PCODE 1='AMPLIFIERS'
                              2='RECEIVERS'
                              3='TURNTABLES'
                              4='TAPE DECKS'
                              5='SPEAKERS'
                              6='OTHER AUDIO';
         RUN;
         PROC TABULATE DATA=REPORT;
            CLASS STORE PRODUCT;
            VAR JAN FEB MAR YTD;
            TABLE (STORE*(PRODUCT ALL='STORE TOTAL')
                  ALL='GRAND TOTAL')*F=COMMA12.2, (JAN FEB MAR YTD)*SUM=' ';
            FORMAT STORE SCODE. PRODUCT PCODE.;
            TITLE 'TABLE WITH FORMATS AND LABELS ADDED';
         RUN;
```

Output 6.10
Another Report Produced
with PROC TABULATE

```
                    TABLE WITH FORMATS AND LABELS ADDED

         ---------------------------------------------------------------
         |          |          |   JAN   |   FEB   |   MAR   |   YTD   |
         |----------+----------+---------+---------+---------+---------|
         |STORE     |PRODUCT   |         |         |         |         |
         |----------+----------|         |         |         |         |
         |MURPHY    |AMPLIFIE- |         |         |         |         |
         |ST.       |RS        | 23,515.21| 28,219.53| 21,531.90| 73,266.64|
         |          |----------+---------+---------+---------+---------|
         |          |RECEIVERS | 22,335.22| 23,312.01| 25,823.35| 71,470.58|
         |          |----------+---------+---------+---------+---------|
         |          |TURNTABL- |         |         |         |         |
         |          |ES        | 11,223.22| 12,122.33| 15,323.23| 38,668.78|
         |          |----------+---------+---------+---------+---------|
         |          |TAPE      |         |         |         |         |
         |          |DECKS     | 25,211.09| 31,233.15| 21,523.51| 77,967.75|
         |          |----------+---------+---------+---------+---------|
         |          |SPEAKERS  | 21,521.00| 22,505.90| 23,531.21| 67,558.11|
         |          |----------+---------+---------+---------+---------|
         |          |OTHER     |         |         |         |         |
         |          |AUDIO     | 22,151.55| 23,559.01| 23,215.19| 68,925.75|
         |          |----------+---------+---------+---------+---------|
         |          |STORE     |         |         |         |         |
         |          |TOTAL     | 125,957.29| 140,951.93| 130,948.39| 397,857.61|
         |----------+----------+---------+---------+---------+---------|
         |APPLETON  |PRODUCT   |         |         |         |         |
         |ST.       |----------|         |         |         |         |
         |          |AMPLIFIE- |         |         |         |         |
         |          |RS        | 24,519.21| 27,210.54| 21,546.00| 73,275.75|
         |          |----------+---------+---------+---------+---------|
         |          |RECEIVERS | 28,349.28| 24,318.06| 29,783.49| 82,450.83|
         |          |----------+---------+---------+---------+---------|
         |          |TURNTABL- |         |         |         |         |
         |          |ES        | 16,283.82| 18,122.33| 19,323.83| 53,729.98|
         |          |----------+---------+---------+---------+---------|
```

		JAN	FEB	MAR	YTD
	TAPE DECKS	29,816.00	31,233.19	26,984.51	88,033.70
	SPEAKERS	21,926.00	22,905.00	24,936.86	69,767.86
	OTHER AUDIO	28,196.59	23,590.06	23,215.10	75,001.75
	STORE TOTAL	149,090.90	147,379.18	145,789.79	442,259.87
MARKET SQ.	PRODUCT				
	AMPLIFIE-RS	15,321.55	12,318.52	21,512.31	49,152.38
	RECEIVERS	23,218.13	21,015.28	15,212.33	59,445.74

(CONTINUED)

TABLE WITH FORMATS AND LABELS ADDED

		JAN	FEB	MAR	YTD
STORE	PRODUCT				
MARKET SQ.	TURNTABL-ES	12,158.12	15,382.52	13,522.33	41,062.97
	TAPE DECKS	31,082.12	31,233.50	32,535.31	94,850.93
	SPEAKERS	30,532.12	32,238.22	25,339.35	88,109.69
	OTHER AUDIO	21,821.38	20,829.53	20,822.23	63,473.14
	STORE TOTAL	134,133.42	133,017.57	128,943.86	396,094.85
CARSON MALL	PRODUCT				
	AMPLIFIE-RS	19,321.55	18,417.52	21,562.41	59,301.48
	RECEIVERS	24,217.14	21,015.27	19,218.33	64,450.74
	TURNTABL-ES	12,157.12	15,378.58	13,582.33	41,118.03
	TAPE DECKS	31,072.68	31,243.90	32,945.31	95,261.89
	SPEAKERS	30,548.12	32,847.22	29,430.45	92,825.79
	OTHER AUDIO	21,726.47	20,720.93	20,722.83	63,170.23
	STORE TOTAL	139,043.08	139,623.42	137,461.66	416,128.16

(continued on next page)

(continued from previous page)

MAIN ST.	PRODUCT				
	AMPLIFIE-RS	23,182.59	15,133.09	11,522.95	49,838.63
	RECEIVERS	23,381.51	23,521.25	20,111.82	67,014.58
	TURNTABL-ES	15,111.38	15,335.89	12,252.22	42,699.49
	TAPE DECKS	33,135.38	31,328.31	30,111.82	94,575.51

(CONTINUED)

TABLE WITH FORMATS AND LABELS ADDED

		JAN	FEB	MAR	YTD
STORE	PRODUCT				
MAIN ST.	SPEAKERS	25,533.31	22,311.09	28,121.01	75,965.41
	OTHER AUDIO	22,582.13	23,532.38	25,112.23	71,226.74
	STORE TOTAL	142,926.30	131,162.01	127,232.05	401,320.36
SALEM BLVD.	PRODUCT				
	AMPLIFIE-RS	24,672.50	19,143.00	16,588.09	60,403.59
	RECEIVERS	23,476.51	24,981.85	20,611.72	69,070.08
	TURNTABL-ES	19,161.47	19,445.70	18,892.28	57,499.45
	TAPE DECKS	34,145.37	31,427.36	30,661.78	96,234.51
	SPEAKERS	25,934.46	28,316.00	27,186.06	81,436.52
	OTHER AUDIO	22,578.63	24,548.37	25,618.23	72,745.23
	STORE TOTAL	149,968.94	147,862.28	139,558.16	437,389.38
GRAND TOTAL		841,119.93	839,996.39	809,933.91	2,491,050.23

FILE and PUT Statements

Although SAS procedures can produce a variety of reports, there may be times when you want a report format that is different from those available from any procedure. You can also produce reports with a SAS DATA step, taking advantage of all the flexibility of DATA step programming statements. Reports generated by DATA steps can be tailored to your precise specifications, for example, listings in which BY groups have separate columns and headings change with every page.

The FILE and PUT statements are the cornerstones of DATA step report writing. The PUT statement writes to the file specified by the preceding FILE statement. For report writing, the file is usually the default SAS output file, called the PRINT file. Output is directed to the PRINT file when the FILE statement specifies PRINT as the fileref.

```
FILE PRINT options;
```

The PUT statement is similar to the INPUT statement. It can include variable names, formats with which to print the variable values, and pointer directions. Unlike the INPUT statement, it can also contain character constants enclosed in quotes.

A DATA Step Report

A small manufacturing company maintains a file that contains the following information for each employee: name, sex, employee number, department number, gross pay, and net pay. Each month, the company produces a payroll report.

The statements below read the employee data and create a SAS data set called PAYROLL. This data set is then sorted by DEPT and printed. The data set is shown in **Output 6.11**.

```
DATA PAYROLL;
   INFILE EMPLOY;
   INPUT DEPT NAME $ NUMBER SEX $ NETPAY GROSSPAY;
RUN;
PROC SORT;
   BY DEPT;
RUN;
PROC PRINT;
RUN;
```

Output 6.11
Employee Data Set

OBS	DEPT	NAME	SAS NUMBER	SEX	NETPAY	GROSSPAY
1	911	HAFER	9764	F	9664	12195
2	911	YOUNG	4589	M	22969	31360
3	911	REYNOLDS	5805	F	13403	17415
4	911	STRIDE	3890	M	27253	38340
5	911	ISSAC	12641	M	21991	31360
6	911	GREEN	12829	M	23804	36560
7	911	SMOTHERS	1782	M	20243	31520
8	911	KRAUSE	3571	F	18209	24240
9	911	POST	455	M	20660	29200
10	911	POWELL	11710	M	16753	24395
11	914	LARSON	11357	F	21547	28392
12	914	ARNOLD	1956	M	35687	44550
13	914	MANHART	11602	M	25034	34478
14	914	VETTER	1895	M	18928	27936
15	914	CURCI	8262	M	21531	37600
16	914	GRECO	7231	M	68523	100400
17	914	RYAN	10961	M	29156	39920
18	914	JOHNSON	10546	M	13523	18072
19	914	THOMSPON	11584	M	22109	29756
20	915	CORNING	2688	F	10343	14616
21	915	WOOD	8113	F	23817	37224
22	915	GREEN	5276	M	72516	112451
23	915	HAYDEN	6843	F	10354	14631
24	915	TAYLOR	2943	F	28722	40172
25	915	CHAPMAN	3624	M	26431	38547
26	915	ROCHE	6781	M	28737	40212
27	915	MOORE	12649	M	55718	72812
28	915	HELMS	3658	M	47926	70126
29	916	FARLOW	10349	M	52719	84203
30	916	SHIRES	10052	F	18712	27922
31	916	RICHARDS	5781	M	21927	35284
32	916	SMITH	6237	F	14709	20188
33	916	MURPHY	6927	M	27266	38511
34	916	FAIRLEY	8846	M	52166	83480

(continued on next page)

```
   35   917   HERZOG      6433   M   69257   104526
   36   917   TALL       11931   M   35519    49226
   37   917   HIGGINS    11658   M   77750   123546
   38   917   MCKAY      10155   M   82144   139227
   39   917   SANFORD    12649   F   28406    40537
   40   917   DOOB       10554   F   16906    27229
   41   918   BRANDON     2200   M   55431    80464
   42   918   EPERT       7716   M   22436    31040
   43   918   CLANCY      6648   M   24537    34712
   44   918   POWELL      8123   F   18939    27154
   45   940   HICKS      15497   M   55387    80731
   46   940   VANCE       1576   M   48703    78900
   47   940   CARTER      1333   M   71289   115822
```

(continued from previous page)

The DATA step below produces the report shown in **Output 6.12**. You can see how different the DATA step report is from the PROC PRINT report. To understand this DATA step, read the explanations that correspond to the SAS statements marked by the circled numbers in the program.

```
DATA _NULL_;
   RETAIN MONTH;
   SET PAYROLL END=EOF;        ❿
❶ BY DEPT;
   IF _N_=1 THEN MONTH=SCAN(PUT(TODAY(),WORDDATE18.),1);  ❹
❷  FILE PRINT HEADER=H LINESLEFT=LL NOTITLES;
❻  IF FIRST.DEPT THEN DO;       ❺
      NETTOT=0;
      GROSSTOT=0;
      IF LL<14 THEN PUT _PAGE_;
      END;
❼ PUT @7 DEPT 3. @19 NAME $15. @32 NUMBER 5. @42 SEX $1.
      @48 NETPAY 8.2 @63 GROSSPAY 9.2;
❽ NETTOT+NETPAY;
   GROSSTOT+GROSSPAY;
   IF LAST.DEPT THEN DO; ❾
      PUT @46 '_____' @62 '_____'
         / 'DEPARTMENT TOTAL' @44 NETTOT DOLLAR12.2
            @60 GROSSTOT DOLLAR12.2 //;
      GRANDNET+NETTOT;
      GRANDGRO+GROSSTOT;
      END;
❿ IF EOF THEN PUT 'OVERALL TOTAL' @43 GRANDNET DOLLAR13.2
      @59 GRANDGRO DOLLAR13.2;
   RETURN;
   H: PUT // @22 'ABC MANUFACTURING COMPANY'
            / @23 'PAYROLL REPORT FOR ' MONTH  ❸
         /// @19 'EMPLOYEE' @31 'EMPLOYEE' @50 'NET' @65 'GROSS'
            / @3  'DEPARTMENT' @21 'NAME' @32 'NUMBER' @41 'SEX'
               @50 'PAY' @66 'PAY' //;
   RETURN;
RUN;
```

1. The report will be divided into BY groups based on departments.
2. The HEADER= option allows you to print headings. At the top of each page, SAS executes the statements following the label H. The NOTITLES option suppresses the printing of the default title, SAS.
3. To customize the heading printed on each page, add the month to the heading.
4. Rather than edit the program each month to put the correct month name in the heading, use SAS functions to insert the information. The TODAY function returns the current date as a SAS date value. The PUT function returns the TODAY value formatted with the WORDDATE. format. The SCAN function then returns the month name from the formatted date value. The month name, assigned to the MONTH variable, is added to the heading.
5. The LINESLEFT= variable, LL, provides a count of the number of lines left for printing on a page. Here, LL is used to check whether or not there is room to list all of a department's employees. If not, go to the top of the next page.
6. The FIRST. variable detects the beginning of BY groups. At the beginning of a department, reset subtotals of net and gross pay to zero and check the number of lines left on the page.
7. Write the values of the data set's variables at the specified columns.
8. Increment the subtotals for net and gross pay with sum statements.
9. The LAST. variable detects the end of BY groups. At the end of each department, print the department totals and add subtotals to the grand total variables.
10. END= on the SET statement tests for the end of the data set. When SAS processes the last observation in the data set, print the grand total line of the report.

All of the DATA step features used in this example are described in detail in the *SAS User's Guide: Basics, Version 5 Edition*.

Output 6.12
A Report Produced by the
DATA Step

```
                            ABC MANUFACTURING COMPANY
                            PAYROLL REPORT FOR JULY


                        EMPLOYEE     EMPLOYEE            NET          GROSS
        DEPARTMENT        NAME        NUMBER    SEX      PAY           PAY


            911          HAFER         9764      F      9664.00      12195.00
            911          YOUNG         4589      M     22969.00      31360.00
            911          REYNOLDS      5805      F     13403.00      17415.00
            911          STRIDE        3890      M     27253.00      38340.00
            911          ISSAC        12641      M     21991.00      31360.00
            911          GREEN        12829      M     23804.00      36560.00
            911          SMOTHERS      1782      M     20243.00      31520.00
            911          KRAUSE        3571      F     18209.00      24240.00
            911          POST           455      M     20660.00      29200.00
            911          POWELL       11710      M     16753.00      24395.00

    DEPARTMENT TOTAL                                $194,949.00   $276,585.00
```

(continued on next page)

(continued from previous page)

914	LARSON	11357	F	21547.00	28392.00
914	ARNOLD	1956	M	35687.00	44550.00
914	MANHART	11602	M	25034.00	34478.00
914	VETTER	1895	M	18928.00	27936.00
914	CURCI	8262	M	21531.00	37600.00
914	GRECO	7231	M	68523.00	100400.00
914	RYAN	10961	M	29156.00	39920.00
914	JOHNSON	10546	M	13523.00	18072.00
914	THOMSPON	11584	M	22109.00	29756.00

DEPARTMENT TOTAL $256,038.00 $361,104.00

915	CORNING	2688	F	10343.00	14616.00
915	WOOD	8113	F	23817.00	37224.00
915	GREEN	5276	M	72516.00	112451.00
915	HAYDEN	6843	F	10354.00	14631.00
915	TAYLOR	2943	F	28722.00	40172.00
915	CHAPMAN	3624	M	26431.00	38547.00
915	ROCHE	6781	M	28737.00	40212.00
915	MOORE	12649	M	55718.00	72812.00
915	HELMS	3658	M	47926.00	70126.00

DEPARTMENT TOTAL $304,564.00 $440,791.00

ABC MANUFACTURING COMPANY
PAYROLL REPORT FOR JULY

DEPARTMENT	EMPLOYEE NAME	EMPLOYEE NUMBER	SEX	NET PAY	GROSS PAY
916	FARLOW	10349	M	52719.00	84203.00
916	SHIRES	10052	F	18712.00	27922.00
916	RICHARDS	5781	M	21927.00	35284.00
916	SMITH	6237	F	14709.00	20188.00
916	MURPHY	6927	M	27266.00	38511.00
916	FAIRLEY	8846	M	52166.00	83480.00

DEPARTMENT TOTAL $187,499.00 $289,588.00

917	HERZOG	6433	M	69257.00	104526.00
917	TALL	11931	M	35519.00	49226.00
917	HIGGINS	11658	M	77750.00	123546.00
917	MCKAY	10155	M	82144.00	139227.00
917	SANFORD	12649	F	28406.00	40537.00
917	DOOB	10554	F	16906.00	27229.00

DEPARTMENT TOTAL $309,982.00 $484,291.00

918	BRANDON	2200	M	55431.00	80464.00
918	EPERT	7716	M	22436.00	31040.00
918	CLANCY	6648	M	24537.00	34712.00
918	POWELL	8123	F	18939.00	27154.00

DEPARTMENT TOTAL $121,343.00 $173,370.00

940	HICKS	15497	M	55387.00	80731.00
940	VANCE	1576	M	48703.00	78900.00
940	CARTER	1333	M	71289.00	115822.00

DEPARTMENT TOTAL $175,379.00 $275,453.00

OVERALL TOTAL $1,549,754.00 $2,301,182.00

Two Reports in One Step

Suppose each department manager needs a detailed listing of salary information for that department. In addition, the payroll department wants a summary of payroll data with department and company totals. Produce both kinds of reports with one pass of the payroll data by making some modifications to the first program.

The changes are indicated by circled numbers in the following program. Refer to the corresponding explanations in the list that follows. The two reports produced by this DATA step are shown in **Output 6.13** (only one page of the departmental report is shown).

```
DATA _NULL_;
   RETAIN MONTH;
   SET PAYROLL END=EOF;
   BY DEPT;
   IF _N_=1 THEN MONTH=SCAN(PUT(TODAY(),WORDDATE18.),1);
   FILE PRINT HEADER=H NOTITLES;  ❸
   IF FIRST.DEPT THEN DO;
      PUT _PAGE_;  ❶
      NETTOT=0;
      GROSSTOT=0;
      END;
   PUT @8 NAME $15. @30 NUMBER 5. @40 SEX $1.
      @46 NETPAY 8.2 @57 GROSSPAY 9.2;
   NETTOT+NETPAY;
   GROSSTOT+GROSSPAY;
   IF LAST.DEPT THEN DO;  ❷
      PUT @44 '_____' @56 '_____' / 'DEPARTMENT TOTAL'
      @42 NETTOT DOLLAR12.2 @54 GROSSTOT DOLLAR12.2 //;
      GRANDNET+NETTOT;
      GRANDGRO+GROSSTOT;
      LINK FOOT;  ❷
      FILE A PRINT HEADER=NEWH NOTITLES;  ❹
      PUT @15 'DEPARTMENT ' DEPT @38 NETTOT DOLLAR12.2
         @55 GROSSTOT DOLLAR12.2 //;
      IF EOF THEN PUT @15 'OVERALL TOTAL' @37 GRANDNET DOLLAR13.2
                       @54 GRANDGRO DOLLAR13.2;
      END;
   RETURN;
H: PUT // @22 'ABC MANUFACTURING COMPANY'
        / @23 'PAYROLL REPORT FOR ' MONTH
        / @28 'DEPARTMENT ' DEPT 3.  ❶
        /// @14 'EMPLOYEE' @29 'EMPLOYEE' @48 'NET' @59 'GROSS'
         / @16 'NAME' @30 'NUMBER' @39 'SEX' @48 'PAY' @61 'PAY' //;
   RETURN;
NEWH: PUT // @22 'ABC MANUFACTURING COMPANY'
           / @23 'SUMMARY PAYROLL REPORT'
         /// @44 'NET' @59 'GROSS'
           / @44 'PAY' @60 'PAY' //;
   RETURN;
FOOT: DATE=TODAY();  ❷
   PUT // @10 '***CONFIDENTIAL REPORT***'
       / @10 DATE WORDDATE18.;
   RETURN;
RUN;
```

1. At the first observation for each department, a new page is started. SAS prints the current department number as part of the heading on each page of the department report. Because each department's list begins on a new page, the LINESLEFT= option is not needed in the FILE statement.
2. At the last observation for each department, the program links to the FOOT subroutine to print a footnote on each page of the report. The footnote contains the current date.
3. The FILE PRINT statement directs the departmental report to the standard SAS PRINT file.
4. The FILE A statement directs the summary report to a separate file; the PRINT option is included so that file A will be written as a print file, that is, with carriage control characters in column one. Without the PRINT option, the HEADER= option would not work properly. Each time LAST.DEPT is 1, SAS executes the statements that print the summary report in file A.

Output 6.13
Two Reports Produced by
One DATA Step

```
                        ABC MANUFACTURING COMPANY
                         PAYROLL REPORT FOR JULY
                            DEPARTMENT 911


              EMPLOYEE       EMPLOYEE            NET         GROSS
                NAME          NUMBER    SEX      PAY          PAY


        HAFER                  9764      F      9664.00     12195.00
        YOUNG                  4589      M     22969.00     31360.00
        REYNOLDS               5805      F     13403.00     17415.00
        STRIDE                 3890      M     27253.00     38340.00
        ISSAC                 12641      M     21991.00     31360.00
        GREEN                 12829      M     23804.00     36560.00
        SMOTHERS               1782      M     20243.00     31520.00
        KRAUSE                 3571      F     18209.00     24240.00
        POST                    455      M     20660.00     29200.00
        POWELL                11710      M     16753.00     24395.00

DEPARTMENT TOTAL                              $194,949.00 $276,585.00


           ***CONFIDENTIAL REPORT***
             JULY 21, 1986
```

```
                    ABC MANUFACTURING COMPANY
                    SUMMARY PAYROLL REPORT


                                   NET            GROSS
                                   PAY            PAY


          DEPARTMENT 911       $194,949.00      $276,585.00


          DEPARTMENT 914       $256,038.00      $361,104.00


          DEPARTMENT 915       $304,564.00      $440,791.00


          DEPARTMENT 916       $187,499.00      $289,588.00


          DEPARTMENT 917       $309,982.00      $484,291.00


          DEPARTMENT 918       $121,343.00      $173,370.00


          DEPARTMENT 940       $175,379.00      $275,453.00


          OVERALL TOTAL      $1,549,754.00    $2,301,182.00
```

Page-at-a-Time Access

Normally, when you print a report, you have access to one line at a time. Once you execute a PUT statement that prints on and releases a line, you cannot return to the line for later printing. This poses a problem for printing some reports, for example, those containing multiple columns of information. The N=PAGESIZE or N=PS option of the FILE statement tells SAS to hold an entire page until the page is full or until you tell SAS to release it.

A multicolumn listing

A typical application of the N=PAGESIZE option is in reports requiring multiple columns, such as a phone book. N=PAGESIZE allows you to print a column at a time; when PUT statements have printed one column, you can return to the top of the next column to continue printing.

Suppose you want to print a listing of employees included in the PAYROLL data set. The multicolumn list is to show the rank order of employees based on gross pay.

The following SAS program first sorts the data set in descending order of gross pay and then prints the two-column report shown in **Output 6.14.**

```
PROC SORT DATA=PAYROLL OUT=SORTPAY;
   BY DESCENDING GROSSPAY;
RUN;
DATA _NULL_;
   FILE PRINT N=PS HEADER=COLUMNS;
   TITLE 'RANK ORDER OF EMPLOYEES BY GROSS SALARY';
   R36=REPEAT('-',35);
   DO C=2, 41;
      DO L=6 TO 25;
         SET SORTPAY;
         PUT #L aC
            NAME $15. +1 '(' DEPT 3. ')' +5 GROSSPAY DOLLAR8.;
         END;
      END;
   PUT _PAGE_;
   RETURN;
   COLUMNS: PUT / a2 'EMPLOYEE' +4 '(DEPARTMENT)' a29 'GROSS PAY'
                  a41 'EMPLOYEE' +4 '(DEPARTMENT)' a68 'GROSS PAY'
                / a2 R36 a41 R36;
   RETURN;
RUN;
```

The program uses both TITLE statements and the HEADER= option of the FILE statement to produce table headings. When TITLE statements are used, PUT statements that are part of a header group of statements print in the "window" remaining after all titles are printed.

The two DO loops in the program represent column and line counters. The variable C, which is the index for the outer DO loop, becomes the value of the horizontal print position where each column of information begins. L, the index for the inner loop, determines the line, or vertical print position. Printing of each column begins at line 6.

PUT _PAGE_ tells SAS to release the output to the print file specified by the FILE statement when both DO loops have been satisfied. SAS then returns to the top of the DATA step for a new execution and a new page. This process continues until all observations in SORTPAY have been read. PUT _PAGE_ also releases the page when the DATA step is complete.

Output 6.14
A Multicolumn Report

```
                    RANK ORDER OF EMPLOYEES BY GROSS SALARY

  EMPLOYEE    (DEPARTMENT)   GROSS PAY   EMPLOYEE    (DEPARTMENT)   GROSS PAY
  ------------------------------------   ------------------------------------

  MCKAY         (917)       $139,227     MURPHY        (916)        $38,511
  HIGGINS       (917)       $123,546     STRIDE        (911)        $38,340
  CARTER        (940)       $115,822     CURCI         (914)        $37,600
  GREEN         (915)       $112,451     WOOD          (915)        $37,224
  HERZOG        (917)       $104,526     GREEN         (911)        $36,560
  GRECO         (914)       $100,400     RICHARDS      (916)        $35,284
  FARLOW        (916)        $84,203     CLANCY        (918)        $34,712
  FAIRLEY       (916)        $83,480     MANHART       (914)        $34,478
  HICKS         (940)        $80,731     SMOTHERS      (911)        $31,520
  BRANDON       (918)        $80,464     YOUNG         (911)        $31,360
  VANCE         (940)        $78,900     ISSAC         (911)        $31,360
  MOORE         (915)        $72,812     EPERT         (918)        $31,040
  HELMS         (915)        $70,126     THOMSPON      (914)        $29,756
  TALL          (917)        $49,226     POST          (911)        $29,200
  ARNOLD        (914)        $44,550     LARSON        (914)        $28,392
  SANFORD       (917)        $40,537     VETTER        (914)        $27,936
  ROCHE         (915)        $40,212     SHIRES        (916)        $27,922
  TAYLOR        (915)        $40,172     DOOB          (917)        $27,229
  RYAN          (914)        $39,920     POWELL        (918)        $27,154
  CHAPMAN       (915)        $38,547     POWELL        (911)        $24,395


                    RANK ORDER OF EMPLOYEES BY GROSS SALARY

  EMPLOYEE    (DEPARTMENT)   GROSS PAY   EMPLOYEE    (DEPARTMENT)   GROSS PAY
  ------------------------------------   ------------------------------------


  KRAUSE        (911)        $24,240
  SMITH         (916)        $20,188
  JOHNSON       (914)        $18,072
  REYNOLDS      (911)        $17,415
  HAYDEN        (915)        $14,631
  CORNING       (915)        $14,616
  HAFER         (911)        $12,195
```

Columns for BY groups

Not all multicolumn listings have columns of equal length, as the preceding example does. Sometimes, you want to print columns based on BY groups having different numbers of observations. The following program prints such a report.

In this example, a listing of employees by department is produced, with employees rank-ordered by gross pay within department:

```
DATA _NULL_;
   FILE PRINT N=PS;
   TITLE 'RANK ORDER OF EMPLOYEES BY GROSS SALARY';
   TITLE2 'WITHIN DEPARTMENT';
   R24=REPEAT('-',23);
   DO C=2, 28, 54;
      DO L=6 TO 15;
         SET SORTPAY;
         BY DEPT;
         IF FIRST.DEPT THEN LINK HEADING;
         PUT #L @C NAME $15. +1 GROSSPAY DOLLAR8.;
         IF LAST.DEPT THEN GO TO NEWCOL;
         END;
```

```
NEWCOL: IF C=54 THEN DO;
    PUT _PAGE_;
    END;
  END;
  END;
 RETURN;
 HEADING: PUT #2 @C +5 'DEPARTMENT ' DEPT  / @C R24 /
             @C 'NAME' @C +15 'GROSS PAY'/;
 RETURN;
RUN;
```

The report is shown in **Output 6.15.**

Output 6.15
A Report with Columns of
Unequal Length

```
                    RANK ORDER OF EMPLOYEES BY GROSS SALARY
                              WITHIN DEPARTMENT

       DEPARTMENT 911              DEPARTMENT 914              DEPARTMENT 915
    ----------------------     ----------------------     ----------------------
    NAME        GROSS PAY      NAME        GROSS PAY      NAME        GROSS PAY

    STRIDE        $38,340      GRECO      $100,400        GREEN      $112,451
    GREEN         $36,560      ARNOLD      $44,550        MOORE       $72,812
    SMOTHERS      $31,520      RYAN        $39,920        HELMS       $70,126
    YOUNG         $31,360      CURCI       $37,600        ROCHE       $40,212
    ISSAC         $31,360      MANHART     $34,478        TAYLOR      $40,172
    POST          $29,200      THOMSPON    $29,756        CHAPMAN     $38,547
    POWELL        $24,395      LARSON      $28,392        WOOD        $37,224
    KRAUSE        $24,240      VETTER      $27,936        HAYDEN      $14,631
    REYNOLDS      $17,415      JOHNSON     $18,072        CORNING     $14,616
    HAFER         $12,195
```

```
                    RANK ORDER OF EMPLOYEES BY GROSS SALARY
                              WITHIN DEPARTMENT

       DEPARTMENT 916              DEPARTMENT 917              DEPARTMENT 918
    ----------------------     ----------------------     ----------------------
    NAME        GROSS PAY      NAME        GROSS PAY      NAME        GROSS PAY

    FARLOW        $84,203      MCKAY      $139,227        BRANDON     $80,464
    FAIRLEY       $83,480      HIGGINS    $123,546        CLANCY      $34,712
    MURPHY        $38,511      HERZOG     $104,526        EPERT       $31,040
    RICHARDS      $35,284      TALL        $49,226        POWELL      $27,154
    SHIRES        $27,922      SANFORD     $40,537
    SMITH         $20,188      DOOB        $27,229
```

```
                    RANK ORDER OF EMPLOYEES BY GROSS SALARY
                              WITHIN DEPARTMENT

       DEPARTMENT 940
    ----------------------
    NAME        GROSS PAY

    CARTER       $115,822
    HICKS         $80,731
    VANCE         $78,900
```

This example is similar to the first example for multicolumn output. However, instead of the HEADER= option in the FILE statement, the program uses a LINK-RETURN group for column titles. It also links to a labeled subroutine outside the DO loop when the last employee for a department has been printed. The subroutine does two things:

☐ It tests the value of C. If C=54, the third column of a page has printed, so the page is released. In the next execution of the DO loops, SAS begins printing a new page.

□ It executes the END statement for the outer DO loop. This causes SAS to reset the column counter in the next execution of the DO loop.

Rearranging Data Sets to Write Reports

Sometimes, the information in a SAS data set is needed for a report, but the data are in the wrong form. For example, instead of printing observations as rows, and variables as columns, you may want variables to form the rows, and observations the columns. You can use the TRANSPOSE procedure to change rows to columns and columns to rows in an output SAS data set and then print the report you want.

Consider this situation. Suppose you need to calculate descriptive statistics from the PAYROLL data set. You use PROC MEANS to get totals and averages of NETPAY and GROSSPAY, by DEPT, then print the output data set, which is shown in **Output 6.16.**

```
PROC MEANS DATA=PAYROLL NOPRINT;
   BY DEPT;
   VAR NETPAY GROSSPAY;
   OUTPUT OUT=DSTAT SUM=NSUM GSUM MEAN=NMEAN GMEAN;
RUN;
PROC PRINT DATA=DSTAT;
   TITLE 'SALARY TOTALS AND AVERAGES FOR EACH DEPARTMENT:';
   TITLE2 'DEPARTMENTS AS ROWS';
RUN;
```

Output 6.16
PROC MEANS Output
Data Set

```
              SALARY TOTALS AND AVERAGES FOR EACH DEPARTMENT:
                            DEPARTMENTS AS ROWS

      OBS    DEPT     NMEAN     GMEAN      NSUM      GSUM

       1      911    19494.9   27658.5    194949    276585
       2      914    28448.7   40122.7    256038    361104
       3      915    33840.4   48976.8    304564    440791
       4      916    31249.8   48264.7    187499    289588
       5      917    51663.7   80715.2    309982    484291
       6      918    30335.8   43342.5    121343    173370
       7      940    58459.7   91817.7    175379    275453
```

The information you want is in the PRINT output, but the report would be easier to read if each column represented a department and each row a statistic. The TRANSPOSE procedure can reverse the table:

```
PROC TRANSPOSE DATA=DSTAT OUT=TPOSE;
   ID DEPT;
   VAR NSUM GSUM NMEAN GMEAN;
RUN;
PROC PRINT DATA=TPOSE;
   TITLE 'SALARY TOTALS AND AVERAGES FOR EACH DEPARTMENT:';
   TITLE2 'DEPARTMENTS AS COLUMNS';
RUN;
```

The transposed data are shown in **Output 6.17**. Notice that each department's statistics are in one column.

```
                    SALARY TOTALS AND AVERAGES FOR EACH DEPARTMENT:
                              DEPARTMENTS AS COLUMNS

    OBS    _NAME_    _911     _914     _915     _916     _917     _918     _940

     1     NSUM     194949   256038   304564   187499   309982   121343   175379
     2     GSUM     276585   361104   440791   289588   484291   173370   275453
     3     NMEAN     19495    28449    33840    31250    51664    30336    58460
     4     GMEAN     27659    40123    48977    48265    80715    43343    91818
```

Enhance the appearance and readability of the report by adding formats for variable values and labels for variables and observations, as in the following program. The formatted and labeled output is shown in **Output 6.18**.

```
PROC FORMAT;
    VALUE $FMT 'NSUM'   = 'TOTAL NET PAYS'
               'GSUM'   = 'TOTAL GROSS PAYS'
               'NMEAN'  = 'MEAN NET PAY'
               'GMEAN'  = 'MEAN GROSS PAY';
RUN;
PROC PRINT DATA=TPOSE SPLIT='*';
    TITLE 'THE TPOSE DATA SET WITH FORMATS AND LABELS';
    ID _NAME_;
    FORMAT _NAME_ $FMT. _911 -- _940 COMMA12.2;
    LABEL _NAME_ = '  '
          _911  = 'DEPARTMENT*    911'
          _914  = 'DEPARTMENT*    914'
          _915  = 'DEPARTMENT*    915'
          _916  = 'DEPARTMENT*    916'
          _917  = 'DEPARTMENT*    917'
          _918  = 'DEPARTMENT*    918'
          _940  = 'DEPARTMENT*    940';
RUN;
```

```
                    THE TPOSE DATA SET WITH FORMATS AND LABELS

    _NAME_            DEPARTMENT    DEPARTMENT    DEPARTMENT    DEPARTMENT
                         911           914           915           916

    TOTAL NET PAYS    194,949.00    256,038.00    304,564.00    187,499.00
    TOTAL GROSS PAYS  276,585.00    361,104.00    440,791.00    289,588.00
    MEAN NET PAY       19,494.90     28,448.67     33,840.44     31,249.83
    MEAN GROSS PAY     27,658.50     40,122.67     48,976.78     48,264.67

    _NAME_            DEPARTMENT    DEPARTMENT    DEPARTMENT
                         917           918           940

    TOTAL NET PAYS    309,982.00    121,343.00    175,379.00
    TOTAL GROSS PAYS  484,291.00    173,370.00    275,453.00
    MEAN NET PAY       51,663.67     30,335.75     58,459.67
    MEAN GROSS PAY     80,715.17     43,342.50     91,817.67
```

Printing Forms

Forms are another kind of report the SAS System can produce using the data in a SAS data set. You can think of a form as any way of printing the information from an observation in a special pattern. Mailing labels, pay stubs, and report cards can all be handled as forms. Use the FORMS procedure for these kinds of applications.

For example, suppose you need to produce pay stubs for each employee from the data in the PAYROLL data set. The pay stub form looks like this:

```
┌──────────────────────────────────────────────────────────────┐
│                                                                │
│        EMPLOYEE PAYROLL SUMMARY FOR _____                │
│                                                                │
│   DEPARTMENT                                                   │
│                                                                │
│     _____                                                     │
│                                                                │
│                                                                │
│   EMPLOYEE: _____      EMPLOYEE NO: _____      │
│                                                                │
│             GROSS PAY:   _____                          │
│                                                                │
│               NET PAY:   _____                          │
│                                                                │
│            DEDUCTIONS: _____                            │
│                                                                │
└──────────────────────────────────────────────────────────────┘
```

The following program fills in the required information for each person. First, find the current date and calculate the amount of the payroll deductions in a DATA step. Then use the new data set as input to PROC FORMS:

```
DATA STUB;
   RETAIN DATE;
   SET PAYROLL;
   IF _N_=1 THEN DATE=TODAY();
   DEDUCT=GROSSPAY-NETPAY;
RUN;
PROC FORMS DATA=STUB DDNAME=OUT LINES=13 SKIP=5 INDENT=2
           WIDTH=60 ALIGN=0;
   LINE 3 DATE / INDENT=40;
   LINE 6 DEPT / INDENT=3;
   LINE 8 NAME NUMBER / INDENT=11;
   LINE 10 GROSSPAY / INDENT=22;
   LINE 11 NETPAY   / INDENT=22;
   LINE 12 DEDUCT   / INDENT=22;
   FORMAT DATE MONYY5. DEPT 3. NAME $30.
          NETPAY GROSSPAY DEDUCT DOLLAR12.2;
RUN;
```

The FORMS procedure reads the SAS data set and writes to an external file. Generally, the output file is defined as a printer, which holds any special paper, for example, blank pay stubs. Thus, as the observations in the input data set are processed, the information is printed on the form. The FORMS procedure can specify the size of each form, the arrangement and spacing of forms, and the lines and columns at which values are printed. Notice that a FORMAT statement is used in the PROC step so that values are printed in a more meaningful way. A sample of a completed pay stub is shown in **Output 6.19**.

Output 6.19
A Form Printed by the
FORMS Procedure

```
          EMPLOYEE PAYROLL SUMMARY FOR JUL86____

DEPARTMENT

   _911_

EMPLOYEE: _YOUNG_____        EMPLOYEE NO: __4589__

              GROSS PAY:   $31,360.00__

                NET PAY:   $22,969.00__

             DEDUCTIONS: _$8,391.00__
```

Summary of System Options and Functions

In addition to the procedures and DATA step statements, certain SAS system options and DATA step functions are useful for report writing. Some of the most commonly used options and functions are listed here. Refer to the *SAS User's Guide: Basics, Version 5 Edition* for details.

System options frequently used in report writing include the following:

CENTER | NOCENTER
DATE | NODATE
LABEL | NOLABEL
LINESIZE=
MISSING=
NUMBER | NONUMBER
PAGESIZE=

SAS functions that are particularly useful for report writing include the following:

Character functions

COMPRESS

LENGTH

REPEAT

REVERSE

RIGHT

LEFT

SCAN

SUBSTR

TRIM

UPCASE

Date and time functions

DATE (also called TODAY)

DAY

HOUR

JULDATE

MINUTE

MONTH

QTR

SECOND

TIME

WEEKDAY

YEAR

State and zip code functions

FIPNAME

FIPNAMEL

FIPSTATE

STNAME

STNAMEL

ZIPNAME

ZIPNAMEL

ZIPSTATE

Special functions

INPUT

PUT

7 Managing SAS Data Libraries

If you work with the same data values repeatedly, you may want to store them in SAS files and use the SAS System to document and manage these files. SAS files are stored as members of *SAS data libraries.*

This chapter generally describes a SAS data library, then discusses how to manage an existing SAS data library using the following SAS utility procedures:

□ PROC CONTENTS documents all members or specific members in a SAS data library.
□ PROC DATASETS lists, renames, and deletes members in a SAS data library.
□ PROC APPEND adds the observations from one SAS data set to the end of another SAS data set.
□ PROC COPY copies an entire SAS data library or selected members.

For information on how to create a SAS data library, how to estimate the amount of space needed to store a SAS data library, or how to transport a SAS data library from one operating system to another, refer to the *SAS Companion* or SAS technical report for your operating system.

SAS Data Libraries

The SAS System is designed to access a SAS data library in order to read or write one or more members. The SAS System determines the structure of individual members of the library. On different operating systems, members are grouped according to the operating system's file structure to form a SAS data library. Refer to the *SAS Companion* or SAS technical report for your operating system to learn more about SAS data library structure.

Referring to SAS Data Libraries

The way you refer to a SAS data library in your SAS program depends on whether the library is permanent or temporary and whether the SAS statement you are coding accesses a member of the library or the entire library.

If the SAS statement accesses a member of a SAS data library, you must specify the member name. If the member is stored in a permanent SAS data library, you must also specify which library. So, to access a member of a permanent SAS data library, use a two-level name:

libref.membername

The *libref* refers to the SAS data library to be accessed. The *membername* identifies a SAS file to be read from or written to that library.

Statements used in the DATA step and most PROC statements access members of SAS data libraries. PROC CONTENTS and PROC APPEND require a two-level name to access a member of a permanent SAS data library, for example,

```
PROC CONTENTS DATA=libref.membername;
PROC APPEND BASE=libref.membername DATA=libref.membername;
```

Before you enter a SAS statement containing a libref, define the SAS data library by associating a libref with the permanent SAS data library.[1] Details on how to define a SAS data library are given in the "Operating System Notes" appendix in the *SAS User's Guide: Basics, Version 5 Edition*, or you can refer to the *SAS Companion* or technical report for your operating system.

Note: if you change the value of the USER= system option from WORK to a libref that refers to a permanent SAS data library, the SAS System refers to that SAS data library each time you use a member name (one-level) in subsequent SAS statements. SAS system options are described in *SAS User's Guide: Basics, Version 5 Edition*.

To read or create a member in the temporary WORK library, you can specify the member name (one-level) only, for example,

```
PROC CONTENTS DATA=membername;
PROC APPEND BASE=membername DATA=membername;
```

The SAS System uses the libref WORK to refer to the member of the WORK library:

```
WORK.membername
```

By default the WORK library is defined for you when you invoke the SAS System and is automatically deleted when you terminate the SAS session.

Note: if you change the value of the WORK= system option from WORK to a libref that refers to a different temporary SAS data library, the SAS System refers to that SAS data library each time you use a member name (one-level) in subsequent SAS statements. SAS system options are described in *SAS User's Guide: Basics, Version 5 Edition*.

Some utility procedures are designed primarily to operate on an entire SAS data library; these require that you specify the libref only. PROC DATASETS and PROC COPY are good examples. In these procedures you use the libref to indicate which library you want to access; you do not specify a member, for example,

```
PROC DATASETS LIBRARY=libref;
PROC COPY IN=libref OUT=libref;
```

To access the WORK library, you specify the libref WORK:

```
PROC DATASETS LIBRARY=WORK;
PROC COPY IN=libref OUT=WORK;
```

Note that PROC DATASETS accesses the WORK library by default if you omit the LIBRARY= option, for example,

```
PROC DATASETS;
```

To select or exclude individual library members in these PROC steps, specify one or more member names in associated procedure statements. For example, suppose you have been working with temporary SAS data sets and decide to copy one of them to a permanent SAS data library. In the following program,

```
PROC COPY IN=WORK OUT=PERMLIB;
   SELECT ONE;
RUN;
```

PROC COPY copies the SAS data set ONE from the WORK library into a permanent SAS data library referenced by libref PERMLIB. If you remove the SELECT statement from the above PROC COPY step, all temporary WORK members are copied into PERMLIB.

Member Types

A SAS data library can contain a number of different types of members. The SAS System assigns a type when it creates the member.

- SAS data sets are created and read by DATA steps and by many SAS procedures. SAS data sets contain observations for which variable values have been recorded.
- SAS catalogs contain templates created by SAS/GRAPH procedures, or function-key profiles or customized screens created by SAS/AF or SAS/FSP procedures.
- Graphics catalogs contain images created by SAS/GRAPH procedures.
- User-written formats contain numeric or character formats created by the FORMAT procedure in base SAS software.[2]
- Work space files contain saved work space created by SAS/IML software.
- Model files contain model programs and model variables and parameters created in SAS/ETS software.

When accessing a member of a SAS data library, you usually do not have to specify the member type because most SAS statements and procedures are designed to access, create, or operate on one type. For example, PROC APPEND operates on SAS data sets only. The following three procedures are exceptions to this rule: PROC COPY, PROC DATASETS, and PROC CONTENTS. These three procedures can operate on all types of library members. You specify which type or types of members using the MEMTYPE= option in the PROC statement. Valid MEMTYPE= values are given in **Table 7.1.**

Table 7.1
SAS Data Library
Member Types

MEMTYPE= values	Refers to
ALL	all member types in a given library
DATA	SAS data sets
CAT	SAS catalogs
GCAT	graphics catalogs
IMLWK	work space files
MODEL	model files
FORMATC*	character formats
FORMATN*	numeric formats

* Member type in a SAS data library under AOS/VS, PRIMOS, and VMS only.

If you do not specify the MEMTYPE= option,

□ PROC DATASETS uses MEMTYPE=ALL
□ PROC COPY uses MEMTYPE=ALL
□ PROC CONTENTS uses MEMTYPE=DATA.**

Refer to procedure descriptions in *SAS User's Guide: Basics, Version 5 Edition* for details on using the MEMTYPE= option with each procedure.

Storing SAS Data Libraries on Tape

SAS data libraries on tape have a different structure from SAS data libraries on disk. Picture the way a tape drive works; only one part of the tape can be read or written at a time. Thus, it is impossible to look at two SAS files on a single tape in one SAS program step. Consider the following DATA step:

```
DATA SAVE2.ONE;
   SET SAVE2.TWO;
   IF X=1;
```

Although this step is possible with SAS data sets on disk, the SAS System cannot create a new data set while reading from another data set stored on the same tape. Instead, you should either store the SAS

** If you are running SAS 5.16 or a later release, PROC CONTENTS uses MEMTYPE=ALL by default.

data sets on separate tapes or create a temporary data set and then copy it to the tape:

```
DATA ONE;
   SET SAVE2.TWO;
   IF X=1;
PROC COPY IN=WORK OUT=SAVE2 MEMTYPE=DATA;
   SELECT ONE;
```

or

```
DATA ONE;
   SET SAVE2.TWO;
   IF X=1;
DATA SAVE2.ONE;
   SET ONE;
```

The PROC COPY approach is slightly more efficient and easier to specify when you are copying several data sets.

When you add a new SAS file to a SAS data library on tape, it is written at the end of the data library.[3] Be careful: if the new file has the same name as an existing file on the tape, you need to be aware of how your operating system handles this situation.[4] If you delete a SAS file from the tape, all files after it are deleted.

Refer to the *SAS Companion* or technical report for your operating system for information on operating system commands required to access a tape and for details on how to position the tape for writing.

Example: Fantasy Motors, Inc.

Fantasy Motors, Inc. collects monthly sales information about cars sold and stores this information in a permanent SAS data library. At the end of each quarter, the company produces quarterly sales reports and copies the sales data for that quarter into a backup SAS data library.

January and February sales data have already been collected and stored. Sales data are currently being collected for March, the last month of the first quarter.

The following sections describe how to

□ create a SAS data set containing monthly sales data
□ correct a SAS variable name
□ concatenate SAS data sets
□ update the SAS data set
□ update the SAS data library
□ document the contents of the SAS data library
□ produce quarterly sales reports
□ back up the SAS data library.

Create a
SAS Data Set
Following are sales data collected for March and stored in an external file:

003496	84	CHEVY	CHEVETTE	2895	3550	31MAR86	26
005008	78	FORD	FAIRMONT	700	868	22MAR86	13
005227	81	FORD	MUSTANG	1750	2254	13MAR86	29
005712	79	CHEVY	CAMARO	1000	1165	24MAR86	.
005970	80	OLDS	CUTLASS	2995	3752	26MAR86	26
005990	85	FORD	ESCORT	7100	8558	15MAR86	13
006019	78	OLDS	CUTLASS	1095	1341	20MAR86	24
006020	79	OLDS	DELTA88	1800	2383	14MAR86	10
006369	82	BUICK	SKYLARK	3995	4749	25MAR86	24
006409	83	CHEVY	CITATION	4950	6427	03MAR86	29
006650	78	CHEVY	IMPALA	525	671	27MAR86	.
006780	79	FORD	LTD	650	872	05MAR86	09
007100	84	BUICK	REGAL	5995	7882	07MAR86	11
007458	79	MERCURY	COUGAR	1500	1952	31MAR86	13
007493	82	CHRYSLER	LEBARON	3700	4576	03MAR86	.
007526	81	BUICK	LIMITED	2695	3456	01MAR86	12
007551	80	DODGE	COLT	700	950	11MAR86	.
007560	79	PLYMOUTH	FURY	2000	2525	01MAR86	13

The sales data contain values for the following variables: INVOICE, YEAR, MAKE, MODEL, COST, PRICE, SALEDATE, and SALECODE.

Each month the following program is used to create a temporary SAS data set containing the current month's sales data. The DATA step also calculates the relative profit from each sale and stores the calculated value in the variable PROFIT.

The sales data are initially stored in a temporary SAS data set so that the data can be checked and sorted before being permanently stored:

```
%LET CURRENT=MAR86;
DATA &CURRENT;
   INFILE MONTH3;
   INPUT INVOICE YEAR @14 MAKE $8. @24 MODEL $12.
         @36 COST @45 PRICE @53 SALEDATE : DATE7. SALECODE;
   IF COST>0 THEN PROFIT=(PRICE-COST)/COST;
   FORMAT COST REVENUE DOLLAR6. PROFIT 4.2 SALEDATE DATE7.
          SALECODE Z2. INVOICE Z6.;
RUN;
```

Before this program is executed each month, you must change the value of the macro variable CURRENT in the %LET statement to the current month; the name of a SAS data set should appropriately indicate its contents.

Also, prior to executing this program, you must define the external file MONTH3 using operating system commands.[5] Refer to the *SAS Companion* or technical report for your operating system for details on defining external files. Refer to Chapter 9, "Working with External Files," for details on reading and creating external files with SAS programs.

After the MAR86 data set is created, you learn that the sales department has additional sales information for March. For your

convenience, Bill, a salesperson, has already stored the additional
sales data in his permanent SAS data library in a SAS data set named
MOREMAR. He furnishes a printed copy of the data set shown in
Output 7.1.

Output 7.1
Additional Sales Data
for March

```
                      ADDITIONAL SALES DATA FOR MARCH

 OBS  INVOICE  YEAR  MAKE   MODEL     COST   REVENUE  SALEDATE  SALECODE  PROFIT

  1   007835   78    OLDS   DELTA    $6,500   $8,640   09MAR86     28     0.33
  2   008233   76    FORD            $2,795   $3,645   20MAR86     29     0.30
  3   008362   78    OLDS   CUTLASS  $6,100   $7,982   14MAR86     30     0.31
  4   008432   67    CHEVY            $350     $444    09MAR86     14     0.27
  5   008544   73    CHEVY  CAPRICE  $2,850   $3,783   13MAR86     28     0.33
  6   008602   63    FORD   FALCON    $695     $919    28MAR86     12     0.32
  7   009019   74    FORD   MUSTANG  $2,000   $2,468   18MAR86     26     0.23
```

You need to concatenate the additional sales data in MOREMAR to
the MAR86 data set that you just created. You can use a DATA step
or PROC APPEND to concatenate SAS data sets. You decide to use
PROC APPEND:

```
PROC APPEND BASE=MAR86 NEW=BILLSLIB.MOREMAR;
RUN;
```

The SAS log output from this PROC APPEND step is shown in
Output 7.2.

Output 7.2
Appending Data Sets with
Mismatched Variables

```
56         PROC APPEND BASE=MAR86 NEW=BILLSLIB.MOREMAR;
57         RUN;
NOTE: THESE VARIABLES ARE IN WORK.MAR86 BUT NOT IN BILLSLIB.MOREMAR: PRICE.
NOTE: THESE VARIABLES ARE IN BILLSLIB.MOREMAR BUT NOT IN WORK.MAR86: REVENUE.
ERROR: NO APPENDING DONE BECAUSE OF ANOMALIES LISTED ABOVE.
NOTE: SAS STOPPED PROCESSING THIS STEP BECAUSE OF ERRORS.
NOTE: THE PROCEDURE APPEND USED 0.10 SECONDS AND 212K.
```

Output 7.2 shows that no observations were appended because the
variable name PRICE in MAR86 does not match the corresponding
variable name REVENUE in MOREMAR. You can use the FORCE
option of PROC APPEND to append observations and assign missing
values to variables from the DATA= data set that do not match
corresponding variables in the BASE= data set. However, you decide
to correct the variable name in MOREMAR so that PROC APPEND
does not generate missing values.

First, copy BILLSLIB.MOREMAR into the WORK library so that you can make the correction in your temporary version of the data set:

```
PROC COPY IN=BILLSLIB OUT=WORK;
    SELECT MOREMAR;
RUN;
```

Correct a SAS Variable Name

You can either use PROC DATASETS to correct the variable name in place or use a DATA step to re-create MOREMAR with the correct variable names. You decide to use PROC DATASETS because correcting the data set in place is more efficient:

```
PROC DATASETS;
    MODIFY MOREMAR;
    RENAME REVENUE=PRICE;
RUN;
```

The SAS log output from this PROC DATASETS step is shown in **Output 7.3.**

Output 7.3
Changing a Variable Name
with PROC DATASETS

```
LIST OF MEMBERS BEFORE UPDATE OF DIRECTORY.
NAME      MEMTYPE
MAR86    /DATA
MOREMAR /DATA
67          PROC DATASETS;
68              MODIFY MOREMAR;
69              RENAME REVENUE=PRICE;
70          RUN;
LIST OF MEMBERS AFTER UPDATE OF DIRECTORY.
NAME      MEMTYPE
MAR86    /DATA
MOREMAR /DATA

NOTE: THE PROCEDURE DATASETS USED 0.08 SECONDS AND 268K.
```

Under some operating systems, PROC DATASETS shows additional information in the list of members, such as the number of observations.

If you are using a full-screen terminal, you can correct the variable name using the full-screen features of PROC DATASETS, instead of using DATASETS without full-screen processing as shown above.[6]

To invoke PROC DATASETS for full-screen processing, submit the PROC DATASETS statement only (with no associated statements):

```
PROC DATASETS;
RUN;
```

When this statement executes, PROC DATASETS displays the Datasets Menu.

The screen contains a list of members and member types in your WORK library. To correct the variable name in member MOREMAR, you first type selection code V in the CMD field adjacent to the member MOREMAR and press ENTER.

Screen 7.1
The Datasets Menu

```
                              Datasets Menu

Command ===>

                             Library: WORK

          CMD   MEMBER    MEMTYPE    OPERAND1   OPERAND2

           _    MAR86     DATA       _____   _____
           _    MOREMAR   DATA       _____   _____
```

The Dataset Contents screen displays data set information for
MOREMAR.*

Screen 7.2
The Dataset Contents Screen

```
                            Dataset Contents

Command ===>
          Library: WORK                      Obs: 7
           Member: MOREMAR            Created On: MARCH 31, 1986
             Type:                  Generated By: DATA
            Label:

  # Variable  Type    Length  Position  Format        Informat
              Label

  1 INVOICE   NUM        8        4      Z6.           .............
              ....................................................
  2 YEAR      NUM        8       12      .............  .............
              ....................................................
  3 MAKE      CHAR       8       20      $             $
              ....................................................
  4 MODEL     CHAR      12       28      $             $
              ....................................................
  5 COST      NUM        8       40      DOLLAR6.      .............
              ....................................................
  6 REVENUE   NUM        8       48      DOLLAR6.      .............
              ....................................................
  7 SALEDATE  NUM        8       56      DATE7.        .............
              ....................................................
  8 SALECODE  NUM        8       64      Z2.           .............
              ....................................................
  9 PROFIT    NUM        8       72      4.2           .............
              ....................................................
```

On this screen simply type the correct variable name PRICE over
REVENUE and press ENTER. Note that on the Dataset Contents
screen you can also change the data set label and variable attributes

---

* If a data set contains more variables than can be displayed on one screen, you can
  issue the FORWARD command to display remaining variables.

in the Format, Informat, and Variable Label fields. Notice that fields containing no variable information are delineated with dots.*

To save the variable name that you just corrected and return to the Datasets Menu, type END on the command line of the Dataset Contents screen and press ENTER, or press the function key defined to execute the END command.

To exit DATASETS full-screen processing and return to your SAS session, type END on the command line of the Datasets Menu and press ENTER, or use the function key defined to execute the END command.

Concatenate SAS Data Sets

Now you can run PROC APPEND to concatenate observations in MOREMAR to MAR86. **Output 7.4** shows the SAS log output from this PROC APPEND step.

Output 7.4
Concatenating SAS Data Sets with PROC APPEND

```
74        PROC APPEND BASE=MAR86 DATA=MOREMAR;
75        RUN;
NOTE: WORK.MAR86 HAS 18 OBSERVATION(S) BEFORE APPENDING.
NOTE: 7 OBSERVATION(S) ADDED.
NOTE: THE PROCEDURE APPEND USED 0.08 SECONDS AND 204K.
```

Output 7.5 shows a printed copy of the sales data concatenated with PROC APPEND.

Output 7.5
Printed Results of Appended Data

```
                      ADDITIONAL DATA APPENDED
                        TO MARCH SALES DATA

OBS INVOICE YEAR MAKE      MODEL     COST   PRICE  SALEDATE SALECODE PROFIT

  1 003496  84  CHEVY     CHEVETTE $2,895 $3,550  31MAR86     26     0.23
  2 005008  78  FORD      FAIRMONT   $700   $868  22MAR86     13     0.24
  3 005227  81  FORD      MUSTANG  $1,750 $2,254  13MAR86     29     0.29
  4 005712  79  CHEVY     CAMARO   $1,000 $1,165  24MAR86      .     0.16
  5 005970  80  OLDS      CUTLASS  $2,995 $3,752  26MAR86     26     0.25
  6 005990  85  FORD      ESCORT   $7,100 $8,558  15MAR86     13     0.21
  7 006019  78  OLDS      CUTLASS  $1,095 $1,341  20MAR86     24     0.22
  8 006020  79  OLDS      DELTA88  $1,800 $2,383  14MAR86     10     0.32
  9 006369  82  BUICK     SKYLARK  $3,995 $4,749  25MAR86     24     0.19
 10 006409  83  CHEVY     CITATION $4,950 $6,427  03MAR86     29     0.30
 11 006650  78  CHEVY     IMPALA     $525   $671  27MAR86      .     0.28
 12 006780  79  FORD      LTD        $650   $872  05MAR86     09     0.34
 13 007100  84  BUICK     REGAL    $5,995 $7,882  07MAR86     11     0.31
 14 007458  79  MERCURY   COUGAR   $1,500 $1,952  31MAR86     13     0.30
 15 007493  82  CHRYSLER  LEBARON  $3,700 $4,576  03MAR86      .     0.24
 16 007526  81  BUICK     LIMITED  $2,695 $3,456  01MAR86     12     0.28
 17 007551  80  DODGE     COLT       $700   $950  11MAR86      .     0.36
 18 007560  79  PLYMOUTH  FURY     $2,000 $2,525  01MAR86     13     0.26
 19 007835  78  OLDS      DELTA    $6,500 $8,640  09MAR86     28     0.33
 20 008233  76  FORD               $2,795 $3,645  20MAR86     29     0.30
 21 008362  78  OLDS      CUTLASS  $6,100 $7,982  14MAR86     30     0.31
 22 008432  67  CHEVY                $350   $444  09MAR86     14     0.27
 23 008544  73  CHEVY     CAPRICE  $2,850 $3,783  13MAR86     28     0.33
 24 008602  63  FORD      FALCON     $695   $919  28MAR86     12     0.32
 25 009019  74  FORD      MUSTANG  $2,000 $2,468  18MAR86     26     0.23
```

---

* The variable attribute fields may not be delineated with dots as shown in **Screen 7.2** depending on the operating system you are using.

Instead of using PROC APPEND, you could have concatenated the additional sales data to MAR86 in a DATA step:

```
DATA MAR86;
    SET MAR86 MOREMAR;
RUN;
```

The SAS log output from this DATA step is shown in **Output 7.6**.

Output 7.6
Concatenating SAS Data
Sets with DATA Steps

```
95          DATA MAR86;
96              SET MAR86 MOREMAR;
97          RUN;

NOTE: DATA SET WORK.MAR86 HAS 25 OBSERVATIONS AND 9 VARIABLES.
NOTE: THE DATA STATEMENT USED 0.06 SECONDS AND 136K.
```

Output 7.7 shows the sales data concatenated using the DATA step, which is identical to the results shown in **Output 7.5**.

Output 7.7
Printed Results of
Concatenated Data

```
                    ADDITIONAL DATA CONCATENATED
                        TO MARCH SALES DATA

 OBS INVOICE YEAR MAKE      MODEL     COST   PRICE SALEDATE SALECODE PROFIT

   1 003496  84  CHEVY     CHEVETTE $2,895 $3,550 31MAR86     26     0.23
   2 005008  78  FORD      FAIRMONT   $700   $868 22MAR86     13     0.24
   3 005227  81  FORD      MUSTANG  $1,750 $2,254 13MAR86     29     0.29
   4 005712  79  CHEVY     CAMARO   $1,000 $1,165 24MAR86      .     0.16
   5 005970  80  OLDS      CUTLASS  $2,995 $3,752 26MAR86     26     0.25
   6 005990  85  FORD      ESCORT   $7,100 $8,558 15MAR86     13     0.21
   7 006019  78  OLDS      CUTLASS  $1,095 $1,341 20MAR86     24     0.22
   8 006020  79  OLDS      DELTA88  $1,800 $2,383 14MAR86     10     0.32
   9 006369  82  BUICK     SKYLARK  $3,995 $4,749 25MAR86     24     0.19
  10 006409  83  CHEVY     CITATION $4,950 $6,427 03MAR86     29     0.30
  11 006650  78  CHEVY     IMPALA     $525   $671 27MAR86      .     0.28
  12 006780  79  FORD      LTD        $650   $872 05MAR86     09     0.34
  13 007100  84  BUICK     REGAL    $5,995 $7,882 07MAR86     11     0.31
  14 007458  79  MERCURY   COUGAR   $1,500 $1,952 31MAR86     13     0.30
  15 007493  82  CHRYSLER  LEBARON  $3,700 $4,576 03MAR86      .     0.24
  16 007526  81  BUICK     LIMITED  $2,695 $3,456 01MAR86     12     0.28
  17 007551  80  DODGE     COLT       $700   $950 11MAR86      .     0.36
  18 007560  79  PLYMOUTH  FURY     $2,000 $2,525 01MAR86     13     0.26
  19 007835  78  OLDS      DELTA    $6,500 $8,640 09MAR86     28     0.33
  20 008233  76  FORD               $2,795 $3,645 20MAR86     29     0.30
  21 008362  78  OLDS      CUTLASS  $6,100 $7,982 14MAR86     30     0.31
  22 008432  67  CHEVY                $350   $444 09MAR86     14     0.27
  23 008544  73  CHEVY     CAPRICE  $2,850 $3,783 13MAR86     28     0.33
  24 008602  63  FORD      FALCON     $695   $919 28MAR86     12     0.32
  25 009019  74  FORD      MUSTANG  $2,000 $2,468 18MAR86     26     0.23
```

In choosing between PROC APPEND or the DATA step, you should consider the size of the data sets being concatenated and whether you want to analyze or manipulate the data.

Compare the amount of time and memory required by PROC APPEND in **Output 7.4** to the amount required by the DATA step in **Output 7.6.** In this example, PROC APPEND uses slightly more time and memory than the DATA step.* However, PROC APPEND is more efficient if the BASE= data set has a large number of observations because PROC APPEND adds observations to the BASE= data set

---

* The exact amount of time required for either method varies with your installation's hardware, operating system, and configuration of SAS software.

without processing existing observations. The DATA step processes observations in both data sets named in the SET statement.

However, combining SAS data sets in the DATA step allows more flexibility. You can program the DATA step to conditionally add observations or to check the data. For example, the following DATA step concatenates the sales data and also checks it for missing values:

```
DATA MAR86;
   SET MAR86 MOREMAR;
* PRINT RECORDS WITH MISSING VALUES;
   IF NMISS(OF INVOICE-NUMERIC-PROFIT) OR MAKE=' ' OR MODEL=' '
       THEN PUT / 'MISSING DATA:' / _ALL_ ;
RUN;
```

If the observation contains missing values for any of the variables, the program prints all information about that sale in the SAS log.

As shown in **Output 7.8,** there are six observations with missing values in the MAR86 data set.

```
MISSING DATA:
INVOICE=005712 YEAR=79 MAKE=CHEVY MODEL=CAMARO COST=$1,000 PRICE=$1,165
SALEDATE=24MAR86 SALECODE=. PROFIT=0.16 _ERROR_=0 _N_=4

MISSING DATA:
INVOICE=006650 YEAR=78 MAKE=CHEVY MODEL=IMPALA COST=$525 PRICE=$671
SALEDATE=27MAR86 SALECODE=. PROFIT=0.28 _ERROR_=0 _N_=11

MISSING DATA:
INVOICE=007493 YEAR=82 MAKE=CHRYSLER MODEL=LEBARON COST=$3,700 PRICE=$4,576
SALEDATE=03MAR86 SALECODE=. PROFIT=0.24 _ERROR_=0 _N_=15

MISSING DATA:
INVOICE=007551 YEAR=80 MAKE=DODGE MODEL=COLT COST=$700 PRICE=$950
SALEDATE=11MAR86 SALECODE=. PROFIT=0.36 _ERROR_=0 _N_=17

MISSING DATA:
INVOICE=008233 YEAR=76 MAKE=FORD MODEL=  COST=$2,795 PRICE=$3,645
SALEDATE=20MAR86 SALECODE=29 PROFIT=0.30 _ERROR_=0 _N_=20

MISSING DATA:
INVOICE=008432 YEAR=67 MAKE=CHEVY MODEL=  COST=$350 PRICE=$444 SALEDATE=09MAR86
SALECODE=14 PROFIT=0.27 _ERROR_=0 _N_=22
NOTE: DATA SET WORK.MAR86 HAS 25 OBSERVATIONS AND 9 VARIABLES.
NOTE: THE DATA STATEMENT USED 0.08 SECONDS AND 148K.
```

You must update the SAS data set by replacing the missing values with correct values. There are several ways to do this.

Update the SAS Data Set

You can update a SAS data set using PROC EDITOR (described in Chapter 5, "Updating and Editing SAS Data Sets") or PROC FSEDIT (described in *SAS/FSP User's Guide, Version 5 Edition*). Both of these procedures edit an existing data set in place; that is, you issue commands to access and change only those observations in which values need to be changed. Choose this method when you need to make a few immediate changes. For example, in the March sales data, you would change only those observations that contain missing values.

When you edit in place, remember that you cannot start over if you save a mistake because you are working with the original data set. Also, you cannot compare values or perform calculations.

Another method is the standard update operation in which sorted transactions are applied to a sorted master file in the DATA step. You decide to use the standard update operation because you have a number of changes to make and because you want to calculate the relative profit for the updated observations and do some additional editing.

First, you sort the sales data by invoice number:

```
PROC SORT DATA=MAR86;
   BY INVOICE;
RUN;
```

PROC SORT produces a sorted version of MAR86 in the WORK library; the original, unsorted version of MAR86 is no longer accessible.

Next, you create a transaction file named CHANGES containing changes to be applied to MAR86, the master file in this example. **Output 7.9** shows a printed copy of the transaction data set CHANGES, which has already been sorted and stored in the WORK library.

Output 7.9
Transaction File for
Updating Master File

```
                    TRANSACTION FILE CONTAINING CHANGES

OBS TRANCODE INVOICE YEAR MAKE    MODEL     COST   PRICE SALEDATE SALECODE

  1     A     004503   83  CHEVY CHEVETTE $1,100 $1,350  04MAR86     29
  2     U     005712    .                      .      .        .     30
  3     A     005790   81  OLDS  CUTLASS  $2,995 $3,752  26MAR86     26
  4     D     005970    .                      .      .        .      .
  5     U     006650    .                      .      .        .     30
  6     U     007493    .        LEBARON       .      .        .     15
  7     U     007551    .                      .      .        .     11
  8     U     008233    .        GRANADA       .      .        .      .
  9     U     008432    .        NOVA          .      .        .      .
 10     D     009019    .                      .      .        .      .
 11     A     009022   83  CHEVY ELCAMINO $2,799 $3,425  28MAR86     11
```

In the transaction file, the variable TRANCODE indicates whether to add a new record (A), change an existing record (U), or delete a record (D).

Output 7.10 shows the DATA step execution that creates an updated version of MAR86 in the WORK library.

```
141        DATA MAR86;
142           UPDATE MAR86 (IN=MASTER)
143                 CHANGES (IN=UPDATES);
144           BY INVOICE;
145           DROP TRANCODE;
146           * DELETIONS;
147           IF TRANCODE='D' THEN DO;
148              PUT /'DELETION OF MASTER RECORD' / _ALL_;
149              IF ¬MASTER
150                 THEN PUT 'INVOICE NUMBER NOT FOUND ON MASTER FILE';
151              DELETE;
152              END;
153           * ADDITION INDICATED, BUT MASTER RECORD ALREADY EXISTS;
154           IF TRANCODE='A' THEN IF MASTER
155              THEN PUT /
156              ' ADDITION REQUESTED, BUT MASTER RECORD ALREADY EXISTS '
157              /_ALL_;
158           * UPDATE INDICATED, BUT MASTER RECORD DOES NOT EXIST;
159           IF TRANCODE='U' THEN IF ¬MASTER
160              THEN PUT /
161              ' UPDATE REQUESTED, BUT MASTER RECORD DOES NOT EXIST '
162              /_ALL_;
163           * RECALCULATE PROFIT IF RECORD WAS UPDATED;
164           IF UPDATES THEN IF LAST.INVOICE
165              THEN PROFIT=(PRICE-COST)/COST;
166           * PRINT RECORDS WITH MISSING VALUES;
167           IF NMISS(OF INVOICE-NUMERIC-PROFIT) OR MAKE= ' ' OR MODEL= ' '
168              THEN PUT / 'MISSING DATA:' / _ALL_ ;
169           RUN;


DELETION OF MASTER RECORD
MASTER=1 INVOICE=005970 YEAR=80 MAKE=OLDS MODEL=CUTLASS COST=$2,995 PRICE=$3,752
SALEDATE=26MAR86 SALECODE=26 PROFIT=0.2527546 UPDATES=1 TRANCODE=D
LAST.INVOICE=1 FIRST.INVOICE=1 _ERROR_=0 _N_=7

DELETION OF MASTER RECORD
MASTER=1 INVOICE=009019 YEAR=74 MAKE=FORD MODEL=MUSTANG COST=$2,000 PRICE=$2,468
SALEDATE=18MAR86 SALECODE=26 PROFIT=0.234 UPDATES=1 TRANCODE=D LAST.INVOICE=1
FIRST.INVOICE=1 _ERROR_=0 _N_=27
NOTE: DATA SET WORK.MAR86 HAS 26 OBSERVATIONS AND 9 VARIABLES.
NOTE: THE DATA STATEMENT USED 0.10 SECONDS AND 188K.
```

The printed results of the update operation appear in **Output 7.11.**

```
                    MASTER FILE WITH CHANGES APPLIED

     OBS INVOICE YEAR MAKE      MODEL     COST   PRICE SALEDATE SALECODE PROFIT

       1 003496   84  CHEVY     CHEVETTE $2,895 $3,550 31MAR86     26     0.23
       2 004503   83  CHEVY     CHEVETTE $1,100 $1,350 04MAR86     29     0.23
       3 005008   78  FORD      FAIRMONT   $700   $868 22MAR86     13     0.24
       4 005227   81  FORD      MUSTANG  $1,750 $2,254 13MAR86     29     0.29
       5 005712   79  CHEVY     CAMARO   $1,000 $1,165 24MAR86     30     0.16
       6 005790   81  OLDS      CUTLASS  $2,995 $3,752 26MAR86     26     0.25
       7 005990   85  FORD      ESCORT   $7,100 $8,558 15MAR86     13     0.21
       8 006019   78  OLDS      CUTLASS  $1,095 $1,341 20MAR86     24     0.22
       9 006020   79  OLDS      DELTA88  $1,800 $2,383 14MAR86     10     0.32
      10 006369   82  BUICK     SKYLARK  $3,995 $4,749 25MAR86     24     0.19
      11 006409   83  CHEVY     CITATION $4,950 $6,427 03MAR86     29     0.30
      12 006650   78  CHEVY     IMPALA     $525   $671 27MAR86     30     0.28
      13 006780   79  FORD      LTD        $650   $872 05MAR86     09     0.34
      14 007100   84  BUICK     REGAL    $5,995 $7,882 07MAR86     11     0.31
      15 007458   79  MERCURY   COUGAR   $1,500 $1,952 31MAR86     13     0.30
      16 007493   82  CHRYSLER  LEBARON  $3,700 $4,576 03MAR86     15     0.24
      17 007526   81  BUICK     LIMITED  $2,695 $3,456 01MAR86     12     0.28
      18 007551   80  DODGE     COLT       $700   $950 11MAR86     11     0.36
      19 007560   79  PLYMOUTH  FURY     $2,000 $2,525 01MAR86     13     0.26
      20 007835   78  OLDS      DELTA    $6,500 $8,640 09MAR86     28     0.33
      21 008233   76  FORD      GRANADA  $2,795 $3,645 20MAR86     29     0.30
      22 008362   78  OLDS      CUTLASS  $6,100 $7,982 14MAR86     30     0.31
      23 008432   67  CHEVY     NOVA       $350   $444 09MAR86     14     0.27
      24 008544   73  CHEVY     CAPRICE  $2,850 $3,783 13MAR86     28     0.33
      25 008602   63  FORD      FALCON     $695   $919 28MAR86     12     0.32
      26 009022   83  CHEVY     ELCAMINO $2,799 $3,425 28MAR86     11     0.22
```

Update the SAS Data Library

Now that you have the sales data organized, you want to store MAR86 in a permanent SAS data library. You use PROC COPY to copy the temporary version into the permanent SAS data library referenced by SALEDATA. With the MOVE option, PROC COPY deletes the temporary version of MAR86 from the WORK library when it copies the permanent version to SALEDATA:

```
PROC COPY IN=WORK OUT=SALEDATA MEMTYPE=DATA MOVE;
    SELECT MAR86;
RUN;
```

Note that before invoking PROC COPY, you must define the permanent SAS data library referenced by libref SALEDATA using operating system control language or the SAS LIBNAME statement.[7]

Document the Contents of the SAS Data Library

Use PROC CONTENTS to list the contents of the newly updated library:

```
PROC CONTENTS DATA=SALEDATA._ALL_ NODS MEMTYPE=ALL;
    TITLE 'CONTENTS OF LIBRARY CONTAINING SALE DATA';
RUN;
```

In the above PROC CONTENTS statement, the member name _ALL_ is a special SAS name that refers to all members of the specified type in the library. In this case, you ask for all types by specifying MEMTYPE=ALL.* The NODS option suppresses detailed CONTENTS output on each SAS data set (DATA type) in the library.

When you specify _ALL_ as the member name, PROC CONTENTS automatically generates a list (or directory) of all members of the specified type. The appearance of the list varies with different operating systems. Following are examples of output produced under each operating system by the above PROC CONTENTS step for the SAS data library referenced by SALEDATA. Notice that the library contains SAS data sets JAN86, FEB86, and MAR86, as well as other types of members.

Output 7.12
*PROC CONTENTS Output Produced under an AOS/VS, PRIMOS, or VMS Operating System.***

```
            CONTENTS OF LIBRARY CONTAINING SALES DATA

                       CONTENTS PROCEDURE
                  SAS DATA LIBRARY DIRECTORY

                    NAME        MEMTYPE

                    AMAP        GCAT
                    CHANGES     DATA
                    FEB86       DATA
                    JAN86       DATA
                    MAR86       DATA
                    MEMO        CAT
                    SCREEN      CAT
```

---

* If you are using SAS 5.16 or a later release, MEMTYPE=ALL is the default; in earlier releases MEMTYPE=DATA is the default.

** If you are running SAS 5.03 or an earlier release under one of these operating systems, PROC CONTENTS lists all DATA types then lists all other types of SAS files in the library.

Output 7.13
PROC CONTENTS Output
Produced under a
CMS or VM/PC
Operating System

```
          CONTENTS OF LIBRARY CONTAINING SALES DATA

                      CONTENTS PROCEDURE
                  SAS DATA LIBRARY DIRECTORY


          NAME        MEMTYPE      #OBS

          AMAP        GCAT
          CHANGES     DATA         11
          FEB86       DATA         26
          JAN86       DATA         28
          MAR86       DATA         26
          MEMO        CAT
          SCREEN      CAT
```

Output 7.14
PROC CONTENTS Output
Produced under an OS or
VSE Operating System

```
          CONTENTS OF LIBRARY CONTAINING SALES DATA

                      CONTENTS PROCEDURE
          PHYSICAL CHARACTERISTICS OF THE OS DATA SET

DSNAME= SALES.DATA.LIB    UNIT=DISK    VOL=SER=ABC123.    DISP=OLD
DEVICE=3380 DISK   MAX BLKSIZE=32760 BYTES    CREATED ON MARCH 13, 1986
10 TRACKS ALLOCATED IN 1 EXTENT(S)    COST IF DATA IS STORED ONLINE= $0.1200/DAY
COST IF DATA IS STORED OFFLINE= $0.0400/DAY


                  SAS DATA LIBRARY DIRECTORY


       NAME       MEMTYPE      #OBS        TRACKS       EXTENTS

       AMAP       GCAT                        1            1
       CHANGES    DATA         11             1            1
       FEB86      DATA         26             1            1
       JAN86      DATA         28             1            1
       MAR86      DATA         26             1            1
       MEMO       CAT                         1            1
       SCREEN     CAT                         1            1

                  TOTAL  TRACKS USED =        8
                  HIGH   TRACKS USED =        8
```

Please refer to the PROC CONTENTS description in *SAS User's Guide: Basics, Version 5 Edition* for details on CONTENTS output produced under your operating system.

Produce Quarterly Sales Reports

At the end of each quarter, you want to produce a summary report using data sets JAN86, FEB86, and MAR86. The following job concatenates these three data sets to create a temporary data set, then uses the CHART procedure with a temporary data set to generate the quarterly sales report:

```
DATA QTR1;
   SET SALEDATA.JAN86
       SALEDATA.FEB86
       SALEDATA.MAR86;
   NET=PRICE-COST;
PROC CHART DATA=QTR1;
   FORMAT NET PRICE COST DOLLAR10. PROFIT 3.2;
   HBAR SALECODE / DISCRETE SUMVAR=NET TYPE=SUM ASCENDING;
   TITLE1 'FANTASY MOTORS, INC.';
   TITLE2 'FIRST QUARTER SALES REPORT';
   TITLE3 "&SYSDATE";
RUN;
```

Output 7.15 shows the quarterly sales report produced by PROC CHART. The horizontal bar chart compares the total net profit (NET SUM) to the total number of sales (FREQ) for each salesman (SALECODE) during the first quarter.

Output 7.15
Quarterly Sales Report
Produced by
PROC CHART

```
                              FANTASY MOTORS, INC.
                           FIRST QUARTER SALES REPORT
                                  31MAR86

                              BAR CHART OF SUMS

      SALECODE                                            FREQ    NET SUM
          23   |*                                           1        $165
               |
          14   |**                                          3        $386
               |
          15   |****                                        1        $876
               |
          30   |*********                                   3      $2,193
               |
          12   |**********                                  4      $2,507
               |
          09   |************                                8      $3,027
               |
          28   |************                                2      $3,073
               |
          10   |*************                               7      $3,311
               |
          24   |********************                       10      $5,000
               |
          26   |*********************                       8      $5,241
               |
          13   |***********************************        14      $8,710
               |
          29   |*****************************************   11     $10,247
               |
          11   |*****************************************    8     $10,476
               |
               --------+-------+-------+-------+-------+--
                   $2,000  $4,000  $6,000  $8,000  $10,000

                                   NET SUM
```

Back Up the SAS Data Library

At the end of each quarter, you want to back up the data sets for that quarter. You use PROC COPY to copy the data sets into a backup SAS data library:

```
PROC COPY IN=SALEDATA OUT=BACKUP;
   SELECT JAN86 FEB86 MAR86;
RUN;
```

The SAS log from the copy operation is shown in **Output 7.16**.

Output 7.16
Using PROC COPY to Back
Up a SAS Data Library

```
NOTE: DATA SET BACKUP.JAN86 HAS 28 OBSERVATIONS AND 9 VARIABLES.
NOTE: DATA SET BACKUP.FEB86 HAS 26 OBSERVATIONS AND 9 VARIABLES.
NOTE: DATA SET BACKUP.MAR86 HAS 26 OBSERVATIONS AND 9 VARIABLES.
NOTE: THE PROCEDURE COPY USED 0.12 SECONDS AND 152K.
```

Notes

1. **CMS:** You do not need to define a SAS data library that is accessible through the search order automatically defined by CMS SAS.

2. **CMS, OS, VM/PC, VSE:** Files containing user-written formats are not stored as members of SAS data libraries.

3. **AOS/VS, VMS:** A SAS data library on tape can contain only SAS data sets, and the tape must be labeled.
   PRIMOS: A SAS data library on tape can contain only SAS data sets, and the tape is always unlabeled.

4. **AOS/VS:** You cannot write the SAS data to tape if the data set has the same name as a SAS data set already on the tape.
   CMS, OS, VM/PC, VSE: The original data set of the same name is overwritten.
   PRIMOS, VMS: The data set is written after the last data set on the tape, which means you have data sets with duplicate names. Be aware when reading the data set from tape that the SAS System reads the first (oldest) data set with that name.

5. **AOS/VS, PRIMOS, VMS:** You do not have to define the file if it is located in your current directory. Under VMS only, the file must be located in your current directory and have a file type of .DAT. You do not have to define the file if you specify its full path name in quotes in the INFILE statement.

6. **AOS/VS, PRIMOS, VMS:** When you invoke a full-screen procedure from a line-mode or noninteractive SAS session, the SAS System prompts you for the device name of your terminal. Device names for supported terminals are given in the *SAS Companion* or technical report for your operating system.

7. **CMS, VM/PC:** You need to define the SAS data library only if SAS System defaults will cause the file to be written to a minidisk that you do not want to use.
   OS: The LIBNAME statement is available in SAS release 5.16 and later.
   VSE: The LIBNAME statement is not available under VSE; you must use the /FILE statement to associate the libref SALEDATA with the SAS data library being accessed.

8 Diagnosing Errors

Whether you are a newcomer to SAS software or a long-time user, chances are you have had some experience in making errors in your SAS programs. You probably know that if you misspell a SAS keyword, forget a semicolon, or make similar mistakes, SAS prints the word ERROR followed by a number and message explaining the error.

The message may tell you exactly how to correct your mistake. Other times, however, a message caused by some previous mistake that went undetected may be difficult to interpret. Some jobs that have errors produce no message at all; they just process your data incorrectly. To find errors like this, you may need to print intermediate data sets in the job or use programming tricks that take advantage of error-checking features in the SAS System.[1]

This chapter discusses some of the most common SAS programming errors and offers suggestions on how to avoid errors in your programs.

How the SAS System Checks Syntax

You can better understand why SAS generates the notes and messages on your SAS log if you understand how SAS works. This section describes in simple terms how SAS checks the statements in your job.

The SAS Supervisor   The SAS supervisor is in charge of the execution of every SAS program. The supervisor handles

- reading your SAS statements and data
- translating your program statements into machine code that can be executed
- creating all your SAS data sets
- calling the SAS procedures you request
- printing error messages
- ending your job.

The supervisor scans the statements in your job. When it sees a DATA statement, it finds the *parsing module* responsible for the DATA step; when it sees a PROC statement, it finds the parsing module for that procedure.

Parsing Module A parsing module is associated with the DATA step and with every SAS procedure. The parsing module knows what statements are allowed in the step. If the step is a DATA step, the parsing module knows the form and type of statements that can be present. If the step is a PROC step, the parsing module knows the options and procedure information statements allowed for that procedure and the output data sets the procedure can create.

The supervisor works with the parsing module to scan the statements in the step. If the supervisor does not recognize something, it prints an error message immediately.

Errors in Syntax

The *SAS User's Guide: Basics, Version 5 Edition* describes the programming statements that may appear in a DATA step. All but two begin with a SAS keyword; all of them end with a semicolon. The two that do not begin with a keyword—the assignment statement and the sum statement—have a very special syntax.

Assignment Statement The assignment statement always begins with the name of a variable followed by an equal sign and an expression:

    variable=expression;

When SAS sees this form, it recognizes the statement as an assignment statement. SAS evaluates the expression following the equal sign and assigns the result to the variable preceding the equal sign.

Sum Statement The sum statement also has a special form—the name of a variable followed by a plus sign and an expression:

    variable+expression;

When SAS sees a statement of this form, it evaluates the expression following the plus, adds it to the variable's value, and retains the value of the variable for the next execution of the DATA step. Because SAS looks for this exact form, you must use the form below to subtract an expression from an accumulator variable:

    variable+(-expression);

SAS does not recognize a statement of this form:

    variable-expression;

Examples   Consider this common error and the results shown in **Output 8.1**:

```
DATA A;
   INPUT X Y;
   X+Y=Z;
   CARDS;
1 2
5 6
8 4
;
```

Output 8.1
Incorrect Assignment
Statement

```
10         DATA A;
11            INPUT X Y;
12            X+Y=Z;
13            CARDS;

NOTE: THE VARIABLE Z IS UNINITIALIZED.
NOTE: DATA SET WORK.A HAS 3 OBSERVATIONS AND 3 VARIABLES. 680 OBS/TRK.
NOTE: THE DATA STATEMENT USED 0.07 SECONDS AND 132K.
```

SAS produces no error message even though the assignment statement
X+Y=Z should be written Z=X+Y. Why does SAS consider this
DATA step correct?

The supervisor sees the statement

```
X+Y=Z;
```

and recognizes a sum statement of the form

variable+expression;

with X the variable and Y=Z the expression. Each time Y equals Z,
the expression Y=Z is "true" and has a value 1. When Y is not equal
to Z, the expression is "false" and has a value 0. Thus, the statement
is valid, although not executed as you intended. As shown in **Output
8.1**, the message

```
NOTE:  THE VARIABLE Z IS UNINITIALIZED.
```

appears in the SAS log for this DATA step.

When you create a new variable in an assignment statement, this
message will not appear. It is printed only when SAS expects a
variable to have a value already, either from input data or from an
earlier assignment or sum statement. You usually get this message if a
variable appears on the right-hand side of an equal sign in an
assignment statement and SAS does not have a value stored for it.

Keywords For statements that begin with keywords, spell the keyword correctly so SAS can recognize it. If you submit the following statements, the SAS log looks like **Output 8.2**:

```
DATA D;
   INPUT X;
   Y=X+1;
   DORP X; ◄── note incorrect keyword
   CARDS;
9
6
4
3
;
```

Output 8.2
Misspelling a SAS
Keyword

```
10        DATA D;
11           INPUT X;
12           Y=X+1;
13           DORP X;
             ----
             180
14           CARDS;


ERROR 180: STATEMENT IS NOT VALID OR IT IS USED OUT OF PROPER ORDER.

NOTE: SAS STOPPED PROCESSING THIS STEP BECAUSE OF ERRORS.
NOTE: SAS SET OPTION OBS=0 AND WILL CONTINUE TO CHECK STATEMENTS.
      THIS MAY CAUSE NOTE: NO OBSERVATIONS IN DATA SET.
NOTE: DATA SET WORK.D HAS 0 OBSERVATIONS AND 2 VARIABLES. 953 OBS/TRK.
NOTE: THE DATA STATEMENT USED 0.03 SECONDS AND 116K.
```

Semicolons Once SAS recognizes a statement, it records the information contained in the statement to use later. SAS knows it has read all the information contained in a statement when it finds a semicolon.

If you omit a semicolon from the end of a statement, SAS continues to scan through the next statement as if it were part of the last. Sometimes SAS does not detect a missing semicolon and tries to execute your statements.

Examples Below are two such DATA steps that SAS tries to execute:

```
DATA A  ◄── note missing semicolon
   INPUT X;
   Y=X+1;
   CARDS;
18
26
95
63
70
;
```

The SAS log for this step is shown in **Output 8.3.**

```
10          DATA A
11             INPUT X;
12             Y=X+1;
13             CARDS;
NOTE: THE VARIABLE X IS UNINITIALIZED.
NOTE: MISSING VALUES WERE GENERATED AS A RESULT OF PERFORMING
      AN OPERATION ON MISSING VALUES.
      EACH PLACE IS GIVEN BY: (NUMBER OF TIMES) AT (LINE):(COLUMN).

      1 AT 12:6

NOTE: DATA SET WORK.A HAS 1 OBSERVATIONS AND 2 VARIABLES. 953 OBS/TRK.
NOTE: DATA SET WORK.INPUT HAS 1 OBSERVATIONS AND 2 VARIABLES. 953 OBS/TRK.
NOTE: DATA SET WORK.X HAS 1 OBSERVATIONS AND 2 VARIABLES. 953 OBS/TRK.
NOTE: THE DATA STATEMENT USED 0.05 SECONDS AND 172K.

19             ;
```

How does SAS process this step? SAS sees the keyword DATA, so it knows to process a DATA step; the names of any data sets to be created in the step follow the word DATA. In this case, SAS stores the information that it is to create three data sets: A, INPUT, and X. The semicolon tells SAS it has reached the end of the statement. SAS recognizes the next statement

```
Y=X+1;
```

as an assignment statement; it stores the fact that X is added to 1 and the result stored in Y. The next statement

```
CARDS;
```

tells SAS that there are no further program statements in the DATA step and that data lines follow.

These statements are now ready to be executed. SAS does not know whether the step makes sense logically, but it recognizes all the statements.

The step is executed once. SAS does not read any data since there is no INPUT statement. It sets up three data sets and creates a variable Y. As in the previous example, SAS looks for an existing X value, and when it does not find one, it prints the first NOTE in **Output 8.3**. The second NOTE in **Output 8.3** is printed since X has a missing value when SAS creates Y.

Consider this step with the missing semicolon on the PUT statement:

```
DATA C;
   INPUT X Y Z;
   PUT X        ←—— note missing semicolon
   M=X+Y;
   CARDS;
 1 2 3
 4 5 6
 ;
```

and the resulting SAS log shown in **Output 8.4**.

```
10          DATA C;
11            INPUT X Y Z;
12            PUT X
13            M=X+Y;
14            CARDS;

NOTE: THE VARIABLE M IS UNINITIALIZED.
 1 M=. 1
 4 M=. 4
NOTE: DATA SET WORK.C HAS 2 OBSERVATIONS AND 4 VARIABLES. 529 OBS/TRK.
NOTE: THE DATA STATEMENT USED 0.05 SECONDS AND 132K.
```

As before, the statements in this step are syntactically correct. The statement

```
PUT X M=X+Y;
```

is a valid SAS statement. We can analyze the parts of this SAS statement as follow:

```
PUT X
```

Print the value of the variable X.

```
    M=
```

Print the variable M using named output.

```
    X
```

Print X again.

```
    +Y;
```

Skip Y columns.

SAS spacing rules are very flexible—special characters can take the place of a space. Since M has no value when the PUT statement is executed, SAS prints the first NOTE. Notice the messages in **Output 8.4** that result from the PUT statement.

In the following example, the first statement after the DATA step has a missing semicolon. SAS thinks the line is part of the data:

```
DATA CC;
   INPUT X Y Z;
   CARDS;
1 2 3
4 5 6
PROC PRINT ◄── note missing semicolon
   VAR X;
RUN;
```

The resulting log is shown in **Output 8.5**.

Output 8.5
Additional Errors When
Semicolon Is Omitted

```
10          DATA CC;
11             INPUT X Y Z;
12             CARDS;
NOTE: INVALID DATA FOR X IN LINE 15 1-4.     11:10
NOTE: INVALID DATA FOR Y IN LINE 15 6-10.    11:12
NOTE: LOST CARD.

RULE:    ----+----1----+----2----+----3----+----4----+----5----+----6----+----7

15          PROC PRINT
X=. Y=. Z=. _ERROR_=1 _N_=3
NOTE: SAS WENT TO A NEW LINE WHEN INPUT STATEMENT
      REACHED PAST THE END OF A LINE.
NOTE: DATA SET WORK.CC HAS 2 OBSERVATIONS AND 3 VARIABLES. 680 OBS/TRK.
NOTE: THE DATA STATEMENT USED 0.04 SECONDS AND 132K.

16             VAR X;
               ---
               180
17          RUN;

ERROR 180: STATEMENT IS NOT VALID OR IT IS USED OUT OF PROPER ORDER.
```

SAS knows that it is no longer reading data following a CARDS statement when it encounters a line that contains a semicolon. Thus, the line

```
PROC PRINT
```

is interpreted as part of the data, and SAS prints messages about invalid data. The lost card message is printed because SAS tries to read PROC as the value of X and PRINT as the value of Y, then goes past the end of the line to find a value for Z. (See **Errors in Input,** later in this chapter, for more about the lost card message.) Since SAS does not recognize the PROC statement, it does not expect the VAR statement, and error message 180 appears in the log.

There is a special situation in which your SAS program may contain statements that are correct but SAS may not be able to read them correctly. If you receive an error message and some of the more obvious errors in syntax, logic, or input do not seem to be the source of your problems, you might consider the problem discussed below.

Normally, SAS reads fixed-length records of 80 characters when scanning the source statements and data lines in your program. You can tell SAS to read a different record length with the S= system option.[2]

If you (or your SAS Software Representative) change the S= value by specifying, for example, S=72, SAS reads only columns 1-72 when it scans your statements and data lines. If S=72 and if the semicolon for a statement appears in columns 73-80, SAS does not detect the semicolon, and an error results, as shown in **Output 8.6.**

```
OPTIONS S=72;
DATA TEST;
   SET PEOPLE;
   KEEP NAME AGE SEX ADDRESS CITY STATE TITLE YEARS DEGREE MARITAL DEPT ;
PROC PRINT;
   VAR NAME AGE SEX;
RUN;
```

```
24         OPTIONS S=72;
25         DATA TEST;
26           SET PEOPLE;
27           KEEP NAME AGE SEX ADDRESS CITY STATE TITLE YEARS DEGREE MARITAL DE
PT ;
28         PROC PRINT;
29           VAR NAME AGE SEX;
                   ────
                   180
30         RUN;


ERROR 180: STATEMENT IS NOT VALID OR IT IS USED OUT OF PROPER ORDER.

ERROR: THE VARIABLE PROC IN THE KEEP LIST HAS NEVER BEEN REFERENCED.
ERROR: THE VARIABLE PRINT IN THE KEEP LIST HAS NEVER BEEN REFERENCED.
NOTE: SAS STOPPED PROCESSING THIS STEP BECAUSE OF ERRORS.
NOTE: SAS SET OPTION OBS=0 AND WILL CONTINUE TO CHECK STATEMENTS.
      THIS MAY CAUSE NOTE: NO OBSERVATIONS IN DATA SET.
NOTE: DATA SET WORK.TEST HAS 0 OBSERVATIONS AND 11 VARIABLES. 226 OBS/TRK.
NOTE: THE DATA STATEMENT USED 0.05 SECONDS AND 128K.
```

SAS begins reading the KEEP statement but does not read the semicolon that appears in column 73. SAS interprets everything from the keyword KEEP to the semicolon after the keyword PRINT as part of the KEEP statement. Since it never sees the PROC PRINT statement, SAS issues an error message when it sees a VAR statement that seems to be out of order.

Comments   Remember that comment statements in your SAS job are just like any other SAS statements; they must end in a semicolon. If you enter the statements

```
DATA A;
  *SUBSET THE DATA  ←── note missing semicolon
  SET B;
  IF X<Y;
PROC PRINT;
RUN;
```

you will get the message shown in **Output 8.7**.

```
10         DATA A;
11           *SUBSET THE DATA
12           SET B;
13           IF X<Y;
NOTE: THE VARIABLE X IS UNINITIALIZED.
NOTE: THE VARIABLE Y IS UNINITIALIZED.
NOTE: DATA SET WORK.A HAS 0 OBSERVATIONS AND 2 VARIABLES. 953 OBS/TRK.
NOTE: THE DATA STATEMENT USED 0.04 SECONDS AND 128K.

14         PROC PRINT;
15           RUN;
NOTE: NO OBSERVATIONS IN DATA SET WORK.A .
NOTE: THE PROCEDURE PRINT USED 0.07 SECONDS AND 216K.
```

SAS interprets the comment as

```
*SUBSET THE DATA SET B;
```

and finds no source of input for the step.

If you use the other form of comment, for example

```
/* Here is a comment */
```

SAS treats everything between the comment indicators /* and */ as part of the comment. If you use the /* to begin a comment and omit the end of comment indicator */, everything after the /* is ignored, and your program executes incorrectly.

Note: if the end of your comment appears after column 72 when the system option S=72 is in effect, SAS does not read the */ and an error results.

Between Keyword and Semicolon

From the time SAS recognizes the type of statement to the time it finds the semicolon ending the statement, SAS makes sure the statement has been coded correctly. For example, KEEP and DROP statements require a list of variable names. SAS does not accept the statement

```
DROP X+Y;
```

but prints the message shown in **Output 8.8.**

Output 8.8
Errors between the
Keyword and Semicolon

```
15          DATA B;
16             SET A;
17             DROP X+Y;
                        -
                        102


     ERROR 102: WORD DOES NOT START WITH A LETTER OR UNDERSCORE.
          SEE USER'S GUIDE, "SAS NAMES".

     NOTE: SAS STOPPED PROCESSING THIS STEP BECAUSE OF ERRORS.
     NOTE: SAS SET OPTION OBS=0 AND WILL CONTINUE TO CHECK STATEMENTS.
          THIS MAY CAUSE NOTE: NO OBSERVATIONS IN DATA SET.
     NOTE: DATA SET WORK.B HAS 0 OBSERVATIONS AND 0 VARIABLES. 4766 OBS/TRK.
     NOTE: THE DATA STATEMENT USED 0.04 SECONDS AND 124K.
```

SAS interprets X, +, and Y as variables. Since you cannot begin a variable name with a plus sign (+), the error message 102 is printed. If you code this KEEP statement

```
KEEP=X;
```

SAS interprets it as an assignment statement and transfers the value of X to a new variable, KEEP. Both KEEP and X (and any other variables mentioned in the step) appear in the data set being created.

IF-THEN Statement

The form of the IF-THEN statement is sometimes confusing:

```
IF expression THEN statement;
```

Expression can include a comparison like X<10 or X LT 10, and
statement must be an executable SAS program statement. Statements
like

DROP	LABEL	LENGTH	ENDSAS
KEEP	RETAIN	FORMAT	%INCLUDE
RENAME	TITLE	ARRAY	X

are not allowed. Some of these statements tell SAS to perform an
action that is independent of a DATA or PROC step. Other statements
give SAS information about the data set being created or the procedure being executed; the information they provide must apply to the
entire step, not just part of it. For example, when you create a SAS
data set, you cannot drop variables from some of the observations and
not others; the DROP statement cannot be executed conditionally. The
rule is: if a statement can be executed conditionally, that is, if it can
apply to some without applying to all of the variables or observations
in the data set, then it is an executable statement. The statement

```
IF X=1 THEN DROP X;
```

results in a message about the DROP statement, shown in **Output 8.9**.

Output 8.9
An IF-THEN Statement
with a Nonexecutable
Statement

```
15          DATA B;
16             SET A;
17             IF X=1 THEN DROP X;
                        ----
                        180


ERROR 180: STATEMENT IS NOT VALID OR IT IS USED OUT OF PROPER ORDER.

NOTE: SAS STOPPED PROCESSING THIS STEP BECAUSE OF ERRORS.
NOTE: SAS SET OPTION OBS=0 AND WILL CONTINUE TO CHECK STATEMENTS.
      THIS MAY CAUSE NOTE: NO OBSERVATIONS IN DATA SET.
NOTE: DATA SET WORK.B HAS 0 OBSERVATIONS AND 2 VARIABLES. 953 OBS/TRK.
NOTE: THE DATA STATEMENT USED 0.04 SECONDS AND 124K.
```

Expressions   In an IF-THEN statement, the expression following the IF can consist
of simple expressions joined by AND or OR, for example,

```
IF X=1 OR X=2 THEN OUTPUT;
```

In this case, if X is either 1 or 2, the observation is output. Do not
make this mistake:

```
IF X=1 OR 2 THEN OUTPUT;
```

The expression in this statement is always true; all the observations
are output. The statement is evaluated as if it were

```
IF X=1 OR 2¬=0 THEN OUTPUT;
```

Only statements are permitted after THEN. Although you can say

```
IF X LT Y THEN Z=1;
```

you cannot say

```
IF X LT Y THEN Z EQ 1;
```

In the first IF-THEN statement, Z=1 is an assignment statement. In the second IF-THEN statement, Z EQ 1 is an expression involving a comparison; the value of Z is compared to the number 1. Similarly, you cannot say

```
IF X<Y THEN Z<Y;
```

or

```
IF X<Y THEN SUM(X,Y);
```

because Z<Y and SUM(X,Y) are expressions, not SAS statements.

The character equivalents for the operators mentioned in the *SAS User's Guide: Basics, Version 5 Edition*, for example LT for < and GT for >, can take the place of comparison operators only in SAS expressions.

Parentheses and Quotes

These mistakes also generate error messages:

□ leaving off one of the parentheses around the arguments of a function or in an expression
□ forgetting a matching quote after a character value
□ omitting quotes around character literals.

SAS can easily spot a missing parenthesis. For example, the statement

```
X=INT((X+Y)/2;     ◄—— note missing parenthesis after 2
```

produces the message shown in **Output 8.10.**

Output 8.10
Omitting a Parenthesis

```
10         DATA B;
11             SET A;
12             X=INT((X+Y)/2;
                            -
                           303


ERROR 303: RIGHT PARENTHESIS FOR FUNCTION EXPECTED.
NOTE: SAS STOPPED PROCESSING THIS STEP BECAUSE OF ERRORS.
NOTE: SAS SET OPTION OBS=0 AND WILL CONTINUE TO CHECK STATEMENTS.
      THIS MAY CAUSE NOTE: NO OBSERVATIONS IN DATA SET.
NOTE: DATA SET WORK.B HAS 0 OBSERVATIONS AND 2 VARIABLES. 953 OBS/TRK.
NOTE: THE DATA STATEMENT USED 0.04 SECONDS AND 124K.
```

Similarly, when SAS sees one quote mark, it looks for a matching one. Anything between the two is considered a character literal. If you omit a quote, SAS keeps looking for the end of the literal; it looks for up to 200 characters, the maximum length of a character value. Here is an example:

```
DATA A;
   INPUT X Y ᚛᚛;
   NEW='YES';
   IF X=5 THEN NEW='NO;  ◄——— note missing quote
   CARDS;
1 4 5 7 9 11
;
PROC PRINT;
   TITLE 'THIS SHOWS WHAT HAPPENS WHEN YOU OMIT A QUOTE';
RUN;
```

The results appear in **Output 8.11**.

Output 8.11
Omitting a Quote

```
10         DATA A;
11            INPUT X Y ᚛᚛;
12            NEW='YES';
13            IF X=5 THEN NEW='NO;
                                   ----------------------------------------------------
-----------
                                    107
14            CARDS;
15            1 4 5 7 9 11
16            ;
17            TITLE 'THIS SHOWS WHAT HAPPENS WHEN YOU OMIT A QUOTE';


ERROR 107: CHARACTER LITERAL HAS MORE THAN 200 CHARACTERS.

ERROR: NO INFILE OR CARDS STATEMENT USED.
NOTE: SAS STOPPED PROCESSING THIS STEP BECAUSE OF ERRORS.
NOTE: SAS SET OPTION OBS=0 AND WILL CONTINUE TO CHECK STATEMENTS.
      THIS MAY CAUSE NOTE: NO OBSERVATIONS IN DATA SET.
NOTE: DATA SET WORK.A HAS 0 OBSERVATIONS AND 3 VARIABLES. 828 OBS/TRK.
NOTE: THE DATA STATEMENT USED 0.04 SECONDS AND 116K.

18         PROC PRINT;
19         RUN;
NOTE: THE PROCEDURE PRINT USED 0.07 SECONDS AND 216K.
```

Error messages result due to the missing quote after the word NO.

Suppose you omit the ending quote in a character string when there are fewer than 200 characters left in your program. When the statements below are executed, data set NEW is created but never printed. SAS reads the statements beginning with the TITLE statement but never sees the PROC PRINT statement because it is still searching for the end of the character string. You may not get any error message indicating a problem. If you submit this job from display manager, you will not be aware of a problem until you submit more statements.

```
DATA NEW;
   INPUT NAME $ AGE;
   CARDS;
ALICE 12
BARBARA 13
BRIAN 15
CARLA 14
;
TITLE 'NEW PEOPLE;  ◄── note missing quote
PROC PRINT; RUN;
```

In the following example, a quote is left off a literal value in a step that contains many. SAS pairs up the quotes but gets out of sync. Although similar messages are printed, none of them point to where the error actually occurs.

```
DATA CARS;
   INPUT TYPE $;
   IF TYPE='A' THEN MAKE='CHEVY';
   IF TYPE='B' THEN MAKE='OLDS;  ◄── note missing quote
   IF TYPE='C' THEN MAKE='FORD';
   CARDS;
A
B
C
;
```

Several error messages result from the omitted quote, as shown in **Output 8.12**.

Output 8.12
Multiple Error Messages
Caused by Omitting a
Quote

```
10        DATA CARS;
11           INPUT TYPE $;
12           IF TYPE='A' THEN MAKE='CHEVY';
13           IF TYPE='B' THEN MAKE='OLDS;
14           IF TYPE='C' THEN MAKE='FORD';
                          -                    --------------------------------
-----------
                          301                  107
15           CARDS;
16        A
17        B
18        C
19        ;
          -
          309

                                              (continued on next page)
```

```
(continued from previous page)

ERROR 107: CHARACTER LITERAL HAS MORE THAN 200 CHARACTERS.

ERROR 301: INVALID SYNTAX, OR MISSING INFIX OPERATOR, ';', ',', OR ')'.

ERROR 309: THE EXPRESSION IS INCOMPLETE.

NOTE: CHARACTER VALUES HAVE BEEN CONVERTED TO NUMERIC
      VALUES AT THE PLACES GIVEN BY: (LINE):(COLUMN).

      13:26

NOTE: NUMERIC VALUES HAVE BEEN CONVERTED TO CHARACTER
      VALUES AT THE PLACES GIVEN BY: (LINE):(COLUMN).

      13:25

ERROR: NO INFILE OR CARDS STATEMENT USED.
NOTE: SAS STOPPED PROCESSING THIS STEP BECAUSE OF ERRORS.
NOTE: SAS SET OPTION OBS=0 AND WILL CONTINUE TO CHECK STATEMENTS.
      THIS MAY CAUSE NOTE: NO OBSERVATIONS IN DATA SET.

NOTE: DATA SET WORK.CARS HAS 0 OBSERVATIONS AND 2 VARIABLES. 1121 OBS/TRK.
NOTE: THE DATA STATEMENT USED 0.04 SECONDS AND 116K.
```

When you refer to the value of a character variable, enclose the value in quotes. Character values without quotes may look like variable names. For example, suppose you specify the following statements:

```
DATA B;
   INPUT X $;
   IF X=A THEN OUTPUT;
   CARDS;
A
B
;
```

When SAS sees X=A, it thinks A is a variable and compares the value of X to the value of A. Since there is no value for A, SAS prints the message shown in **Output 8.13.**

Output 8.13
Omitting a Quote with a Character Value

```
10          DATA B;
11             INPUT X $;
12             IF X=A THEN OUTPUT;
13             CARDS;

NOTE: THE VARIABLE A IS UNINITIALIZED.
NOTE: DATA SET WORK.B HAS 0 OBSERVATIONS AND 2 VARIABLES. 953 OBS/TRK.
NOTE: THE DATA STATEMENT USED 0.05 SECONDS AND 132K.

16          ;
```

Errors in Logic

Even though the statements in your SAS job may be syntactically correct, your program may not execute properly because of logic errors. When you look for errors, remember that SAS normally executes statements in a DATA step one by one. Follow your statements as the supervisor does and be sure they will execute the way you want.

Deleting before FIRST. and LAST. Variables

Logic errors occur when you delete observations in a DATA step before you refer to FIRST. or LAST. variables. Consider data set CLASS, sorted by SEX, shown in **Output 8.14**.

Output 8.14
Data Set Class

```
                            DATA SET CLASS

        OBS     NAME      SEX    AGE    HEIGHT    WEIGHT

          1     ALICE      F      13     56.5      84.0
          2     BARBARA    F      13     65.3      98.0
          3     CAROL      F      14     62.8     102.5
          4     JANE       F      12     59.8      84.5
          5     JANET      F      15     62.5     112.5
          6     JOYCE      F      14     11.0      51.3
          7     JUDY       F      14     64.3      90.0
          8     LOUISE     F      12     56.3      77.0
          9     MARY       F      15     66.5     112.0
         10     ALFRED     M      14     69.0     112.5
         11     HENRY      M      14     63.5     102.5
         12     JAMES      M      12     57.3      83.0
         13     JEFFREY    M      13     62.5      84.0
         14     JOHN       M      12     59.0      99.5
         15     PHILIP     M      16     72.0     150.0
         16     ROBERT     M      12     64.8     128.0
         17     RONALD     M      15     67.0     133.0
         18     THOMAS     M      11     57.5      85.0
         19     WILLIAM    M      15     66.5     112.0
```

You want to count the students of each sex that are less than thirteen years old, so you enter the following statements:

```
DATA NEW;
    SET CLASS;
    BY SEX;
    IF AGE<13;
    N+1;
    IF LAST.SEX THEN DO;
        OUTPUT;
        N=0;
        END;
    KEEP SEX N;
```

The subsetting IF statement deletes observations where AGE is 13 or greater. In the CLASS data set, both the last female (MARY) and the last male (WILLIAM) are deleted, and no further statements are executed for these observations. None of the remaining observations are the last in a BY group, so no observations are output.

These statements give you the results shown in **Output 8.15:**

```
DATA NEW;
   SET CLASS;
   BY SEX;
   IF AGE<13 THEN N+1;
   IF LAST.SEX THEN DO;
      OUTPUT;
      N=0;
      END;
   KEEP SEX N;
PROC PRINT;
   TITLE 'DATA SET NEW';
RUN;
```

Output 8.15
Reordering Statements to
Produce Correct Results

```
                    DATA SET NEW

               OBS    SEX    N

                1      F     2
                2      M     4
```

Compound Expressions in IF-THEN Statements

Be careful when you use compound expressions in an IF-THEN statement. Suppose you want to create a data set that contains only observations with X values of 1 or 2. You code

```
IF X¬=1 OR X¬=2 THEN DELETE;
```

All the observations are deleted. The statement above is equivalent to the statement:

```
IF NOT(X=1 AND X=2) THEN DELETE;
```

Since X cannot be both 1 and 2, the expression is always true. If you code

```
IF X¬=1 AND X¬=2 THEN DELETE;
```

you get the desired result.

Calculated Values

Calculated values involving fractions can create problems in your programs. When SAS performs numeric variable calculations, it uses the floating point instructions provided by the hardware. The machine stores floating point numbers only to a fixed precision. Thus, fractional values that cannot be represented exactly in binary or hexadecimal are not stored exactly. Because SAS is used for many different types of calculations, there is no best way to round fractions for all uses. If fractional values are critical to the accuracy of your analysis, use the INT or ROUND functions to tell SAS the precision you need.

The example below illustrates a situation in which the logic in the program is valid, but the results are not necessarily what you intended because of the way values are calculated and stored using SAS:

```
DATA A;
   INPUT X Y;
   Z=X/Y*3;
   IF Z=1 THEN OUTPUT;
   CARDS;
1 3
;
```

If you were to perform the calculation without using a computer, you would obtain the value of Z using fractional arithmetic. Thus, by substituting the data values 1 and 3 into the SAS statement Z=X/Y*3, the result would be Z=1/3*3=1. Since the condition posed in the IF-THEN statement is true (that is, Z=1), the observation is output.

When SAS reads the data, it divides 1 by 3 and the result is the fraction 1/3 expressed as the decimal value .33333 . . . . When this value is multiplied by 3, the result (.99999 . . .) is assigned to Z. Because Z is not equal to 1 (although it is very close), no observation is output.

Errors in Input

When SAS encounters an invalid character in a numeric field, this message is printed in the SAS log:

```
NOTE: INVALID DATA FOR variable IN LINE line column.
```

giving the data line and column location of the invalid field. SAS does not stop processing the step; the special variable _ERROR_ is set to 1, and the invalid variable to missing.

Other errors that occur in input have to do with how SAS executes the INPUT statement.

Past the End of a Line
If your data lines do not contain all the values SAS expects, or if the INPUT statement causes SAS to read past the end of a line to find a value for a variable, the data set it creates may be rather unusual. The following statements produce the log and data set shown in **Output 8.16:**

```
DATA LINE;
   INPUT X Y Z;
   CARDS;
1 2 3
4 5
7 8 9
;
PROC PRINT;
   TITLE 'DATA SET LINE';
RUN;
```

Output 8.16
Reading Past the End of a
Line and the Resulting
Data Set

```
10          DATA LINE;
11            INPUT X Y Z;
12          CARDS;
NOTE: SAS WENT TO A NEW LINE WHEN INPUT STATEMENT
      REACHED PAST THE END OF A LINE.
NOTE: DATA SET WORK.LINE HAS 2 OBSERVATIONS AND 3 VARIABLES. 680 OBS/TRK.
NOTE: THE DATA STATEMENT USED 0.04 SECONDS AND 132K.

16          PROC PRINT;
17            TITLE 'DATA SET LINE';
18          RUN;
NOTE: THE PROCEDURE PRINT USED 0.08 SECONDS AND 216K
      AND PRINTED PAGE 1.
```

```
                    DATA SET LINE

              OBS    X    Y    Z

               1     1    2    3
               2     4    5    7
```

In this example, SAS uses list input to read the data lines. The first data line is read correctly because there are values for each of the variables in the INPUT statement. For the second line read, SAS goes past the end of the line and on to the next before it finds a nonblank field; it assigns the value 7 to Z.

MISSOVER option

You can prevent SAS from going past the end of a line to read values by using the MISSOVER option in the INFILE statement. If you repeat the example above but specify the MISSOVER option in the INFILE statement (as shown below), the log and data set shown in **Output 8.17** are produced.

```
DATA LINE;
   INFILE CARDS MISSOVER;
   INPUT X Y Z;
   CARDS;
1 2 3
4 5
7 8 9
;
PROC PRINT;
   TITLE 'DATA SET LINE USING MISSOVER OPTION';
RUN;
```

```
9            DATA LINE;
10               INFILE CARDS MISSOVER;
11               INPUT X Y Z;
12               CARDS;
NOTE: DATA SET WORK.LINE HAS 3 OBSERVATIONS AND 3 VARIABLES. 680 OBS/TRK.
NOTE: THE DATA STATEMENT USED 0.04 SECONDS AND 132K.

16           :
17               PROC PRINT;
18               TITLE 'DATA SET LINE USING MISSOVER OPTION';
19               RUN;
NOTE: THE PROCEDURE PRINT USED 0.08 SECONDS AND 216K
            AND PRINTED PAGE 1.
```

```
                     DATA SET LINE USING MISSOVER OPTION

                          OBS    X    Y    Z

                           1     1    2    3
                           2     4    5    .
                           3     7    8    9
```

The MISSOVER option tells SAS to assign missing values to those variables for which no values appear on the current input line.

STOPOVER option

If you want to stop processing when you have variables for which no values appear on the current input line, specify the STOPOVER option in the INFILE statement. Use the example above but specify STOPOVER instead of MISSOVER:

```
DATA LINE;
    INFILE CARDS STOPOVER;
    INPUT X Y Z;
    CARDS;
1 2 3
4 5
7 8 9
;
PROC PRINT;
    TITLE 'DATA SET LINE USING STOPOVER OPTION';
RUN;
```

SAS stops building the data set when it runs out of values on the current line, as shown in **Output 8.18**.

Output 8.18
DATA Step Using
STOPOVER Option

```
9              DATA LINE;
10               INFILE CARDS STOPOVER;
11               INPUT X Y Z;
12             CARDS;

ERROR: INPUT STATEMENT EXCEEDED RECORD LENGTH.
       INFILE 'CARDS' OPTION STOPOVER SPECIFIED.

RULE:     ----+----1----+----2----+----3----+----4----+----5----+----6----+----7

14        4 5
X=4 Y=5 Z=. _ERROR_=1 _N_=2
NOTE: SAS SET OPTION OBS=0 AND WILL CONTINUE TO CHECK STATEMENTS.
      THIS MAY CAUSE NOTE: NO OBSERVATIONS IN DATA SET.
NOTE: DATA SET WORK.LINE HAS 1 OBSERVATIONS AND 3 VARIABLES. 680 OBS/TRK.
NOTE: THE DATA STATEMENT USED 0.04 SECONDS AND 132K.

16             ;
17             PROC PRINT;
18               TITLE 'DATA SET LINE USING STOPOVER OPTION';
19             RUN;
NOTE: THE PROCEDURE PRINT USED 0.07 SECONDS AND 216K.
```

Here is another example in which SAS reads past the end of a line.

```
DATA LINE2;
    INPUT (X1-X10) (9.);
    CARDS;
11111111122222222233333333344444444455555555556666666667777777778888888889999999990000000
11111111122222222233333333344444444455555555556666666667777777778888888889999999990000000
    ;
PROC PRINT;
    TITLE 'DATA SET LINE2';
RUN;
```

The log and the resulting data set are shown in **Output 8.19.**

Output 8.19
Another Example of
Reading Past the End of a
Line and the Resulting
Data Set

```
10             DATA LINE2;
11               INPUT (X1-X10) (9.);
12             CARDS;

NOTE: SAS WENT TO A NEW LINE WHEN INPUT STATEMENT
      REACHED PAST THE END OF A LINE.
NOTE: DATA SET WORK.LINE2 HAS 1 OBSERVATIONS AND 10 VARIABLES. 226 OBS/TRK.
NOTE: THE DATA STATEMENT USED 0.05 SECONDS AND 136K.

15             ;
16             PROC PRINT;
17               TITLE 'DATA SET LINE2';
18             RUN;
NOTE: THE PROCEDURE PRINT USED 0.08 SECONDS AND 216K
      AND PRINTED PAGE 1.
```

		DATA SET LINE2			
OBS	X1	X2	X3	X4	X5
1	111111112	222222233	333333444	444445555	555566666
OBS	X6	X7	X8	X9	X10
1	666777777	778888888	899999999	111111112	222222233

The example above uses formatted input to read the data lines, which contain ten 8-character fields. The format 9. instead of 8. is incorrectly coded. The INPUT statement must go past the end of the line to read ten variables each of length 9. After SAS reads the variable X8, the pointer is ready to begin reading X9 at column 73. SAS knows that reading X9 will take the pointer past the end of the line. It goes to the beginning of the next line to read a value for X9; it does not try to read columns 73-80 of one line and column 1 of the next.

Lost Card Message

When SAS reads data lines and unexpectedly comes to the end of the data, it prints a lost card message on the log. Here are some examples:

```
DATA A;
   INPUT X Y #2 Z A;
   CARDS;
1 2
3 4
5 6
;
```

The log is shown in **Output 8.20**.

Output 8.20

Lost Card Message When Data Lines Exhausted

```
10          DATA A;
11             INPUT X Y #2 Z A;
12             CARDS;

NOTE: LOST CARD.

RULE:     ----+----1----+----2----+----3----+----4----+----5----+----6----+----7

14          3 4
15          5 6
X=5 Y=6 Z=. A=. _ERROR_=1 _N_=2
NOTE: DATA SET WORK.A HAS 1 OBSERVATIONS AND 4 VARIABLES. 529 OBS/TRK.
NOTE: THE DATA STATEMENT USED 0.04 SECONDS AND 132K.
```

On the second execution of the step, SAS finds only one line of data; the INPUT statement indicates that there should be two. Then SAS prints the lost card message.

In the next example, when SAS reads the second line of data, it goes past the end of a line to find the value of Z. Since there are no more data lines, SAS prints the lost card message shown in **Output 8.21**.

```
DATA B;
   INPUT X Y Z;
   CARDS;
1 2 3
4 5
;
```

Output 8.21
Lost Card Message at the
End of a Data Line

```
10              DATA B;
11                  INPUT X Y Z;
12              CARDS;

NOTE: LOST CARD.

RULE:       ----+----1----+----2----+----3----+----4----+----5----+----6----+----7

14       4 5
X=4 Y=5 Z=. _ERROR_=1 _N_=2
NOTE: SAS WENT TO A NEW LINE WHEN INPUT STATEMENT
      REACHED PAST THE END OF A LINE.
NOTE: DATA SET WORK.B HAS 1 OBSERVATIONS AND 3 VARIABLES. 680 OBS/TRK.
NOTE: THE DATA STATEMENT USED 0.04 SECONDS AND 132K.
```

LOSTCARD Statement

The examples above show some simple situations that result in a lost card message. In each case, SAS does not know there is a lost data line until it reaches the end of the data. The example below uses a LOSTCARD statement to handle missing data lines for each observation:

```
DATA QUESTN;
    INPUT ID 1-4 C1 6 @11 (Q1-Q3) (1.)
       #2 ID2 1-4 C2 6 @11 (Q4-Q6) (1.);
    IF ID NE ID2 OR C1 NE 1 OR C2 NE 2 THEN LOSTCARD;
    CARDS;
0001 1    354
0001 2    223
0002 1    414
0003 1    534
0003 2    122
0004 1    422
0004 2    232
0005 1    454
0005 2    223
;
```

Only one line of data is available for the observation with ID=0002.

When SAS executes the LOSTCARD statement, it stops building the current observation. The INPUT statement returns to the start of the DATA step, ignores the first line in the group it was reading, and reads a new group of lines beginning with the second line previously read. These lines are then used for the current observation. Thus, when the input buffer contains these lines:

```
0002 1    414
0003 1    534
```

the LOSTCARD statement is executed, and SAS gets these lines:

```
0003 1
0003 2
```

No observation is output for ID=0002.

Checking for Data Errors

The LOSTCARD statement in the example above gives you a way to check for possible missing data lines or lines out of order. These SAS statements also provide error-checking tools:

□ STOP
□ ABORT

The statements are described in the *SAS User's Guide: Basics, Version 5 Edition*.

PROC FORMAT   In addition to the tools SAS provides especially for error checking, you can use SAS programming statements to validate your data. The example below uses PROC FORMAT as a data editor. In this example, the data to be edited have these variables and valid values:

Variable	Valid Values
AGE	1-100
SEX	1,2
NAME	BROWN, SMITH, WHITE, GREEN

If any of these variables contains invalid data, you want to set its value to missing and print an error message. PROC FORMAT sets valid values to X. The DATA step then checks for values not equal to X, counts them, sets them to missing, and prints the resulting data set. The following SAS code can be used to validate your data:

```
PROC FORMAT;
   VALUE AGEFMT 1-100='X';
   VALUE SEXFMT 1='X' 2='X';
   VALUE $NAMEFMT 'SMITH'='X' 'GREEN'='X' 'WHITE'='X' 'BROWN'='X';
DATA TEST;
   LENGTH NAME $ 15;
   INFILE CARDS EOF=ENDFILE;
   INPUT NAME $ SEX AGE;
   CARD+1;                  *COUNT INPUT RECORDS;
   IF PUT(NAME,$NAMEFMT.)¬='X' THEN DO;
      PUT 'ERROR IN NAME ON CARD ' CARD ' NAME IS: ' NAME;
      NAME=' ';
      ERRORN+1;
      END;
   IF PUT(AGE,AGEFMT.)¬='X' THEN DO;
      PUT 'ERROR IN AGE ON CARD ' CARD ' AGE IS: ' AGE;
      AGE=.;
      ERRORA+1;
      END;
```

```
              IF PUT(SEX,SEXFMT.)¬='X' THEN DO;
                 PUT 'ERROR IN SEX ON CARD ' CARD ' SEX IS: ' SEX;
                 SEX=.;
                 ERRORS+1;
                 END;
              RETURN;
              ENDFILE: PUT  'NUMBER OF CARDS READ WAS:  ' CARD
                 / 'NAME ERRORS FOUND: ' ERRORN
                 / 'AGE ERRORS FOUND:  ' ERRORA
                 / 'SEX ERRORS FOUND:  ' ERRORS;
              DROP CARD ERRORN ERRORA ERRORS;
              STOP;
              CARDS;
          SMITH 1 56
          GREEN 2 78
          YELLOW 3 56
          WHITE 3 112
          SMITH 2 34
          BROWN 1 56
          BROWN 1 666
          GREEN 1 0
          ;
          PROC PRINT;
              TITLE 'DATA AFTER EDIT';
          RUN;
```

The log shown in **Output 8.22** lists the errors found in the variable values.

Output 8.22
Using PROC FORMAT to
Find Invalid Data Values

```
10 PROC FORMAT;
11
NOTE: FORMAT AGEFMT HAS BEEN OUTPUT.
  11    VALUE AGEFMT 1-100='X';
  12
NOTE: FORMAT SEXFMT HAS BEEN OUTPUT.
  12    VALUE SEXFMT 1='X' 2='X';
  13
NOTE: FORMAT $NAMEFMT HAS BEEN OUTPUT.
  13    VALUE $NAMEFMT 'SMITH'='X' 'GREEN'='X' 'WHITE'='X' 'BROWN'='X';

14 DATA TEST;
15    LENGTH NAME $ 15;
16    INFILE CARDS EOF=ENDFILE;
17    INPUT NAME $ SEX AGE;
18    CARD+1;                    *COUNT INPUT RECORDS;
19    IF PUT(NAME,$NAMEFMT.)¬='X' THEN DO;
20       PUT 'ERROR IN NAME ON CARD ' CARD ' NAME IS: ' NAME;
21       NAME=' ';
22       ERRORN+1;
23       END;
24    IF PUT(AGE,AGEFMT.)¬='X' THEN DO;
25       PUT 'ERROR IN AGE ON CARD ' CARD ' AGE IS: ' AGE;
26       AGE=.;
27       ERRORA+1;
28       END;
29    IF PUT(SEX,SEXFMT.)¬='X' THEN DO;
30       PUT 'ERROR IN SEX ON CARD ' CARD ' SEX IS: ' SEX;
31       SEX=.;
32       ERRORS+1;
33       END;
34    RETURN;
35    ENDFILE: PUT 'NUMBER OF CARDS READ WAS:  ' CARD
36       / 'NAME ERRORS FOUND: ' ERRORN
37       / 'AGE ERRORS FOUND: ' ERRORA
38       / 'SEX ERRORS FOUND: ' ERRORS;
```

```
39    DROP CARD ERRORN ERRORA ERRORS;
40    STOP;
41    CARDS;
ERROR IN NAME ON CARD 3  NAME IS: YELLOW
ERROR IN SEX ON CARD 3   SEX IS: 3
ERROR IN AGE ON CARD 4   AGE IS: 112
ERROR IN SEX ON CARD 4   SEX IS: 3
ERROR IN AGE ON CARD 7   AGE IS: 666
ERROR IN AGE ON CARD 8   AGE IS: 0
NUMBER OF CARDS READ WAS:  8
NAME ERRORS FOUND: 1
AGE ERRORS FOUND: 3
SEX ERRORS FOUND: 2
NOTE: DATA SET WORKS1.TEST HAS 8 OBSERVATIONS AND 3 VARIABLES. 531 OBS/TRK.

50  ;
51 PROC PRINT;
52    TITLE 'DATA SET AFTER EDIT';
53 RUN;
```

After editing, you get the data set shown in **Output 8.23.**

Output 8.23
Data Set with Invalid Data
Values Removed

```
                      DATA AFTER EDIT

         OBS    NAME    SEX    AGE

          1    SMITH     1     56
          2    GREEN     2     78
          3              .     56
          4    WHITE     .      .
          5    SMITH     2     34
          6    BROWN     1     56
          7    BROWN     1      .
          8    GREEN     1      .
```

ABORT Statement

Suppose you want to abort a batch or noninteractive program if you encounter data errors but still print the error messages from the log before ending the job. The following statements show how to do it:

```
DATA ONE ERROR;
    SET TEST;
    IF NAME=' ' OR SEX=. OR AGE=. THEN OUTPUT ERROR;
    ELSE OUTPUT ONE;
DATA _NULL_;
    SET ERROR END=LAST;
    FILE PRINT;
    PUT _ALL_;
    IF LAST THEN DO;
        PUT 'ERRORS ON DATA--TERMINATE RUN';
        ABORT;
        END;
RUN;
additional PROC and DATA steps
```

If data set ERROR contains any observations, SAS will not execute any further steps, as shown in **Output 8.24.**

Output 8.24

Using an ABORT
Statement to Terminate
the Program

```
NAME=   SEX=. AGE=56 LAST=0 _ERROR_=0 _N_=1
NAME=WHITE SEX=. AGE=. LAST=0 _ERROR_=0 _N_=2
NAME=BROWN SEX=1 AGE=. LAST=0 _ERROR_=0 _N_=3
NAME=GREEN SEX=1 AGE=. LAST=1 _ERROR_=0 _N_=4
ERRORS ON DATA--TERMINATE RUN
```

Notes

1. **AOS/VS, PRIMOS, VMS:** When you make a syntax error in your program, the error is flagged in the SAS log with overprinted lines using carriage control. If you list the SAS log at your terminal, the overprinting obscures the line of your program that is in error. To avoid this, always use the system option NOOVP to prevent SAS from overprinting characters.

2. **AOS/VS, PRIMOS, VMS:** The S= option is not recognized. If you specify the S= option, SAS prints a note indicating that the option is ignored.

9 Working with External Files

Introduction

In preceding chapters, you have seen how to work with SAS data sets—building data sets, subsetting and combining data sets, and storing and maintaining them. The SAS System also has many features for working with *external files* on disk, tape, and, under some operating systems, cards. This chapter illustrates a number of techniques for processing external files. You may be able to use the SAS System to perform many functions that you have been performing with utility programs.

External files are not SAS files. Before you can read an external file in a SAS program, you must identify it in an INFILE statement that specifies a fileref and describes its characteristics to the SAS System. Likewise, to write to an external file in a SAS program, you must define the file in a FILE statement that specifies a fileref.[1]

Most of the DATA steps in this chapter use the reserved name, _NULL_. Using DATA _NULL_ saves CPU time and space when you do not need to create a SAS data set. Another technique common to some of the examples is the use of the INPUT statement without operands and the use of _INFILE_ in the PUT statement. An INPUT statement that does not specify any variable names reads the entire record without creating any variables. The PUT _INFILE_ statement writes the entire record that was read by the INPUT statement.

Copying Records from a Disk File

Suppose that you want to copy the records from one disk file to another. Use these statements:

```
DATA _NULL_;
   INFILE STUDY;
   INPUT;
   FILE DISK;
   PUT _INFILE_;
RUN;
```

The INPUT statement does not name any variables but still reads in the entire record so that it can be written, exactly as it is, by the PUT _INFILE_ statement.[2]

Making a Subset of a File

There may be occasions when you need to process only part of an external file. In this example, the SAS System reads each record from the file and copies the record to the output file if the value in columns 21 and 22 is NC:

```
DATA _NULL_;
   INFILE IN;
   FILE OUT;
   INPUT STATE $ 21-22;
   IF STATE='NC' THEN PUT _INFILE_;
RUN;
```

The records with NC in columns 21-22 are written to the file referenced with the fileref OUT.

Writing a Literal in Every Record

In this example, as part of a statewide study of universities, you are collecting some data relating to the university where you work. The data are to be written to a disk file, coded with an identifying number unique to your university, and then sent to the person conducting the study.

Your data are currently on 70-byte records in a disk file with a fileref of STUDY1. These statements write your university's code number, 242424, in columns 1 through 6 in each output record, and then copy each input record, starting in column 11. Columns 7 through 10 of each output record are blank.

```
DATA _NULL_;
   INFILE STUDY1;
   INPUT;
   FILE OUT;
   PUT '242424' @11 _INFILE_;
RUN;
```

Adding Sequence Numbers While Copying Records

If you want to write records to a file and at the same time add sequence numbers in the last eight columns, use these statements:

```
DATA _NULL_;
   INFILE DISKIN;
   INPUT;
   FILE DISKOUT;
   N=_N_*100;
   PUT _INFILE_ a73 N Z8.;
RUN;
```

The variable N, which is the automatic variable _N_ multiplied by 100, becomes the sequence number that appears on the records produced. The automatic variable _N_ is the number of times the DATA step is executed. In this case, _N_ is automatically incremented each time a new record is read. The sequence number is written on the record beginning in column 73, using the Z. format that prints leading zeros. The sequence numbers replace any information contained in columns 73-80 of the original data records.

Updating the Same Field on Records in a File

Suppose you want to change a particular field in some of the records in a file. The following example copies the entire input record and then, depending on the value of the variable LOC in columns 10 through 12, updates the field:

```
DATA _NULL_;
   INFILE IN;
   FILE OUT;
   INPUT a10 LOC 3.;
   IF LOC=121 THEN DO;
      LOC=212;
      PUT _INFILE_ a10 LOC 3.;
      END;
   ELSE PUT _INFILE_;
RUN;
```

The SAS System copies the _INFILE_ line to the new file exactly as it is in the old file; then it writes the new value of LOC over the old value.

Copying Part of a Record

You can use the LENGTH= option and the START= option in the INFILE statement to copy part of a record. The LENGTH= option specifies a variable (L in this example) that SAS sets automatically to the length of each record read with the INPUT statement. The assignment statement redefines the length of the record so that the PUT _INFILE_ statement accesses all but the last twenty columns of the record. Thus, the output record is 20 bytes shorter.

```
DATA _NULL_;
   INFILE IN LENGTH=L;
   INPUT;
   L=L-20;
   FILE OUT;
   PUT _INFILE_;
RUN;
```

To begin reading the input record from a position other than column 1, use the START= option. The following job writes each record of the file IN (beginning with column 20) to the output file:

```
DATA _NULL_;
   INFILE IN START=S;
   INPUT;
   S=20;
   FILE OUT;
   PUT _INFILE_;
RUN;
```

Use the LENGTH= and START= options together when you want to copy from the middle of each INFILE record:

```
DATA _NULL_;
   INFILE INDATA START=S LENGTH=L;
   INPUT;
   S=11;
   L=60;
   FILE OUTDATA;
   PUT _INFILE_;
RUN;
```

This example copies only columns 11-60 of the input file to the output file. The START= variable, S, specifies the starting position for the input file and is given a value of 11. The LENGTH= variable, L, specifies the length of the record and is given a value of 60.

Listing a Subset of Records from a Tape

It is easy to print any number of records you want from a tape[3] with the LIST statement and the OBS= and FIRSTOBS= options. The LIST statement causes the SAS System to list the contents of the current INFILE record. The advantage of writing the record with the LIST statement instead of a PUT statement is that any unprintable characters included in the data will automatically print in hex.

In the statements below, the OBS= option specifies the number of the last input line that you want listed. The first 100 records of the tape are listed in the SAS log.

```
DATA _NULL_;
   INFILE TAP1 OBS=100;
   INPUT;
   LIST;
RUN;
```

You can also select the first record that you want from the file with the FIRSTOBS= option in the INFILE statement. Thus, you can choose a subset of records from anywhere in the file by using the FIRSTOBS= and OBS= options together.

Note: OBS= always counts from the first observation in the data set, not from the FIRSTOBS= value. That is, if OBS= is less than FIRSTOBS=, zero observations will be processed.

Refer to the appropriate *SAS Companion* for your operating system for specifics about accessing tape files.

Printing a File with Control Characters

Operating systems: CMS, OS, VM/PC, and VSE

If you want to print a file that already contains carriage control characters in the first column of every line, for example when you are reading in output that has been routed to a file with PROC PRINTTO, use the NOPRINT option in the FILE statement. Without the NOPRINT option, new carriage control characters are used, and the original carriage control characters are printed in your output.

```
DATA _NULL_;
   INFILE IN;
   FILE PRINT NOPRINT;
   INPUT;
   PUT _INFILE_;
RUN;
```

The FILE statement specifies the fileref for the SAS procedure output file, PRINT.

Copying to a File with Different Characteristics

You can use the following method to write records to an output file with a different logical record length than the input file. The following job reads in 80-byte records, pairs them, and writes them to a file already defined with a logical record length of 160:

```
DATA _NULL_;
   INFILE IN;
   FILE OUT;
   INPUT LINE1 $CHAR80.;
   INPUT LINE2 $CHAR80.;
   PUT @1 LINE1 $CHAR80. @81 LINE2 $CHAR80.;
RUN;
```

You can easily modify this example to remove extra spaces by using the $80. format instead of $CHAR80. Or, you can concatenate the two input lines into a variable and use the TRIM function before writing the output record.

A more efficient version of this program can be run under CMS, OS, VM/PC, and VSE. The following program is more efficient because it does not create any variables:

```
*CMS, OS, VM/PC, AND VSE;
DATA _NULL_;
   INFILE IN;
   FILE OUT;
   INPUT;
   PUT _INFILE_ @;
   INPUT;
   PUT @81 _INFILE_;
RUN;
```

Methods for Reading Variable-Length Records

The next three sections discuss different methods for reading a file with variable-length records.

With the $VARYING. Informat

Suppose you have directed the SAS log to a disk file, and you need to read information from it. In the following example, the INFILE statement specifies the fileref LOGFILE, a data set containing the SAS log saved from a previous execution. The example assumes that carriage control characters are in column 1. The program creates and prints a SAS data set containing the data set names, number of observations, and the variables associated with each data set created during the prior SAS execution.

Here are a few of the records from LOGFILE (containing the SAS log output) used as input to the example below.

```
NOTE: 4 LINES WERE WRITTEN TO FILE PRINT.
NOTE: THE DATA STATEMENT PRINTED PAGE 1.

NOTE: DATA SET WORK.MASTER HAS 3 OBSERVATIONS AND 4 VARIABLES. 529 OBS/TRK.

NOTE: 4 CYLINDERS DYNAMICALLY ALLOCATED ON RIO FOR EACH OF 3 SORT WORK DATA SETS.

NOTE: DATA SET WORK.TRANSACT HAS 4 OBSERVATIONS AND 3 VARIABLES. 680 OBS/TRK.

NOTE: THE PROCEDURE PRINT PRINTED PAGE 2.
```

In this example the LENGTH= option specifies a variable L that is set automatically to the length of each record. The INPUT statement reads each record into the variable LINE with the $VARYING. informat. The $VARYING. informat specifies the maximum length of the record, and variable L specifies the actual length of each record.

```
DATA READLOG(KEEP=OBS VARS DSNAME LIBREF);
    INFILE LOGFILE LENGTH=L;
    INPUT @1 LINE $VARYING137. L;
    IF SUBSTR(LINE,2,5)='NOTE:' AND
        INDEX(LINE,'OBSERVATIONS') THEN DO;
        LINE=SUBSTR(LINE,INDEX(LINE,'DATA SET'));
        LIBREF=SCAN(LINE,3);
        DSNAME=SCAN(LINE,4);
        OBS=SCAN(LINE,6);
        VARS=SCAN(LINE,9);
        OUTPUT;
        END;
```

With Repeating Fields

The following example illustrates a method of reading a file with varying length records without using the $VARYING. informat. The program creates one observation for each time an automatic banking machine is accessed. The program expects the input records to be in the following format:

```
AA 08:01 08:08 08:20 08:31 08:36 08:47 08:50 08:56 09:04
BB 12:11 12:45 12:58
CC 08:22 08:30 08:46 08:52 08:59
DD 08:15 08:37
```

The first field, TELLER, is an identification field. The rest of the record contains an unknown number of time values. The number of these values to be read is determined by the length of the record. After each time value is read, a TELLER and TIME pair is output.

```
DATA HISTORY;
   INFILE TELLDATA LENGTH=L;
   FORMAT TIME TIME5.;
   INPUT @1 TELLER $2. @;   *** INPUT 24HR TELLER ID;
   DO I=1 TO (L-2)/6;   *** INPUT EACH ACCESS AND OUTPUT;
      INPUT TIME : TIME5. @;
      OUTPUT;
      END;
   DROP I;
RUN;
```

With the ARRAY Statement

The next example illustrates another method of reading variable-length records. This method uses the ARRAY statement and does not depend on the length of the record. The program reads records from a personnel employee file that keeps track of whether the employee is married and how many offspring each employee has. The employees are identified by an identification number. Here are a few example input records:

```
754749292 1 0 JOHN JAMES SMITH
MARY JANE DOE
213449999 1 3 RICHARD RAYMOND RICHFIELD
JUDITH MCDERMIT
RICHARD RAYMOND
MARY BETH
ALICE MAY
549210184 0 2 CHRISTINE LYNN JOHNSON
NICK JAY
RUTH ANNE
```

This example program expects the input record to contain the employee's identification number, a value of 1 or 0 that indicates whether or not the employee is married, the number of offspring, and the employee's name. If the value following the identification number is 1, the program expects to read a second record containing the spouse's name. The spouse's first, middle, and last names are read into three variables, SPFIRST, SPMID, and SPLAST. If the value is 0, the employee does not have a spouse. If the value of OFFNUM is not 0, the program expects to read records containing the names of the employee's offspring. Here is the DATA step that reads the input records:

```
DATA EMPLOYEE (KEEP=IDNUM EMP1-EMP3 SPFIRST SPMID SPLAST
              FIRST1-FIRST10 MIDDL1-MIDDL10);
   ARRAY OFFSPRG1{10} $ FIRST1-FIRST10;
   ARRAY OFFSPRG2{10} $ MIDDL1-MIDDL10;
   INFILE EMPLOY MISSOVER;
   INPUT @1 IDNUM 9. @11 SP 1. @12 OFFNUM 2.
         EMP1 : $12. EMP2 : $12. EMP3 : $20. @;
   IF SP THEN INPUT / SPFIRST : $12. SPMID : $12. SPLAST : $20. @;
   IF OFFNUM THEN DO I=1 TO OFFNUM;
      INPUT / OFFSPRG1{I} : $12. OFFSPRG2{I}: $12. @;
      END;
   IF SPLAST=' ' THEN SPLAST=EMP3;
RUN;
```

Inserting Records into an Existing External File

Suppose you need to transport a series of programs to another installation. You decide to concatenate the programs into one large file to reduce the number of transport operations. In the program that concatenates the source data sets, each of the original programs is delimited by the following statement:

```
./      ADD NAME=procname
```

where *procname* is the name of the data set containing a program. You want to add a header to each program. The following program searches for the delimiting statement and writes a header after each occurrence:

```
DATA _NULL_;
   INFILE IN;
   FILE OUT;
   LENGTH NAME $ 8;
   DATE=TODAY();
   FORMAT DATE DATE7.;
   INPUT @1 STRING $40.;
   PUT _INFILE_;
   IF SUBSTR(STRING,1,2)='./' THEN DO;
      NAME=SCAN(STRING,2,'=');
      PUT @2 '/****************************************/'
       / @2 '/*   NAME:  ' NAME
       / @2 '/*   AUTHOR:   JOHN SMITH'
       / @2 '/*   DATE:  ' DATE
       / @2 '/*   LANG:   SAS'
       / @2 '/*   DEVELOPMENT SYSTEM:  XXX'
       / @2 '/****************************************/';
      END;
   RUN;
```

After the concatenated file is transported to the other installation, you can use another program to separate the programs. This time the original programs will be preceded by a program header.

Notes

1. **VSE:** Special requirements exist for accessing external files. See the *SAS Companion for the VSE Operating System* for specifics.
2. **CMS, OS, VM/PC,** and **VSE:** You can create a copy of a file that has different physical attributes than the original file by specifying the new attributes in the FILE statement with the RECFM=, LRECL=, and BLKSIZE= options. See the *SAS Companion* for your operating system for more information.
3. **AOS/VS:** With labeled tape files, specify the RECFM= option in the FILE statement to let the SAS System know the output file's record format. On labeled tape files the value for RECFM= must be F (for fixed) or V (for variable). You must also specify the logical record length with the LRECL= option in the FILE statement for tape files that have RECFM=F. The LRECL= option can be used only with RECFM=F files.

   CMS and VM/PC: You must assign a fileref of TAP*n* in a FILEDEF command for external tape files. You must also specify the logical record length, block size, and record format either in the FILEDEF command or in the INFILE statement for labeled tapes.

   PRIMOS: Specify the RECFM= option in the INFILE and FILE statements to let the SAS System know the input and output file's record format. The value for RECFM= must be F (for fixed) for tape files. You must also specify the logical record length with the LRECL= option in the INFILE and FILE statements for tape files.

   VMS: For an unlabeled tape, specify the RECFM= option in the INFILE and FILE statements to let the SAS System know the input and output file's record format. The value for RECFM= must be F (for fixed) for tape files. You must also specify the logical record length with the LRECL= option in the INFILE and FILE statements for tape files.

   OS: In the control language that precedes your SAS statements, describe both the input tape file and the data set on disk where you want the records written. When filerefs are used in the INFILE and FILE statements, the SAS System looks for the matching name in the control language and copies the records from or to that file.

   VSE: The last three digits of a tape fileref must specify the programmer logical unit.

10 Processing Large Data Sets with SAS® Software

As long as your SAS job involves only a small amount of data, you do not need to worry about the computer resources involved in running the job. But since complex applications involving large amounts of data are so easy to write with SAS software, the use of computer resources sometimes becomes a real consideration.

For the SAS System to be an effective tool for processing large files, you need to exercise good judgment in selecting the applications to be written in SAS software and in choosing the best approach to write them. This chapter describes some characteristics of the SAS System to consider when the use of computer resources is important and makes some recommendations for using SAS software to process large data sets.

Characteristics of SAS Software

SAS software is easy to use, but sometimes you must expend a little effort to make your SAS programs process large data sets efficiently. Three characteristics are particularly troublesome when processing large amounts of data:

□ SAS tends to pass the data many times.
□ SAS data sets may end up larger than the original data file.
□ Your application may require frequent sorting of the data.

Multiple Passes of Data

In a simple job, SAS usually makes at least three input/output passes through the data: reading the raw data, outputting the SAS data set, and inputting the SAS data set to the procedure. If you want to use a SAS procedure to analyze a subset of the data, you usually go through a DATA step to select the observations you want.

To decrease the number of passes through your data, you can use the following techniques:

□ Build data sets containing different subsets of the data in a single DATA step.
□ Use the FIRSTOBS= and OBS= data set options to perform limited data selection in procedures.
□ Use the APPEND procedure rather than a DATA step to concatenate SAS data sets when you do not need to modify the data values in them.

Data Expansion

When you write an INPUT statement, which gives the specifications and formats for reading the raw data, you tend to code every field defined in the data, whether or not those fields are needed in the SAS data set. In addition, a simple number that occupies 1 byte in the input data is stored in 8 bytes (as a floating point number) in the SAS data set. Thus, a reasonably-sized input file can easily result in a SAS data set that needs several times as much space as the original raw data.

You can avoid the problem of data expansion if you use these techniques when building your SAS data sets:

☐ Input only the fields you need.
☐ Subset variables with KEEP and DROP statements or KEEP= and DROP= data set options.
☐ Store numbers as character variables when the numbers represent classifications.
☐ Use a LENGTH statement to specify the size of data fields in the SAS data set.

Frequent Sorting

Sorting large data sets is time-consuming—about $n(\log (n))$ comparisons must be made for each sort. In addition, if you want to process the data set by several different subgroups, you may have to sort the data several times.

Use the following techniques to reduce the number of times you sort your data:

☐ When you use a BY statement to process a data set in subsets, SAS expects the observations to be in the same order as though the SORT procedure had been used. If the observations are already in the correct order, you do not have to use a PROC SORT step.
☐ If observations with the same BY value are grouped, but the groups are not in alphabetical or numeric order, use the NOTSORTED option in the BY statement.
☐ Whenever possible, use procedures like SUMMARY, FREQ, and CHART that collect statistics on subgroups of data without requiring you to sort the data set first.
☐ If you use the UPDATE statement, your data set must be sorted by the matching variable; but if you use the EDITOR procedure, you can edit the data directly.

In addition, keep in mind that SAS does not sort a data set "in place." Instead, it makes a new copy of the data set. There must be space to store both the new and the old data sets at least momentarily.

The SAS System is easy to use, but it is also easy to abuse. When you have large amounts of data to process, you should know all the SAS features that let you process that data efficiently.

Plan Your SAS Job

If you have ever run a SAS job that required a large amount of computer resources but did not finish because of an error, then you know how important it is to plan before you run the job.

Examine your SAS statements and data for obvious mistakes and use these checklists to avoid additional problems:

Computer Resources Checklist

☐ Investigate any operating system restrictions, such as memory region, sort work space, CPU time, or disk quota, that might cause the job to fail.

☐ Store your data in the form of a SAS data set instead of reading the raw data with each analysis.

☐ Save intermediate files created in your job. If the job fails in the middle, you will not need to run it from the beginning.

☐ Make test runs with small amounts of sample data.

SAS Programming Checklist

☐ Place subsetting IF statements as close to the beginning of a DATA step as possible. Keep in mind that when an observation does not meet the subsetting condition, SAS returns to the beginning of the DATA step immediately and does not execute statements following the subsetting IF for that observation.

☐ In a series of nested IF-THEN/ELSE statements or in a SELECT group, order the conditions so that the ones most likely to be true come first. SAS skips the remaining statements in the series or group after it finds a true condition.

☐ Include code in your SAS statements to check for and reject data that could invalidate your results.

☐ If you need an expression in only one statement, write the expression. If you need it in more than one statement, assign the result of the expression to a variable and use the variable in later statements.

☐ Assign values to constants in a RETAIN statement rather than in an assignment statement.

☐ If you are working from a permanent SAS data set, you may be able to start your program with a PROC step, as in this example:

```
PROC REG DATA=IN.HUGE(KEEP=Y X1-X10);
   MODEL Y=X1-X10;
RUN;
```

It is not necessary to start every program with a DATA step.

Create Subsets

If you repeatedly use the same subset of variables from a large data file, you can reduce the amount of input and output by creating subsets of your data file to use as working files. Chapter 3, "Reshaping Your Data," describes several ways to create subsets of SAS data sets. The next example subsets variables in a PROC step.

Subset of Variables Suppose your data set contains 10,000 observations and 300 variables, and you want to do a regression on ten of the variables using a BY variable. It is much less expensive to sort only the variables you need for the analysis, rather than the whole data set:

```
PROC SORT DATA=IN.HUGE(KEEP=ID X1-X10) OUT=LITTLE;
   BY ID;
PROC REG DATA=LITTLE;
   BY ID;
   MODEL X1=X2-X10;
```

Remember to use the OUT= option in this case. Otherwise, the SORT procedure attempts to replace data set IN.HUGE with the new, smaller version!

Space Considerations Space limitations sometimes make it necessary to input a subset of variables from a very large external file. The length of the program data vector, which contains the current values for the observation being processed, must be less than 32,088 bytes. All numeric variables have a length of 8 in the program data vector; the length of character variables depends on lengths specified in a LENGTH statement or implied in an INPUT statement. Thus, a SAS data set can contain approximately 4000 variables of length 8, or more variables with shorter lengths.

Take Random Samples

In many cases, you can select a random sample of a large data set and analyze the sample. The precision is not noticeably affected, and the cost can be cut dramatically. In fact, some SAS procedures limit the number of observations you can analyze, thus making it necessary to select a random sample.

The examples in this section use the records in data set CLASS (shown in Chapter 3, "Reshaping Your Data"). Some examples assume that you have already created data set CLASS; others assume that you are reading the data from an external file named CLASFILE (since one of the reasons for selecting a random sample is to avoid reading all the records in a file into a SAS data set).

Decisions about Your Sample One of the first decisions you must make in selecting a random sample is whether to sample with or without replacement. An introductory statistics text explains the properties of both kinds of samples. If you decide to sample without replacement, you can choose among the methods described under **Sampling without Replacement**. If you sample with replacement, use the direct-access method described in **Sampling with Replacement**.

Another decision is the size of sample to take. For example, suppose you want to estimate a mean to within .01 of the true value with 95% confidence. The formula is as follows:

$$d = t_{.95}\sigma_{\bar{x}}$$

where $\sigma_{\bar{x}}$, the standard error of the mean, can be used to find the sample size you need. In this example

$$.01 = 1.96\sigma_{\bar{x}}$$

and

$$\sigma_{\bar{x}} = .0051 \quad .$$

A preliminary estimate of the standard deviation of x is .22, and since

$$\sigma_{\bar{x}} = \sigma_x / \sqrt{n}$$

the resulting sample size n is

$$n = (.22 / .0051)^2 = 1860.8 \quad .$$

You need a sample of 1861 observations.

Standard statistics texts give methods for determining the proper sample size for other types of analyses.

Sampling without Replacement

DATA steps SAMPLE1-SAMPLE7 below show relatively economical ways to select a random sample without replacement. For comparison, DATA steps SAMPLE8 and SAMPLE9 show methods that are conceptually simpler and more flexible in the selection process but are much more expensive than the others. In addition, if the original file is large and you plan to sample a fairly small proportion of the observations, the method given in **Sampling with Replacement** may be acceptable since the probability of duplicating sample units is small when the size of the population is very large relative to the size of the sample. Under those conditions, the method in **Sampling with Replacement** is also the most economical method for sampling without replacement.

Approximate random sample

When the exact size of your sample is not important, it is easy to select an approximate portion of the total population. Select an observation when a uniformly distributed random number (with limits 0 and 1) is less than the portion you want. To select approximately 20% of the nineteen observations in CLASFILE, use the following SAS statements:

```
DATA SAMPLE1;
   INFILE CLASFILE;
   INPUT NAME $ SEX $ AGE HEIGHT WEIGHT;
   IF RANUNI(0)<=.20;
PROC PRINT;
   TITLE 'DATA SET SAMPLE1';
RUN;
```

The RANUNI function returns a (pseudo) random number that is less than X about X x 100% of the time. The subset selected is different each time unless you supply a nonzero "seed" argument to RANUNI. The sample drawn is shown in **Output 10.1**.

Output 10.1
Approximate Random
Sample

```
                        DATA SET SAMPLE1

        OBS     NAME     SEX   AGE    HEIGHT    WEIGHT

         1     JEFFREY    M     13     62.5       84
         2     JUDY       F     14     64.3       90
         3     LOUISE     F     12     56.3       77
         4     MARY       F     15     66.5      112
         5     PHILIP     M     16     72.0      150
```

Exact-sized random sample

If you know how many observations are in the data set, it is easy to randomly select a specified number. Select observations according to probabilities conditional on the number of observations remaining in the data set and the number needed to complete the sample. If fifty observations remain in the data set and you need five more in your sample, you select the next observation with probability 5/50.

In the following examples, N is the number of observations left in CLASS, and K is the number left to select for the sample. To draw a sample containing four observations, initialize K to 4 in the RETAIN statement. N is decremented by 1 at each execution of the DATA step, and K is decremented by 1 for each observation selected. The sample is shown in **Output 10.2**.

```
DATA SAMPLE2;
    RETAIN K 4 N;
    DROP N K;
    IF _N_=1 THEN N=NUMOBS;
    SET CLASS POINT=_N_ NOBS=NUMOBS;
    IF RANUNI(0)<K/N THEN DO;
        OUTPUT;
        K=K-1;
        END;
    N=N-1;
    IF N=0 OR K=0 OR _N_=NUMOBS THEN STOP;
PROC PRINT;
    TITLE 'DATA SET SAMPLE2';
RUN;
```

Output 10.2
Exact-Sized Random
Sample

```
                        DATA SET SAMPLE2

        OBS     NAME     SEX   AGE    HEIGHT    WEIGHT

         1     ALICE      F     13     56.5      84.0
         2     JEFFREY    M     13     62.5      84.0
         3     JOHN       M     12     59.0      99.5
         4     ROBERT     M     12     64.8     128.0
```

Another way to code the example above is to initialize N to the number of observations in CLASS plus 1; a subsetting IF statement deletes observations not selected. This example reads observations from CLASFILE. **Output 10.3** shows the result.

```
DATA SAMPLE3;
   RETAIN K 4 N 20;
   DROP N K;
   INFILE CLASFILE;
   INPUT NAME $ SEX $ AGE HEIGHT WEIGHT;
   N=N-1;
   IF RANUNI(0)<K/N;
   K=K-1;
PROC PRINT;
   TITLE 'DATA SET SAMPLE3';
RUN;
```

Output 10.3
Another Exact-Sized
Random Sample

```
                        DATA SET SAMPLE3

         OBS   NAME      SEX   AGE   HEIGHT   WEIGHT

          1    ALFRED     M     14    69.0    112.5
          2    JANE       F     12    59.8     84.5
          3    JOHN       M     12    59.0     99.5
          4    WILLIAM    M     15    66.5    112.0
```

If the data are already in a SAS data set, you can obtain the number of observations in the data set from the NOBS= option as in SAMPLE2. If you are reading from an external file, you must specify the number of observations in the file (for example, in the RETAIN statement as shown in SAMPLE3).

Exact-sized sample using direct access

This method is more economical than the methods given in SAMPLE1-SAMPLE3. However, the data must be in a SAS data set, not an external file, and the size of the sample cannot exceed the maximum number of variables in the program data vector (about 4000, as discussed in **Space Considerations** earlier in this chapter).

DATA step RANDOM determines the observations to select. Then DATA step SAMPLE4 reads an observation from RANDOM and uses the value of INDEX in that observation to select the observation in CLASS to be processed. In this case you want to select a sample of four observations. **Output 10.4** shows data sets RANDOM and SAMPLE4.

```
DATA RANDOM(KEEP=INDEX);
   ARRAY SAMP(4) S1-S4;
   IF 4>TOTOBS THEN STOP;
   DO N=1 TO 4;
      REPLACE: SAMP(N)=INT(RANUNI(0)*TOTOBS+1);
      IF N>1 THEN DO I=1 TO N-1;
         IF SAMP(I)=SAMP(N) THEN GO TO REPLACE;
         END;
      INDEX=SAMP(N);
      OUTPUT;
      END;
   STOP;
   SET CLASS POINT=_N_ NOBS=TOTOBS;
DATA SAMPLE4(DROP=INDEX);
   SET RANDOM;
   SET CLASS POINT=INDEX;
PROC PRINT DATA=RANDOM;
   TITLE 'DATA SET RANDOM';
PROC PRINT DATA=SAMPLE4;
   TITLE 'DATA SET SAMPLE4';
RUN;
```

Output 10.4
Exact-Sized Random
Sample Drawn by Direct
Access

```
                    DATA SET RANDOM

                    OBS     INDEX

                     1       16
                     2        4
                     3        1
                     4        5
```

```
                    DATA SET SAMPLE4

        OBS    NAME    SEX    AGE    HEIGHT    WEIGHT

         1    ROBERT    M     12      64.8     128.0
         2    CAROL     F     14      62.8     102.5
         3    ALFRED    M     14      69.0     112.5
         4    HENRY     M     14      63.5     102.5
```

RANDOM first creates an array of variables, SAMP, to contain the random integers selected. As each random integer is generated, it is assigned to the member of the array currently being processed and is checked against the numbers already placed into variables in the array. If the random integer duplicates an existing number, it is replaced with a new random integer, and the checking begins again. When the number has been checked against all existing numbers, RANDOM assigns the number to variable INDEX and outputs an observation. The STOP statement causes RANDOM to cease execution before it reads any observations from CLASS; the SET statement simply provides the number of observations in CLASS through the NOBS= option.

Stratified random sample

If you want to select a certain number of observations from each of several BY groups, first count the observations in each group, then select from within the BY group. In this example, which selects two observations from each SEX value, the PROC FREQ step counts the number in each SEX category; the DATA step selects the sample. **Output 10.5** shows the two data sets created.

```
PROC FREQ DATA=CLASS ORDER=DATA;
   TABLES SEX / OUT=BYCOUNT NOPRINT;
DATA SAMPLE5;
   MERGE CLASS BYCOUNT (RENAME=(COUNT=N) DROP=PERCENT);
   BY SEX;
   RETAIN K;
   DROP N K;
   IF FIRST.SEX THEN K=2;
   IF RANUNI(0)<K/N THEN DO;
      OUTPUT;
      K=K-1;
      END;
   N=N-1;
PROC PRINT DATA=BYCOUNT;
   TITLE 'DATA SET BYCOUNT';
PROC PRINT DATA=SAMPLE5;
   TITLE 'DATA SET SAMPLE5';
RUN;
```

Output 10.5
Stratified Random Sample
with Same Number of
Observations from Each
BY Group

```
                      DATA SET BYCOUNT

         OBS      SEX     COUNT     PERCENT

          1        F        9       47.3684
          2        M       10       52.6316
```

```
                     DATA SET SAMPLE5

      OBS    NAME      SEX    AGE    HEIGHT    WEIGHT

       1     JANET      F      15     62.5     112.5
       2     JOYCE      F      11     51.3      50.5
       3     PHILIP     M      16     72.0     150.0
       4     WILLIAM    M      15     66.5     112.0
```

For each BY group, the value of N comes from the BYCOUNT data set; K's value is set when FIRST.SEX is 1.

Or, you can interleave a data set with itself and select the sample in one DATA step. The sample selected appears in **Output 10.6.**

```
DATA SAMPLE6;
   RETAIN N K;
   DROP N K;
   SET CLASS(IN=IN1) CLASS;
   BY SEX;
   IF IN1 THEN DO;
      N+1;
      K=2;
      END;
   ELSE DO;
      IF RANUNI(0)<K/N THEN DO;
         OUTPUT;
         K=K-1;
         END;
      N=N-1;
      END;
PROC PRINT;
   TITLE 'DATA SET SAMPLE6';
RUN;
```

Output 10.6
Another Stratified Random Sample with Same Number of Observations from Each BY Group

```
                      DATA SET SAMPLE6

     OBS    NAME      SEX    AGE    HEIGHT    WEIGHT

      1     CAROL      F      14     62.8     102.5
      2     JUDY       F      14     64.3      90.0
      3     HENRY      M      14     63.5     102.5
      4     WILLIAM    M      15     66.5     112.0
```

To select a fixed portion (say 20%) rather than a fixed number, replace K=2 with K=CEIL(N*.2) in the example above.

Suppose you want to select a different number of observations from each BY group. First create a SAS data set, say NSELECT, that contains the total number in each group and the number to select in that group. If you know the number of observations you want from each group (for example, six females and three males), input the numbers:

```
DATA NSELECT;
   SET CLASS(KEEP=SEX);
   BY SEX;
   N+1;
   IF LAST.SEX;
   INPUT K;
   OUTPUT;
   N=0;
   CARDS;
6
3
;
```

If you want a fixed portion, such as 20%, rather than an exact number, calculate the number of observations required:

```
DATA NSELECT2;
   SET CLASS(KEEP=SEX);
   BY SEX;
   N+1;
   IF LAST.SEX;
   K=CEIL(N*.2);
   OUTPUT;
   N=0;
RUN;
```

Then merge NSELECT or NSELECT2 with CLASS to select the sample. **Output 10.7** shows data sets NSELECT and SAMPLE7.

```
DATA SAMPLE7;
   MERGE CLASS NSELECT;
   BY SEX;
   DROP N K;
   IF RANUNI(0)<K/N THEN DO;
      OUTPUT;
      K=K-1;
      END;
   N=N-1;
PROC PRINT DATA=NSELECT;
   TITLE 'DATA SET NSELECT';
PROC PRINT DATA=SAMPLE7;
   TITLE 'DATA SET SAMPLE7';
RUN;
```

Output 10.7
Stratified Random Sample with Different Number of Observations from Each BY Group

```
                    DATA SET NSELECT

           OBS     SEX     N     K

            1       F      9     6
            2       M     10     3
```

```
                    DATA SET SAMPLE7

    OBS     NAME      SEX   AGE   HEIGHT   WEIGHT

     1      ALICE      F     13    56.5     84.0
     2      BARBARA    F     13    65.3     98.0
     3      CAROL      F     14    62.8    102.5
     4      JANET      F     15    62.5    112.5
     5      JUDY       F     14    64.3     90.0
     6      MARY       F     15    66.5    112.0
     7      HENRY      M     14    63.5    102.5
     8      JEFFREY    M     13    62.5     84.0
     9      JOHN       M     12    59.0     99.5
```

SAS reads values for N and K from data set NSELECT at the beginning of each BY group. Their values are retained within the BY group.

A nonsequential method

This method is more flexible in the selection process than the sequential methods, but it may not be feasible for very large data sets. You must have enough disk space available to store and sort the entire set of data as a SAS data set, and SAS must read and write the entire data set twice before you take the sample.

Suppose you want to sample ten observations from a large external file. In the first DATA step, assign a random number to each observation. Then sort the SAS data set by the random numbers. Finally, select the first ten observations from the sorted data set. **Output 10.8** shows the sample.

```
DATA TEMP;
    INFILE CLASFILE;
    INPUT NAME $ SEX $ AGE HEIGHT WEIGHT;
    RANNO=RANUNI(0);
PROC SORT;
    BY RANNO;
DATA SAMPLE8;
    SET TEMP(OBS=10);
    DROP RANNO;
PROC PRINT;
    TITLE 'DATA SET SAMPLE8';
RUN;
```

Output 10.8
Nonsequential Method for
Selecting an Exact Number

```
                          DATA SET SAMPLE8

        OBS    NAME      SEX    AGE    HEIGHT    WEIGHT

         1     BARBARA    F     13      65.3      98.0
         2     JAMES      M     12      57.3      83.0
         3     JEFFREY    M     13      62.5      84.0
         4     PHILIP     M     16      72.0     150.0
         5     JANE       F     12      59.8      84.5
         6     WILLIAM    M     15      66.5     112.0
         7     ROBERT     M     12      64.8     128.0
         8     JOYCE      F     11      51.3      50.5
         9     LOUISE     F     12      56.3      77.0
        10     HENRY      M     14      63.5     102.5
```

If you want to use this approach to select a sample of, say, 20% of the observations, you can replace the DATA SAMPLE8 step with the following one. **Output 10.9** shows the result.

```
DATA SAMPLE9;
    SET TEMP POINT=_N_ NOBS=N;
    IF _N_ > CEIL(.2*N) THEN STOP;
    DROP RANNO;
PROC PRINT;
    TITLE 'DATA SET SAMPLE9';
RUN;
```

Output 10.9
Nonsequential Method for
Selecting a Portion

```
                          DATA SET SAMPLE9

        OBS     NAME      SEX    AGE    HEIGHT    WEIGHT

         1     BARBARA     F      13     65.3       98
         2     JAMES       M      12     57.3       83
         3     JEFFREY     M      13     62.5       84
         4     PHILIP      M      16     72.0      150
```

Sampling with Replacement

For very large SAS data sets on disk, the direct access feature of the SET statement allows you to read observations directly rather than sequentially. This reduces input and output considerably since you do not have to read through the whole data set. The following example samples five observations directly, with replacement, from data set CLASS. You do not need to know the number of observations in CLASS. **Output 10.10** shows the data set produced.

```
DATA SAMPLE10;
   DROP I;
   DO I=1 TO 5;
      IOBS=INT(RANUNI(0)*N)+1;
      SET CLASS POINT=IOBS NOBS=N;
      OUTPUT;
      END;
   STOP;
PROC PRINT;
   TITLE 'DATA SET SAMPLE10';
RUN;
```

Output 10.10
Sample Drawn with
Replacement

```
                          DATA SET SAMPLE10

        OBS     NAME      SEX    AGE    HEIGHT    WEIGHT

         1     PHILIP      M      16     72.0     150.0
         2     MARY        F      15     66.5     112.0
         3     JANE        F      12     59.8      84.5
         4     JOHN        M      12     59.0      99.5
         5     PHILIP      M      16     72.0     150.0
```

Since you are sampling five of the nineteen observations in CLASS, there is a high probability of obtaining a sample in which observations are repeated, as shown in **Output 10.10**. As the size of the population increases with respect to the size of the sample, the probability of repeating observations in the sample decreases.

Replicating a Sample

Using a seed of 0 in a random number function such as RANUNI causes the function to select a different sample each time the program is run. To select a sample you can replicate, do either of the following:

□ Use a nonzero seed for the function so that the function selects the same random sample each time the program is executed.
□ Save the sample in a permanent SAS data set.

Use Summary Statistics

Many analyses of large data sets can be performed from a small set of summary statistics. For example, you can collect these statistics and use them in later analyses:

☐ frequency counts for categorical data (data that can assume only a limited number of discrete values)
☐ means and other moments for continuous numeric data
☐ correlations and crossproducts for continuous numeric data.

Frequencies Suppose you want to analyze variables AGE, RACE, SEX, and INCOME in data set HUGE. Each variable has a limited number of levels. Read data set HUGE once:

```
PROC FREQ DATA=HUGE;
   TABLES AGE*RACE*SEX*INCOME / OUT=STATS;
```

Use data set STATS with FREQ:

```
PROC FREQ DATA=STATS;
   WEIGHT COUNT;
   TABLES AGE*INCOME / CHISQ;
```

and CHART:

```
PROC CHART DATA=STATS;
   HBAR AGE / GROUP=SEX FREQ=COUNT;
```

and CATMOD:

```
PROC CATMOD DATA=STATS;
   WEIGHT COUNT;
   MODEL INCOME=AGE SEX AGE*SEX;
```

Means In data set HUGE, HEIGHT and WEIGHT contain continuous numeric values. Read HUGE:

```
PROC SUMMARY DATA=HUGE NWAY;
   VAR HEIGHT WEIGHT;
   CLASS AGE SEX;
   OUTPUT OUT=LITTLE MEAN=HEIGHT WEIGHT N=NH NW;
```

Use LITTLE in later analyses:

```
PROC CHART DATA=LITTLE;
   HBAR HEIGHT / GROUP=AGE FREQ=NH;
```

Correlations Read HUGE:

```
PROC CORR DATA=HUGE NOMISS OUTP=CR;
   VAR HEIGHT WEIGHT;
```

Use the correlations in regression:

```
PROC REG DATA=CR;
   MODEL WEIGHT=HEIGHT;
```

Recommendations

Some specific recommendations for input/output, report writing, and statistical analyses are given below. To run the most efficient SAS jobs when you process large data sets, follow these suggestions.

Input/Output

□ If you use a numeric field only for classifying values, you save space and CPU time if you read the field as a character variable. Then SAS does not need to convert the field to internal numeric representation.

□ Use a LENGTH statement for numeric variables when you do not need double precision accuracy (seventeen significant digits). For small integers, reduce the length from eight to the minimum available for SAS software under your operating system (discussed with the LENGTH statement in *SAS User's Guide: Basics, Version 5 Edition*).

□ DROP or KEEP statements and DROP= or KEEP= data set options eliminate unnecessary variables from a data set.

□ If you do not need to create a SAS data set but need a DATA step for programming, use DATA _NULL_.

□ Use conditional INPUT techniques when you can: read in a field with a trailing @ and check its value; if you want the record, read in the rest of the variables.

□ Use PROC EDITOR instead of the UPDATE statement when you have only a few observations to correct.

□ Avoid sorting; use PROC SUMMARY rather than PROC MEANS with a BY statement. If you must sort, sort by as many variables as you will ever need.

□ Choose float binary formats to store data in an external form. With RB4. or RB8. formats, SAS does not need to convert the data to another format.

Report Writing

□ Use PUT statements rather than PROC PRINT.

□ Use a FORMAT statement with PROC PRINT. When you do not specify formats, PRINT takes extra time to search for the best format for each variable. When formats are given, the printout is uniform from page to page.

Statistical Analysis

□ In PROC CORR, never request Kendall's tau-b when your data set is large.

□ In SAS/IML software, use array operations rather than loops with element operations.

□ For regression, REG is less expensive than GLM or STEPWISE. With REG, you can save the crossproducts matrix for later use.

□ In analysis of variance of balanced designs, PROC ANOVA is less expensive than PROC GLM.

□ PROC FASTCLUS is much less expensive for large data sets than PROC CLUSTER. PROC CLUSTER should never be used on data sets with a large number of observations.

Use the suggestions above for more efficient SAS programs. You do not need to worry about the style of the INPUT statement; there is no difference in column versus formatted input. Do not worry about computations in the DATA step either; adding two variables is much less expensive than inputting them. If you have a long series of mutually exclusive conditions, a SELECT group makes the program easier to read and debug than a series of IF-THEN/ELSE statements. Array processing in the DATA step saves you time in programming and makes a program more flexible; it does not save computer time.

11 Writing Programs That Write Other Programs

Introduction

This chapter shows how you can use a SAS program to write the code for another program. A program that writes another program is called a *second-order program* or *program generator*. You can use SAS programs to write

□ other SAS programs
□ programs in your operating system's control language
□ programs in other programming languages, such as FORTRAN or PL/I
□ programs combining control language, SAS steps, and/or other programming languages.

A generated program may execute immediately after it is generated, or it can be written to a file and executed at some other time.

Program generators are useful when information collected by one program is needed in order to write a second program. A program generator allows you to collect the necessary information and add it to the other program in one step. Otherwise, you would have to write one program to collect the information you need, examine the output from that program, and write the second program yourself.

A program generator is also useful when you write a number of programs that are similar but not identical. In these cases, a program generator can automate program writing and execution.

For example, at most computing installations large batch programs are executed overnight rather than during the work day. Many such batch programs are programs that are run on a regular basis, daily or weekly, but with minor modifications reflecting changing conditions in data or output requirements. Program generators are used in these situations to make the necessary alterations to the batch programs. This automated approach to program creation has two important advantages: the batch programs are modified in a routine fashion, reducing the possibility of introducing errors; and personnel work loads are reduced because a program instead of a person edits the other programs.*

The examples that follow are SAS applications using program generators as a solution to some typical programming problems.

---

* The program generators discussed in this context are different from the SAS macro facility. A program generator can write statements to any file you name (temporary or permanent), whereas a macro normally generates code for immediate use by the SAS System. A program generator can generate code in any language, but the macro facility can generate only SAS statements and commands. These program generators are also different from SAS/AF software, which allows you to build front-ends for SAS applications. SAS/AF software has all the capabilities of the program generator and more.

Examples

Preprocessing an External File

Suppose you have a group of external files and you want to create a SAS data set from each file. You do not know the names of the variables in the external files. Instead, the number and names of the variables are stored in each file in records preceding the actual data. Therefore, before you can create SAS data sets from these external files, you need to preprocess some records of each file to obtain variable names. Only then can you write the INPUT statement to read the data.

You can write one program generator that first preprocesses an external file to obtain the variable names and then writes the SAS program to create a SAS data set. The same program generator can write all the programs you need to create SAS data sets from the external files.

This example makes the following assumptions about the structure of these external files:

□ The first record contains an identifier (ID) for the file and the number of variables (NVAR).
□ The next few records contain variable names. There are six variable names in each of the records except the last. The number of records containing variable names is equal to

```
INT((NVAR+5)/6)
```

where NVAR is the number of variables.
□ The remaining records contain the data, all numeric values in free-field format.

Here is one such external file. The sample file's identifier is GRP54, and it has seven variables: AGE, WEIGHT, OXY, RUNTIME, RSTPULSE, RUNPULSE, and MAXPULSE.

```
GRP54 7
AGE WEIGHT OXY RUNTIME RSTPULSE RUNPULSE
MAXPULSE
44   89.47   44.609   11.37   62   178   182
40   75.07   45.313   10.07   62   185   185
42   68.15   59.571    8.17   40   166   172
38   89.02   49.874    9.22   55   178   180
47   77.45   44.811   11.63   58   176   176
49   81.42   49.156    8.95   44   180   185
51   69.63   40.836   10.95   57   168   172
51   77.91   46.672   10.00   48   162   168
48   91.63   46.774   10.25   48   162   164
51   73.71   45.790   10.47   59   186   188
49   76.32   48.673    9.40   56   186   188
```

The DATA step below performs the preprocessing on the external file. It reads the records containing the ID and number of variables and the names of the variables. Then, the program writes another SAS program to an output file. The generated program reads only the data records from the external file to create a SAS data set:

```
DATA _NULL_;
   INFILE IN;
   FILE OUT;
   INPUT ID $ NVAR;
   PUT 'DATA ' ID ';'/
       '    INFILE IN;'/
       '    IF _N_=1 THEN INPUT ' @;
   DO I=1 TO INT((NVAR+5)/6);
      PUT '/' @;
      END;
   PUT ';'/
       '    INPUT ' @;
   DO I=1 TO NVAR;
      INPUT NAME $ @;
      PUT NAME @;
      END;
   PUT ';' /
       'RUN;'/
       'PROC PRINT DATA=' ID ';'/
       'RUN;';
   STOP;
RUN;
```

When the sample external file is processed by the program generator, the SAS statements shown in **Output 11.1** are written to FILE OUT.

Output 11.1
Generated Program to
Read External File

```
DATA GRP54 ;
   INFILE IN;
   IF _N_=1 THEN INPUT //;
   INPUT AGE WEIGHT OXY RUNTIME RSTPULSE RUNPULSE MAXPULSE ;
RUN;
PROC PRINT DATA=GRP54 ;
RUN;
```

Notice that the first INPUT statement in the generated program contains two slashes (//). These force the step to skip from the first record of the external file to the records containing data, thereby avoiding the records that list the variable names.

Output 11.2 shows the output from executing the generated program with the sample file.

Output 11.2
Results of a Generated
Program

```
                              SAS
OBS    AGE    WEIGHT    OXY    RUNTIME   RSTPULSE   RUNPULSE   MAXPULSE

 1     44     89.47    44.609   11.37      62         178        182
 2     40     75.07    45.313   10.07      62         185        185
 3     42     68.15    59.571    8.17      40         166        172
 4     38     89.02    49.874    9.22      55         178        180
 5     47     77.45    44.811   11.63      58         176        176
 6     49     81.42    49.156    8.95      44         180        185
 7     51     69.63    40.836   10.95      57         168        172
 8     51     77.91    46.672   10.00      48         162        168
 9     48     91.63    46.774   10.25      48         162        164
10     51     73.71    45.790   10.47      59         186        188
11     49     76.32    48.673    9.40      56         186        188
```

Building a Report Writing Program

Suppose you are responsible for producing weekly reports for all the SAS data sets in a large SAS data library. The library is updated frequently, so you need to execute PROC CONTENTS to get a list of the data set names each week. Then you write the PROC PRINT steps to print the data sets. You can incorporate both steps, collecting the list of data set names and writing the appropriate PRINT steps, in one SAS program generator. An example of this kind of program generator follows:

```
PROC CONTENTS DATA=BIGLIB._ALL_ OUT=MEMINFO NOPRINT;
RUN;
DATA _NULL_;
   FILE PRNTPROG;
   SET MEMINFO;
   BY MEMNAME;
   IF _N_=1 THEN PUT 'OPTIONS DQUOTE;';
   IF FIRST.MEMNAME AND NOBS GT 0 THEN DO;
      PUT 'PROC PRINT DATA=BIGLIB.' MEMNAME ';';
      PUT 'TITLE "LISTING OF DATA SET ' MEMNAME '";';
      PUT 'RUN;';
      END;
RUN;
```

The generator makes use of PROC CONTENT's OUT= option, which creates a SAS data set containing information on all the SAS data sets in the library. The output data set, MEMINFO, has one observation for each variable in each data set in the library. Two of the variables in MEMINFO include MEMNAME (the data set's name) and NOBS (the number of observations in the data set).

Next, the DATA step reads the MEMINFO output data set and conditionally executes PUT statements that write PROC PRINT steps to the file PRNTPROG. PRINT steps are written only when

□ the observation being read from MEMINFO is the first observation for a data set (FIRST.MEMNAME=1). FIRST.MEMNAME is checked so there will be only one PROC PRINT for each data set in the library.

□ NOBS is greater than zero. NOBS is checked so that PRINT steps will not be created for data sets with no observations.

The program written to the PRNTPROG file can be executed to produce the weekly report on the data sets in the library. **Output 11.3** shows a program produced by this program generator.

```
OPTIONS DQUOTE;
PROC PRINT DATA=BIGLIB.CLASS ;
TITLE "LISTING OF DATA SET CLASS ";
RUN;
PROC PRINT DATA=BIGLIB.CLASS2 ;
TITLE "LISTING OF DATA SET CLASS2 ";
RUN;
PROC PRINT DATA=BIGLIB.CLASS3 ;
TITLE "LISTING OF DATA SET CLASS3 ";
RUN;
PROC PRINT DATA=BIGLIB.CLASS4 ;
TITLE "LISTING OF DATA SET CLASS4 ";
RUN;
PROC PRINT DATA=BIGLIB.CONOUT ;
TITLE "LISTING OF DATA SET CONOUT ";
RUN;
PROC PRINT DATA=BIGLIB.CURRENT ;
TITLE "LISTING OF DATA SET CURRENT ";
RUN;
PROC PRINT DATA=BIGLIB.CURRENT2 ;
TITLE "LISTING OF DATA SET CURRENT2 ";
RUN;
PROC PRINT DATA=BIGLIB.DAILY ;
TITLE "LISTING OF DATA SET DAILY ";
RUN;
PROC PRINT DATA=BIGLIB.EDCLASS ;
TITLE "LISTING OF DATA SET EDCLASS ";
RUN;
PROC PRINT DATA=BIGLIB.JOIN ;
TITLE "LISTING OF DATA SET JOIN ";
RUN;
PROC PRINT DATA=BIGLIB.JOINMERG ;
TITLE "LISTING OF DATA SET JOINMERG ";
RUN;
PROC PRINT DATA=BIGLIB.JOINUPDT ;
TITLE "LISTING OF DATA SET JOINUPDT ";
RUN;
PROC PRINT DATA=BIGLIB.JOIN2 ;
TITLE "LISTING OF DATA SET JOIN2 ";
RUN;
PROC PRINT DATA=BIGLIB.MASTER ;
TITLE "LISTING OF DATA SET MASTER ";
RUN;
PROC PRINT DATA=BIGLIB.MAY19 ;
TITLE "LISTING OF DATA SET MAY19 ";
RUN;
PROC PRINT DATA=BIGLIB.MAY20 ;
TITLE "LISTING OF DATA SET MAY20 ";
RUN;
PROC PRINT DATA=BIGLIB.NEW ;
TITLE "LISTING OF DATA SET NEW ";
RUN;
PROC PRINT DATA=BIGLIB.NEWMASTR ;
TITLE "LISTING OF DATA SET NEWMASTR ";
RUN;
PROC PRINT DATA=BIGLIB.OLD ;
TITLE "LISTING OF DATA SET OLD ";
RUN;
PROC PRINT DATA=BIGLIB.TODAY ;
TITLE "LISTING OF DATA SET TODAY ";
RUN;
PROC PRINT DATA=BIGLIB.TRANS ;
TITLE "LISTING OF DATA SET TRANS ";
RUN;
PROC PRINT DATA=BIGLIB.TRANSACT ;
TITLE "LISTING OF DATA SET TRANSACT ";
RUN;
```

Generating a PROC FORMAT Program

In the next example, a DATA step generates a PROC FORMAT program. The DATA step reads an external file that includes fields for ID numbers and last names:

```
186000001   BRINSFIELD
186000002   MCGILLIS
186000003   BROWN
186000004   SAFFER
186000005   FISHER
186000006   LUDWICK
186000007   CAPPY
286000001   HOLT
286000002   NEWBERRY
286000003   PARKER
286000004   HEALY
286000005   GARRET
286000006   SCHROEDER
286000007   PANKY
386000001   MONTGOMERY
386000002   LOUD
386000003   SCHMIDT
386000004   GROGER
386000005   JONES
386000006   EDWARDS
386000007   DALTON
486000001   CASEY
486000002   MORGAN
486000003   FIELDS
486000004   BELL
486000005   CAHILL
486000006   WISE
486000007   MAPLES
```

The DATA step then writes a PROC FORMAT program to another file. The generated program creates a format in which each ID number is formatted as the corresponding last name:

```
DATA _NULL_;
   INFILE EMPLOY END=EOF;
   INPUT @1 ID 9. @12 LASTNAME $20.;
   FILE PFORMAT;
   IF _N_=1 THEN PUT @1 'OPTIONS DQUOTE;'
                   / @1 'PROC FORMAT;'
                   / @3 'VALUE NAMES ';
   PUT @6  ID '="' LASTNAME '"';
   IF EOF THEN PUT @6 ' OTHER ="INVALID";'
                   / 'RUN;';
RUN;
```

The program generated by the DATA step is shown in **Output 11.4.**

Output 11.4
Generated FORMAT
Program

```
OPTIONS DQUOTE;
PROC FORMAT;
  VALUE NAMES
      186000001 ="BRINSFIELD "
      186000002 ="MCGILLIS "
      186000003 ="BROWN "
      186000004 ="SAFFER "
      186000005 ="FISHER "
      186000006 ="LUDWICK "
      186000007 ="CAPPY "
      286000001 ="HOLT "
      286000002 ="NEWBERRY "
      286000003 ="PARKER "
      286000004 ="HEALY "
      286000005 ="GARRET "
      286000006 ="SCHROEDER "
      286000007 ="PANKY "
      386000001 ="MONTGOMERY "
      386000002 ="LOUD "
      386000003 ="SCHMIDT "
      386000004 ="GROGER "
      386000005 ="JONES "
      386000006 ="EDWARDS "
      386000007 ="DALTON "
      486000001 ="CASEY "
      486000002 ="MORGAN "
      486000003 ="FIELDS "
      486000004 ="BELL "
      486000005 ="CAHILL "
      486000006 ="WISE "
      486000007 ="MAPLES "
       OTHER ="INVALID";
RUN;
```

Index

A

ABORT statement
   printing messages before executing   211
ALL specification
   CONTENTS procedure   183
ampersand (&) format modifier   8
ANOVA procedure   237
APPEND procedure   169–170, 175, 178
   compared to DATA step   179
array   12
   efficiency   238
   recoding variables   39, 47
array processing
   INPUT statement   12
   SET statement   16
assignment statement
   syntax   188
at sign
   trailing (@)   19
   double trailing (@@)   19

B

BY statement
   more than one BY variable (example)   77
   PRINT procedure   132
   SET statement   67

C

CARDS statement   2
   with SET statement   232
CEIL function   232
CENTER option
   SAS system options   166
character comparisons   37
CLUSTER procedure   237
colon (:) format modifier   6
column input   4
COMPRESS function   167
concatenation
   example   38
   SAS data sets   66
   several copies of a data set   66
   three data sets   184
   with APPEND procedure   178
   with DATA step   179
CONTENTS procedure   169–170, 183
   MEMTYPE= option   172
COPY procedure   169–170
   backing up a SAS data library   185
   MEMTYPE= option   172
   MOVE option   183
   SELECT statement   171
CORR procedure   237

D

data errors
   checking for with ABORT statement   209
   checking for with FORMAT procedure   209
   checking for with STOP statement   209
DATA step   1
   compared to APPEND procedure   179
   efficiency of computations   238
   report writing   131, 152
Dataset Contents screen
   DATASETS procedure   177
Datasets Menu
   DATASETS procedure   176
DATASETS procedure   169–170
   Dataset Contents screen   177
   Datasets Menu   176
   full-screen example   176
   MEMTYPE= option   172
   renaming variables   176
DATE function   167
DATE option
   SAS system options   166
DAY function   167
DELETE statement   52
diagnosing errors   187
direct access
   more than one SET statement   75
   SAS data set   74
DOUBLE option
   PRINT procedure   132
DROP statement
   errors   195
   RENAME statement   60
   subsetting variables   56
DROP= option
   data set option for input data set   57
   data set option for output data set   57

E

editing SAS data sets   124, 180
   batch PROC EDITOR example   127
   example   129
   interactive PROC EDITOR example   124
EDITOR procedure   109, 124
   compared to FSEDIT procedure   124
   compared to UPDATE statement   124
ELSE statement   30
END= option
   INFILE statement   10
   outputting a total with the SET statement   80
   SET statement   78, 155
   using its value before SET statement   80
EOF= option
   INFILE statement   10

Proofreading and text entry support are performed in the **Technical Writing Department** by **Amy E. Ball, Kimberly I. Barber, Gina A. Eatmon, Rebecca A. Fritz, Lisa K. Hunt, Caroline T. Powell, Beth L. Puryear, Drew T. Saunders, W. Robert Scott,** and **Harriet J. Watts** under the supervision of **David D. Baggett. Gigi Hassan** is index editor.

Production is performed in the **Graphic Arts Department.** Composition was provided by **Joseph H. Moore, Jr.** Text composition programming was provided by **Pamela A. Troutman.**

Creative Services artist **Michael J. Pezzoni** provided illustrations under the direction of **Jennifer A. Davis.**

Your Turn

If you have comments about SAS software or the *SAS Applications Guide, 1987 Edition*, please send them to us on a photocopy of this page.

Please return the photocopy to the Publications Division (for comments about this book) or the Technical Support Division (for suggestions about the software) at SAS Institute Inc., SAS Campus Drive, Cary, NC 27513.

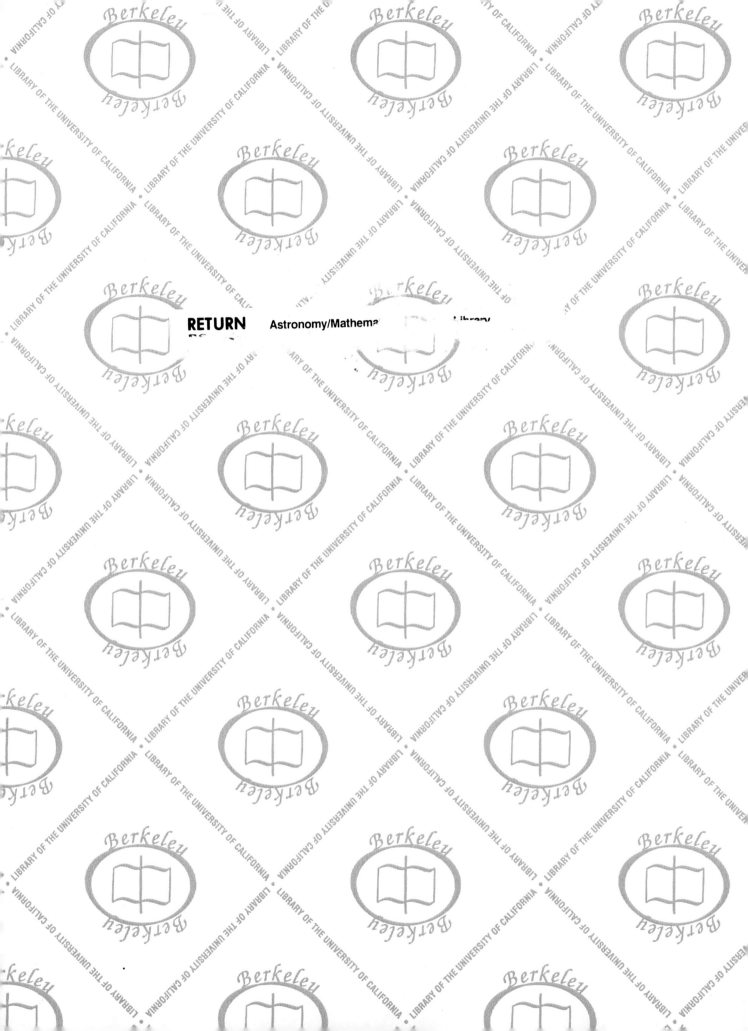